TEACHER EDITIO

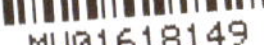

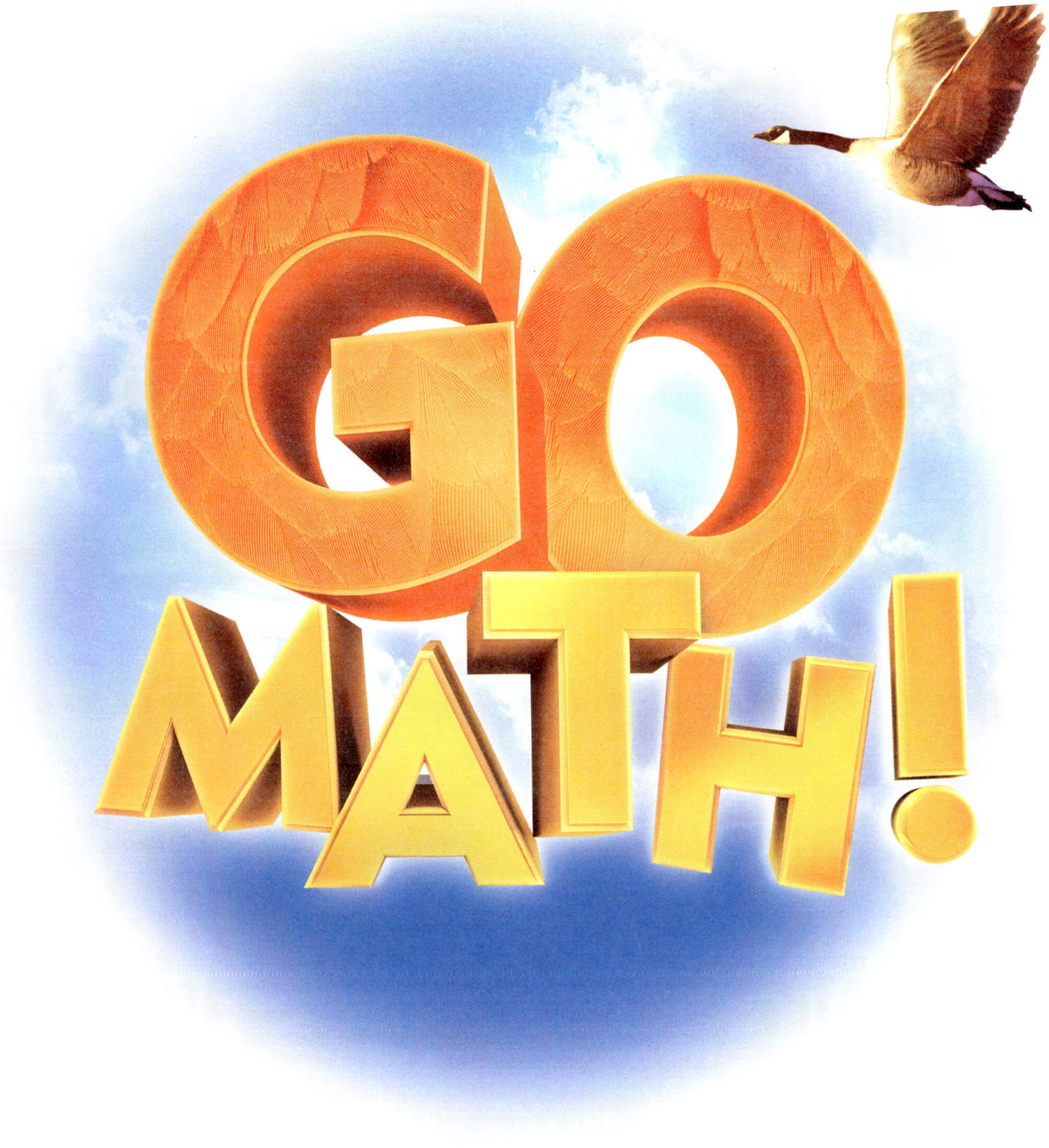

GO MATH!

Carmen Sandiego™ is a trademark of HMH Consumer Company.

Copyright © 2012 by Houghton Mifflin Harcourt Publishing Company.

All rights reserved. No part of this work may be reproduced or transmitted in any form or by any means, electronic or mechanical, including photocopying or recording, or by any information storage and retrieval system, without the prior written permission of the copyright owner unless such copying is expressly permitted by federal copyright law. Requests for permission to make copies of any part of the work should be addressed to Houghton Mifflin Harcourt Publishing Company, Attn: Contracts, Copyrights, and Licensing, 9400 South Park Center Loop, Orlando, Florida 32819.

Common Core State Standards © Copyright 2010. National Governors Association Center for Best Practices and Council of Chief State School Officers. All rights reserved.

This product is not sponsored or endorsed by the Common Core State Standards Initiative of the National Governors Association Center for Best Practices and the Council of Chief State School Officers.

Printed in the U.S.A.

ISBN 978-0-547-59179-7

6 7 8 9 10 0877 20 19 18 17 16 15 14 13 12

4500352741 C D E F G

If you have received these materials as examination copies free of charge, Houghton Mifflin Harcourt Publishing Company retains title to the materials and they may not be resold. Resale of examination copies is strictly prohibited.

Possession of this publication in print format does not entitle users to convert this publication, or any portion of it, into electronic format.

Geometry, Measurement, and Data

CRITICAL AREA Understanding that geometric figures can be analyzed and classified based on their properties, such as having parallel sides, perpendicular sides, particular angle measures, and symmetry

Chapter 10 **Two-Dimensional Figures** 379

Chapter 11 **Angles** 415

Chapter 12 **Relative Sizes of Measurement Units** 443

Domain: Measurement and Data CC.4.MD

Lessons	Grade 4 Common Core State Standards
12.1–12.4, 12.6–12.8, 12.11	**Solve problems involving measurement and conversion of measurements from a larger unit to a smaller unit.** CC.4.MD.1 Know relative sizes of measurement units within one system of units including km, m, cm; kg, g; lb, oz.; l, ml; hr, min, sec. Within a single system of measurement, express measurements in a larger unit in terms of a smaller unit. Record measurement equivalents in a two-column table.
12.5	**Represent and interpret data.** CC.4.MD.4 Make a line plot to display a data set of measurements in fractions of a unit (1/2, 1/4, 1/8). Solve problems involving addition and subtraction of fractions by using information presented in line plots.
12.7, 12.9, 12.10	**Solve problems involving measurement and conversion of measurements from a larger unit to a smaller unit.** CC.4.MD.2 Use the four operations to solve word problems involving distances, intervals of time, liquid volumes, masses of objects, and money, including problems involving simple fractions or decimals, and problems that require expressing measurements given in a larger unit in terms of a smaller unit. Represent measurement quantities using diagrams such as number line diagrams that feature a measurement scale.

Chapter 13 **Algebra: Perimeter and Area** 495

Table of Contents

Chapter 12 Relative Sizes of Measurement Units

Domain:
Measurement and Data CC.4.MD

Mathematical Practices:
CC.K–12.MP.2 Reason abstractly and quantitatively.
CC.K–12.MP.4 Model with mathematics.

Planning	Page
Chapter At A Glance	443A
Teaching for Depth	443E
Daily Classroom Management	443F
Review Prerequisite Skills	443G
Developing Math Language	443H
Introduce the Chapter	443
Show What You Know	443
Vocabulary Builder	444

Lessons		Common Core State Standards	Page
12.1	Measurement Benchmarks	CC.4.MD.1	445A
12.2	Customary Units of Length	CC.4.MD.1	449A
12.3	Customary Units of Weight	CC.4.MD.1	453A
12.4	Customary Units of Liquid Volume	CC.4.MD.1	457A
12.5	Line Plots	CC.4.MD.4	461A
	Mid-Chapter Checkpoint		465
12.6	Investigate • Metric Units of Length	CC.4.MD.1	467A
12.7	Metric Units of Mass and Liquid Volume	CC.4.MD.1, CC.4.MD.2	471A
12.8	Units of Time	CC.4.MD.1	475A
12.9	Problem Solving • Elapsed Time	CC.4.MD.2	479A
12.10	Mixed Measures	CC.4.MD.2	483A
12.11	Algebra • Patterns in Measurement Units	CC.4.MD.1	487A
	Chapter 12 Review/Test ★ Test Prep		491–492
	Chapter 12 Test		494A

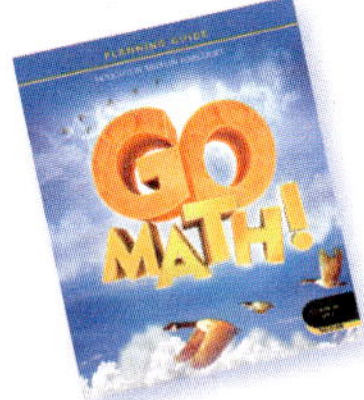

Use the Chapter Planner in the *Go Math! Planning Guide* for pacing.

Chapter At A Glance

Domain: **Measurement and Data**

Chapter Essential Question How can you use relative sizes of measurements to solve problems and to generate measurement tables that show a relationship?

Lesson At A Glance

	LESSON 12.1 CC.4.MD.1	LESSON 12.2 CC.4.MD.1	LESSON 12.3 CC.4.MD.1
	Measurement Benchmarks 445A	Customary Units of Length. 449A	Customary Units of Weight.. . . . . 453A
Essential Question	How can you use benchmarks to understand the relative sizes of measurement units?	How can you use models to compare customary units of length?	How can you use models to compare customary units of weight?
Objective	Use benchmarks to understand the relative sizes of measurement units.	Use models to compare customary units of length.	Use models to compare customary units of weight.
Vocabulary	**kilometer**, **mile**, benchmark	foot, inch, weight, yard	**ounce**, **pound**, **ton**
Materials	MathBoard, Counting Tape	MathBoard, scissors, tape, 1-Inch Grid Paper (see *eTeacher Resources*), Counting Tape	MathBoard, color pencils, Counting Tape

Print Resources

12.1	12.2	12.3
12.1 Student Edition	12.2 Student Edition	12.3 Student Edition
12.1 Standards Practice Book	12.2 Standards Practice Book	12.3 Standards Practice Book
12.1 Reteach	12.2 Reteach	12.3 Reteach
12.1 Enrich	12.2 Enrich	12.3 Enrich
Grab-and-Go™ Centers Kit	Grab-and-Go™ Centers Kit	Grab-and-Go™ Centers Kit
ELL **Strategy** • Explore Context	ELL **Strategy** • Explore Concepts	ELL **Strategy** • Model Language

Digital Path

12.1	12.2	12.3
12.1 *e*Student Edition	12.2 *e*Student Edition	12.3 *e*Student Edition
12.1 *e*Teacher Edition	12.2 *e*Teacher Edition	12.3 *e*Teacher Edition
HMH Mega Math	Animated Math Models	Animated Math Models
	*i*Tools	*i*Tools
	HMH Mega Math	HMH Mega Math

RtI Response to Intervention

Before the Chapter	During the Lesson	After the Chapter
Show What You Know	**Share and Show**	**Chapter Review/Test**
• Prerequisite Skills Activities • Soar to Success Math	• RtI Activities • Mid-Chapter Checkpoint • Soar to Success Math	• RtI Activities • Soar to Success Math

Use every day to develop computational fluency.
Visit www.greatsource.com/everydaycounts

Assess Depth of Knowledge

See Chapter 12 Performance Task and *Assessment Guide*

LESSON 12.4 CC.4.MD.1	LESSON 12.5 CC.4.MD.4	LESSON 12.6 CC.4.MD.1
Customary Units of Liquid Volume 457A	**Line Plots 461A**	**Investigate • Metric Units of Length 467A**
How can you use models to compare customary units of liquid volume?	How can you make and interpret line plots with fractional data?	How can you use models to compare metric units of length?
Use models to compare customary units of liquid volume.	Make and interpret line plots with fractional data.	Use models to compare metric units of length.
cup, **fluid ounce**, **gallon**, **half gallon**, **liquid volume**, **pint, quart**	**line plot**	**decimeter**, **millimeter**, centimeter, kilometer, meter
MathBoard, Counting Tape	MathBoard, Counting Tape	MathBoard, scissors, tape, Ruler (meterstick) (see *eTeacher Resources*), Counting Tape

12.4	12.5	12.6
12.4 Student Edition	12.5 Student Edition	12.6 Student Edition
12.4 Standards Practice Book	12.5 Standards Practice Book	12.6 Standards Practice Book
12.4 Reteach	12.5 Reteach	12.6 Reteach
12.4 Enrich	12.5 Enrich	12.6 Enrich
Grab-and-Go™ Centers Kit	Grab-and-Go™ Centers Kit	Grab-and-Go™ Centers Kit
ELL Strategy • Draw	ELL Strategy • Draw	ELL Strategy • Draw

12.4	12.5	12.6
12.4 *e*Student Edition	12.5 *e*Student Edition	12.6 *e*Student Edition
12.4 *e*Teacher Edition	12.5 *e*Teacher Edition	12.6 *e*Teacher Edition
Animated Math Models	*i*Tools	Animated Math Models
*i*Tools	HMH Mega Math	HMH Mega Math
HMH Mega Math		

GREAT ON INTERACTIVE WHITEBOARD!

Digital Path

- Animated Math Models
- Assessment
- CARMEN SANDIEGO™
- HMH Mega Math
- *i*Tools
- Multimedia *e*Glossary
- Professional Development Video Podcasts
- Real World Videos
- Soar to Success Math

Chapter At A Glance

Domain: Measurement and Data

Lesson At A Glance

	LESSON 12.7 CC.4.MD.1, CC.4.MD.2	LESSON 12.8 CC.4.MD.1	LESSON 12.9 CC.4.MD.2
	Metric Units of Mass and Liquid Volume . . . 471A	Units of Time 475A	Problem Solving • Elapsed Time 479A
Essential Question	How can you use models to compare metric units of mass and liquid volume?	How can you use models to compare units of time?	How can you use the strategy *draw a diagram* to solve elapsed time problems?
Objective	Use models to compare metric units of mass and liquid volume.	Use models to compare units of time.	Use the strategy *draw a diagram* to solve elapsed time problems.
Vocabulary	**milliliter**, gram, kilogram, liter	**second**, day, hour, minute, month, week, year	A.M., elapsed time, P.M.
Materials	MathBoard, Counting Tape	MathBoard, Counting Tape	MathBoard, Counting Tape

Print Resources

12.7	12.8	12.9
12.7 Student Edition 12.7 Standards Practice Book 12.7 Reteach 12.7 Enrich Grab-and-Go™ Centers Kit ELL **Strategy** • Explore Concepts	12.8 Student Edition 12.8 Standards Practice Book 12.8 Reteach 12.8 Enrich Grab-and-Go™ Centers Kit ELL **Strategy** • Draw	12.9 Student Edition 12.9 Standards Practice Book 12.9 Reteach 12.9 Enrich Grab-and-Go™ Centers Kit ELL **Strategy** • Creative Grouping

12.7	12.8	12.9
12.7 *e*Student Edition 12.7 *e*Teacher Edition Animated Math Models HMH Mega Math	12.8 *e*Student Edition 12.8 *e*Teacher Edition Animated Math Models *i*Tools	12.9 *e*Student Edition 12.9 *e*Teacher Edition Animated Math Models *i*Tools HMH Mega Math

Diagnostic	Formative	Summative
• Show What You Know • Diagnostic Interview Task • Soar to Success Math	• Lesson Quick Check • Mid-Chapter Checkpoint	• Chapter Review/Test • Performance Assessment • Chapter Test • Online Assessment

LESSON 12.10 CC.4.MD.2

Mixed Measures 483A

How can you solve problems involving mixed measures?

Solve problems involving mixed measures.

MathBoard, Counting Tape

12.10 Student Edition
12.10 Standards Practice Book
12.10 Reteach
12.10 Enrich
Grab-and-Go™ Centers Kit
ELL Strategy • Explore Context

12.10 *e*Student Edition
12.10 *e*Teacher Edition
Real World Video, Ch. 12
*i*Tools
HMH Mega Math

LESSON 12.11 CC.4.MD.1

Algebra • Patterns in Measurement Units 487A

How can you use patterns to write number pairs for measurement units?

Use patterns to write number pairs for measurement units.

MathBoard, Counting Tape

12.11 Student Edition
12.11 Standards Practice Book
12.11 Reteach
12.11 Enrich
Grab-and-Go™ Centers Kit
ELL Strategy • Identify Patterns

12.11 *e*Student Edition
12.11 *e*Teacher Edition
Chapter 12 Test
*i*Tools

Teacher Notes

Teaching for Depth

by Matt Larson
Curriculum Specialist for Mathematics
Lincoln Public Schools
Lincoln, Nebraska

Underlying Concepts

Results of international comparisons indicate that U.S. students struggle with measurement concepts (Gonzales, Williams, Jocelyn, Roey, Kastberg, & Brenwald, 2008). Teachers should emphasize the essential concepts and meanings that underlie the procedural process of determining a measure (Beckmann, 2008 & Van De Walle, 2004).

- In order to compare the sizes of objects or situations, the attribute of comparison must be clearly identified, e.g. weight vs. volume.
- Measurement of a quantity is about comparison of that quantity with a fixed reference amount of that quantity, or unit.
- Developing personal benchmarks for frequently used units of measure helps students both develop meaning for units and make comparisons.
- There is an inverse relationship between the size of the unit and the numeric measure. Measuring objects with different sized units, building tables comparing units, and discussing the appropriate unit to measure a quantity, can all help build this essential understanding.

Systems of Measurement

Any fixed amount of a measurable quantity can be used as a unit. A system of measurement is nothing more than a collection of agreed upon standard units (Beckmann, 2008). In the United States, two different collections of standard units are used: the customary units and the metric units.

From the Research

"Students should become familiar with the common units in these systems [customary and metric] and establish mental images or benchmarks for judging and comparing size" (NCTM, 2000, p. 172).

Comparing Measurements

Students need to see time as nothing more than another attribute to be measured.

- In order to successfully solve elapsed time problems, students first need considerable time working with the relationship between minutes and hours and the two cycles of 12 hours in a day (Van de Walle, 2004).
- Making connections to how long things typically take in everyday life can help students check the reasonableness of their elapsed time calculations.
- Frequently having students "schedule" activities throughout the school day, e.g., "How long before we go to music?" can help students develop deeper understanding of elapsed time.

Mathematical Practices

Working with measurement concepts gives students multiple opportunities to **attend to precision**. They may use the relative sizes of units to evaluate the reasonableness of their results. Or, they may use benchmark measures to estimate length, weight, and volume.

Professional Development Video Podcasts

Measurement and Geometry: Perimeter, Area, and Volume, Grades 3–6, Segments 1, 2, and 3

Daily Classroom Management

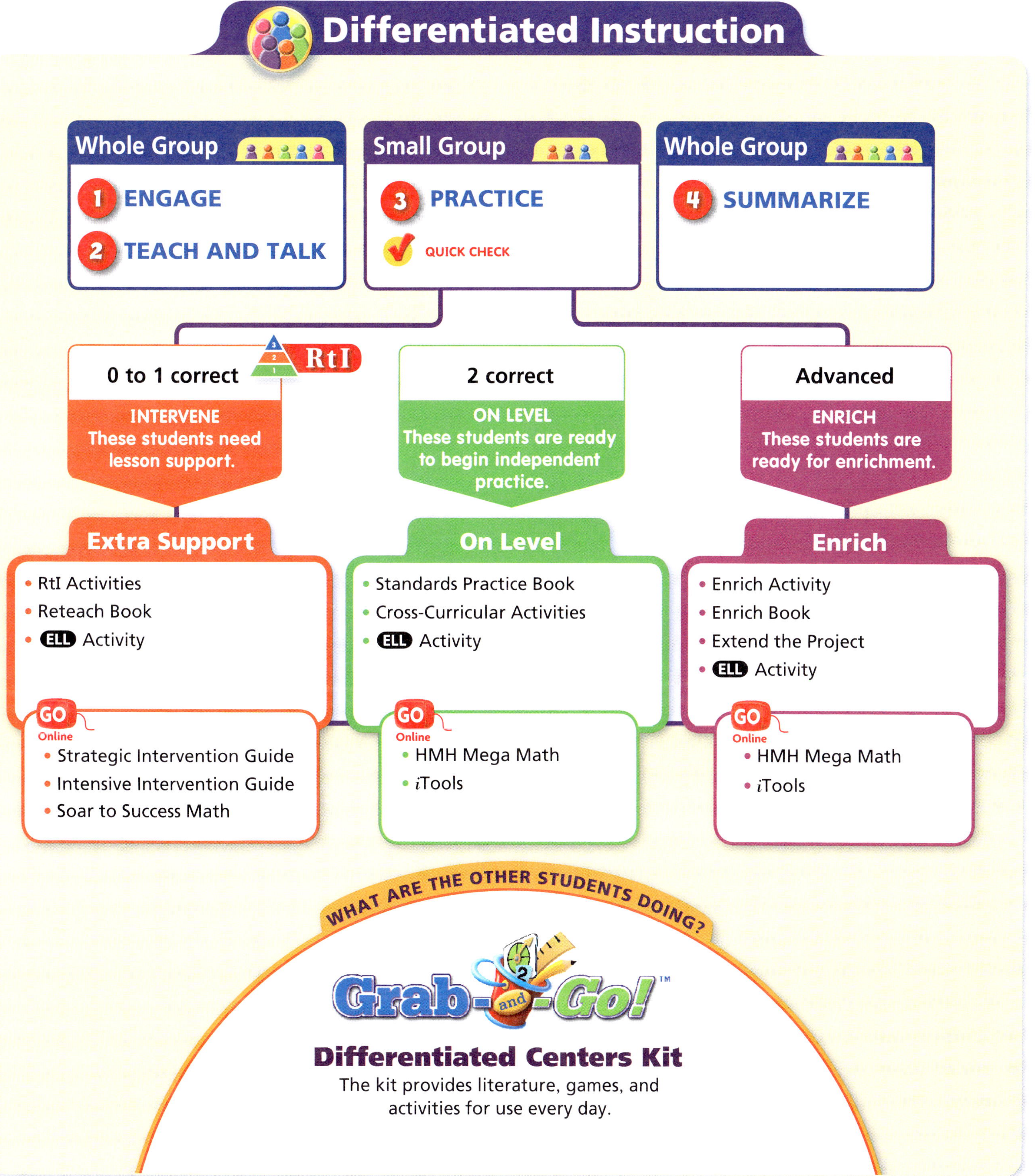

Review Prerequisite Skills

Measure It!

TIER 2

Objective Measure length to the nearest inch and half inch.

Materials inch ruler

Discuss what it means to measure to the nearest inch. Then have students measure the length of their math books to the nearest inch. Possible answer: 11 in.

Now discuss what it means to measure to the nearest half inch. Then have students measure the length of their math books to the nearest half inch. Possible answers: $10\frac{1}{2}$ in.; 11 in.

- **Is it possible to get the same answer when measuring to the nearest inch and half inch? Explain.** Yes; possible explanation: when the actual length is closer to a whole inch than a half inch, you get the same answer.
- **Is it more precise to measure to the nearest inch or to the nearest half inch? Explain.** the nearest half inch; possible explanation: half-inch increments are smaller, and with smaller increments you can get closer to the actual measure.

Have students measure other objects to the nearest inch and half inch and compare their measurements.

Show It!

TIER 3

Objective Show time on an Analog Clock.

Materials Analog Clockfaces (see *eTeacher Resources*)

Show students the face of a clock. Make sure students understand that the numbers on the clock indicate hours and the tic marks indicate minutes.

Remind students that a clock face shows 12 hours and it shows 60 minutes.

Ask students what time they do some common daily tasks, and have them draw on the clock faces to record the times. For example:

- **At what time do you get up in the morning?** Possible answer: 6:30
- **Show the time on the clock.**

Make sure students can identify the hour hand and minute hand in their drawings.

Common Core State Standards Across the Grades

Before	Grade 4	After
Domain: Measurement and Data Solve problems involving measurement and estimation of intervals of time, liquid volumes, and masses of objects. **CC.3.MD.1, CC.3.MD.2** Represent and interpret data. **CC.3.MD.4**	**Domain: Measurement and Data** Solve problems involving measurement and conversion of measurements from a larger unit to a smaller unit. **CC.4.MD.1, CC.4.MD.2** Represent and interpret data. **CC.4.MD.4**	**Domain: Measurement and Data** Convert like measurement units within a given measurement system. **CC.5.MD.1** Represent and interpret data. **CC.5.MD.2**

Developing Math Language

Chapter Vocabulary

cup a customary unit used to measure liquid volume

decimeter a metric unit for measuring length or distance

fluid ounce the smallest customary unit for measuring liquid volume

gallon a customary unit used to measure liquid volume

half gallon a customary unit used to measure liquid volume

line plot a graph that shows the frequency of data along a number line

milliliter a metric unit used to measure liquid volume

millimeter a metric unit used to measure length

ounce a customary unit used to measure weight

pint a customary unit used to measure liquid volume

pound a customary unit used to measure weight

quart a customary unit used to measure liquid volume

second a small unit of time

ton a customary unit used to measure weight

Multimedia eGlossary

ELL Vocabulary Activity

Objective Develop vocabulary for measurement

Materials ruler (metric), measuring tape

Show students a ruler and measuring tape. Explain that these are tools used to measure length.

Draw a line segment on the board that is 1 meter long. Draw tic marks to show 1 millimeter and 1 decimeter. Explain that 1 decimeter is equivalent to one tenth of a meter. Explain that one millimeter is one thousandth of a meter.

Point to different objects as you ask the following questions to practice vocabulary:

Beginning

- Do we measure the length of a fingernail in millimeters or meters? millimeters

Intermediate

- What units can we use to measure the length of this book? decimeters, centimeters

Advanced

- What school objects can you measure in centimeters? Answers will vary. Possible answers: books, pencils, paper sheets, pictures

See ELL Activity Guide for leveled activities.

Vocabulary Strategy • Graphic Organizer

Materials list of new vocabulary terms: cup, decimeter, fluid ounce, gallon, half gallon, milliliter, millimeter, ounce, pint, pound, quart, ton

Brainstorm with the class ways to sort the words in the list. Possible responses: by quantity measured, by what the units measure, by system

Word Sort:

Length	Liquid Volume	Weight
decimeter	cup	ounce
millimeter	gallon	pound
	half gallon	ton
	fluid ounce	
	pint	
	quart	
	milliliter	

Introduce the Chapter

Assessing Prior Knowledge

Use **Show What You Know** to determine if students need intensive or strategic intervention.

In this **Math Detective**, students use what they know about fractions and volume measurement units to determine if enough cups of water were poured to fill a half-gallon bucket.

Ask:

- **Look at the line plot. What do you need to do first?** Add the fractions to get the total number of cups.
- **How many cups did the team squeeze?** 5 cups
- **Describe how you solved the problem after adding the fractions.** Possible answer: I compared the number of cups in a half gallon, 8 cups, to the sum. Since 5 cups < 8 cups, I know the team did not squeeze enough water.

CARMEN SANDIEGO™ Math Detective Activities

Show What You Know

Check your understanding of important skills.

Name ________________

Time to the Half Hour Read the clock. Write the time.

1.  1:30
2. 6:30
3.  12:30

Multiply by 1-Digit Numbers Find the product.

4. 84×7 = 588
5. 536×8 = 4,288
6. 748×5 = 3,740
7. $2,524 \times 2$ = 5,048
8. 360×9 = 3,240
9. 296×3 = 888
10. $\$1,428 \times 4$ = $5,712
11. 64×5 = 320

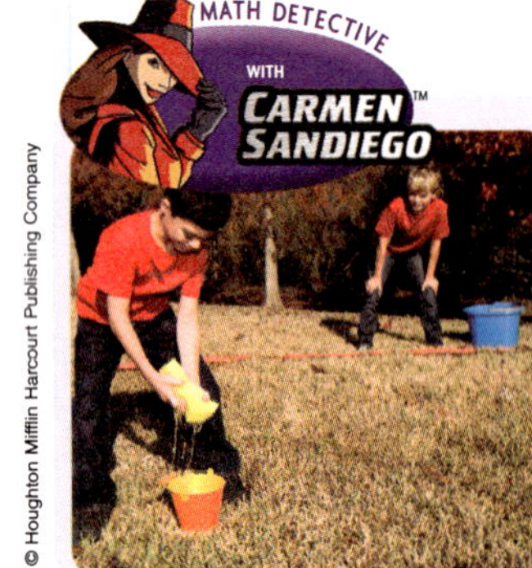

A team was given a bucket of water and a sponge. The team had 1 minute to fill an empty half-gallon bucket with water using only the sponge. The line plot shows the amount of water squeezed into the bucket. Be a Math Detective. Did the team squeeze enough water to fill the half-gallon bucket?

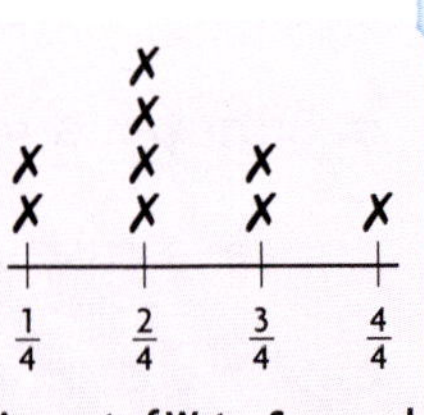

Amount of Water Squeezed into the Bucket (in cups)

No. The team squeezed a total of 5 cups of water. A half gallon is 8 cups, so the team did not squeeze enough water to fill the bucket.

© Houghton Mifflin Harcourt Publishing Company

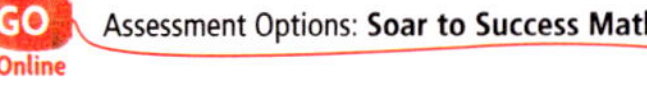

Show What You Know • Diagnostic Assessment

Use to determine if students need intervention for the chapter's prerequisite skills.

Were students successful with Show What You Know?

If NO...then INTERVENE

If YES...then use INDEPENDENT ACTIVITIES

	Skill	Missed More Than	Intervene With	Soar to Success Math
TIER 3	Time to the Half Hour	1	*Intensive Intervention* Skill 50; *Intensive Intervention User Guide* Activity 12	Warm-Up 51.10
TIER 2	Multiply by 1-Digit Numbers	2	*Strategic Intervention* Skill 12	Warm-Up 12.58

Grab-and-Go!™ **Differentiated Centers Kit**

Use the *Enrich Book* or the independent activities in the *Grab-and-Go™ Differentiated Centers Kit.*

For Diagnostic Interview Tasks for Show What You Know skills, see *Assessment Guide.*

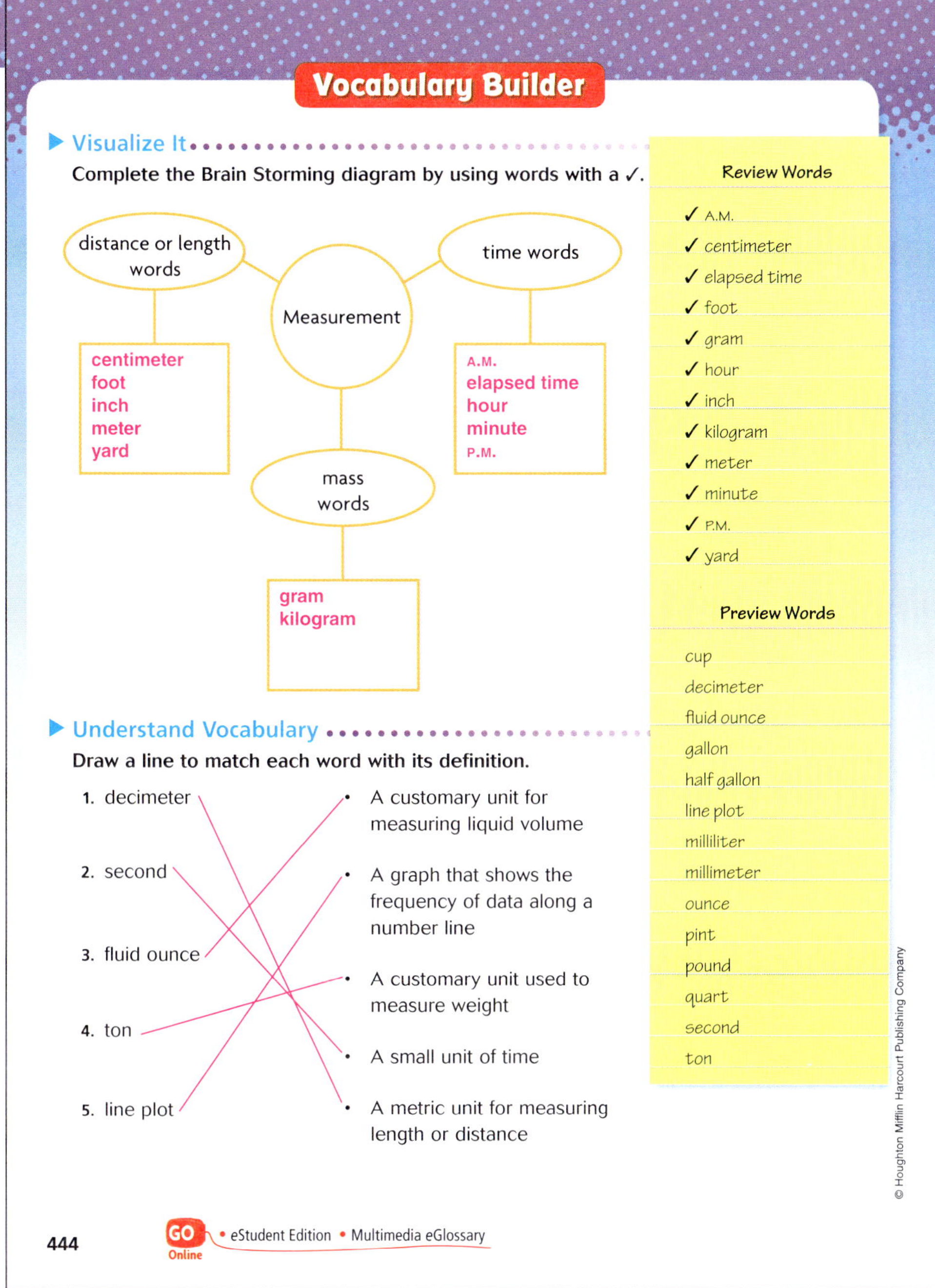

Vocabulary Builder

▶ Visualize It

Complete the Brain Storming diagram by using words with a ✓.

Review Words

✓ A.M.
✓ centimeter
✓ elapsed time
✓ foot
✓ gram
✓ hour
✓ inch
✓ kilogram
✓ meter
✓ minute
✓ P.M.
✓ yard

Preview Words

cup
decimeter
fluid ounce
gallon
half gallon
line plot
milliliter
millimeter
ounce
pint
pound
quart
second
ton

▶ Understand Vocabulary

Draw a line to match each word with its definition.

1. decimeter
2. second
3. fluid ounce
4. ton
5. line plot

- A customary unit for measuring liquid volume
- A graph that shows the frequency of data along a number line
- A customary unit used to measure weight
- A small unit of time
- A metric unit for measuring length or distance

© Houghton Mifflin Harcourt Publishing Company

GO Online • eStudent Edition • Multimedia eGlossary

Vocabulary Builder

Have students complete the activities on this page by working alone or with partners.

▶ Visualize It

The Brain Storming diagram helps you group related measurement terms together. In the left box are the words *centimeter, foot, inch, meter,* and *yard,* which are units used to measure distance or length. In the middle box are the words *gram* and *kilogram,* which are related to the measurement of mass. And in the right box are the words *A.M. elapsed time, hour, minute,* and *P.M.,* which are related to the measurement of time.

▶ Understand Vocabulary

Introduce new words for this chapter.

1. A **fluid ounce** is the smallest customary unit for measuring liquid volume.
2. A **line plot** is a graph that shows the frequency of data along a number line.
3. A **ton** is a customary unit used to measure weight.
4. A **second** is a small unit of time.
5. A **decimeter** is a metric unit for measuring length or distance.

School-Home Letter available in English and Spanish, *Standards Practice Book*, pp. P219–P220

Intervention Options RtI Response to Intervention

Use Show What You Know, Lesson Quick Check, and Assessments to diagnose students' intervention levels.

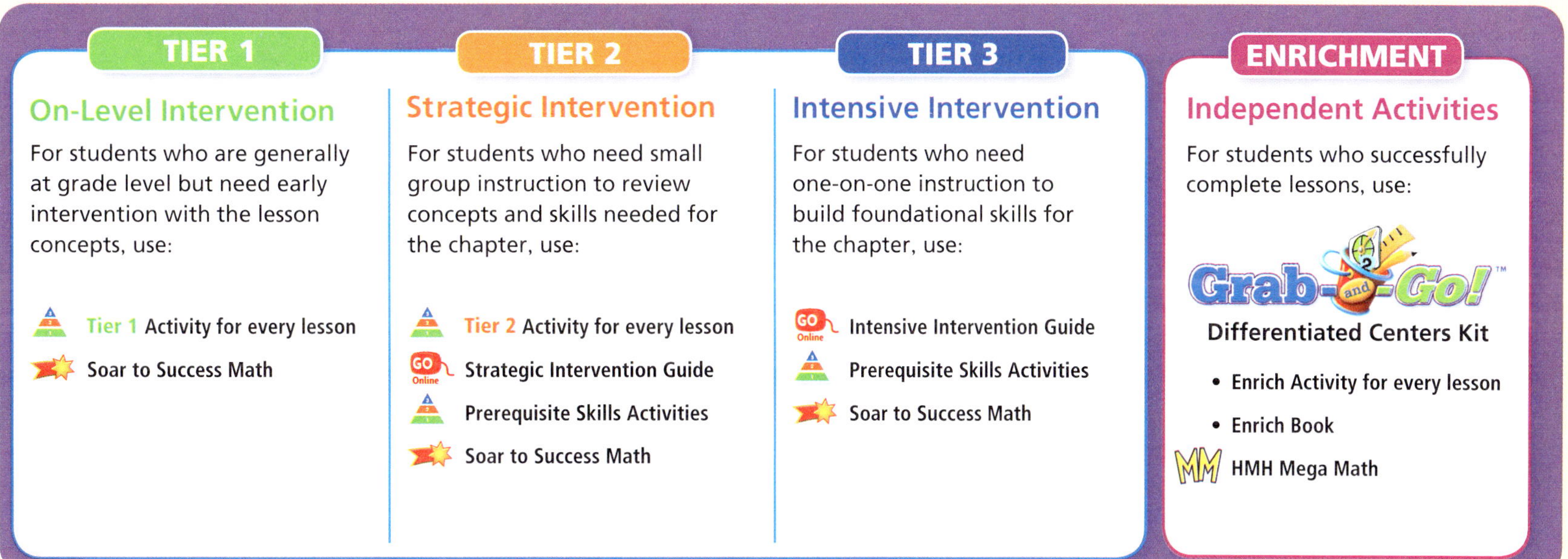

TIER 1

On-Level Intervention

For students who are generally at grade level but need early intervention with the lesson concepts, use:

- Tier 1 Activity for every lesson
- Soar to Success Math

TIER 2

Strategic Intervention

For students who need small group instruction to review concepts and skills needed for the chapter, use:

- Tier 2 Activity for every lesson
- Strategic Intervention Guide
- Prerequisite Skills Activities
- Soar to Success Math

TIER 3

Intensive Intervention

For students who need one-on-one instruction to build foundational skills for the chapter, use:

- Intensive Intervention Guide
- Prerequisite Skills Activities
- Soar to Success Math

ENRICHMENT

Independent Activities

For students who successfully complete lessons, use:

Grab-and-Go!™ Differentiated Centers Kit

- Enrich Activity for every lesson
- Enrich Book

HMH Mega Math

LESSON 12.1

Measurement Benchmarks

LESSON AT A GLANCE

Common Core Standard

Solve problems involving measurement and conversion of measurements from a larger unit to a smaller unit.

CC.4.MD.1 Know relative sizes of measurement units within one system of units including km, m, cm; kg, g; lb, oz.; l, ml; hr, min, sec. Within a single system of measurement, express measurements in a larger unit in terms of a smaller unit. Record measurement equivalents in a two-column table.

Materials

MathBoard

Lesson Objective

Use benchmarks to understand the relative sizes of measurement units.

Essential Question

How can you use benchmarks to understand the relative sizes of measurement units?

Vocabulary

kilometer, **mile**

Digital Path

HMH Mega Math

eStudent Edition

COMMON CORE PROFESSIONAL DEVELOPMENT

About the Math

Why Teach This Lesson 1 explores the concept of using benchmarks. A benchmark is an informal standard that is used to gain a sense of a measurement.

Using benchmarks correctly is a valuable skill for students. In many careers and real-world activities, using benchmarks can help make measurement easier. For example, a baker might know that a flour scoop holds about 1 cup, so she can find the volume of a mixing bowl by counting the number of scoops it takes to fill the bowl.

In this lesson, students will work with units of length, liquid volume, weight, and mass. The goal is for students to use benchmarks to understand the relative sizes of measurement units.

Professional Development Video Podcasts

Daily Routines

Common Core

SPIRAL REVIEW

Problem of the Day

eTransparency 12.1

Test Prep Carlos had $20. He bought a DVD for $13.86. How much money does Carlos have left?

Ⓐ $5.14
Ⓑ $6.14
Ⓒ $6.86
Ⓓ $33.86

Vocabulary Builder

	mile	kilometer
customary unit	Y	N
metric unit	N	Y
used to measure length	Y	Y

Semantic Feature Analysis helps students develop a link between words they know and conceptually similar words. Students should take new vocabulary words and use the chart to analyze similarities and differences between them. Y (yes), N (no), true, or false can be used in each cell to indicate whether the attribute is associated with the term or to answer a question about the term.

Literature

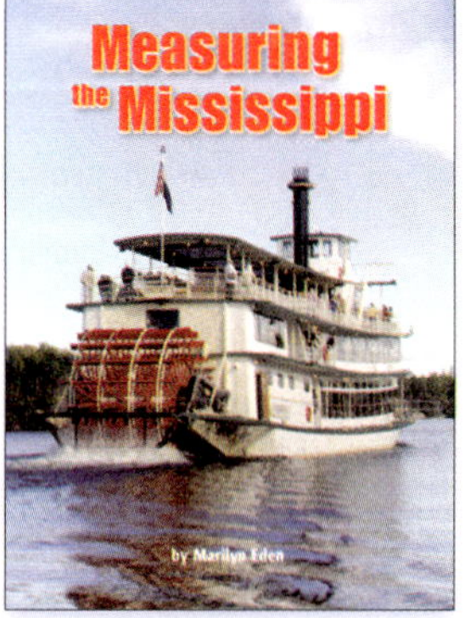

Measuring the Mississippi

From the Grab-and-Go™ Differentiated Centers Kit

Students read about the different measurements that can be observed on a paddleboat trip down the Mississippi river.

Differentiated Instruction Activities

ELL Language Support

Auditory / Kinesthetic
Small Group

Strategy: Explore Context

Materials 12-inch rulers, yardstick

- Students may not be familiar with customary units of measure if they previously lived in another country.
- Show students customary tools for measuring length.

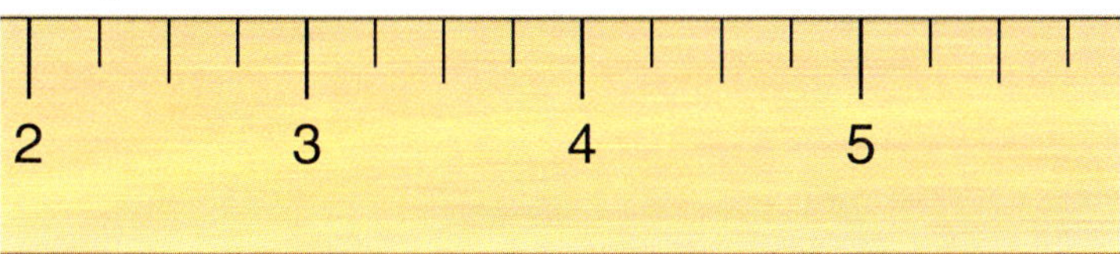

- Have students find benchmarks that are meaningful to them for estimating the size of an inch, foot, and yard.
- Have students use their benchmarks to estimate the lengths of objects in the room. Then measure to see how close they are.

See ELL Activity Guide for leveled activities.

Enrich

Visual / Kinesthetic
Individual

Materials rulers, scales, poster boards, markers

- Students should choose a type of measurement, like length, mass, weight, or liquid volume. For their measurement, they should list 5 common units, such as a pound, gram, foot, or ton.
- They should then find three objects that have the same or about half of that measure.

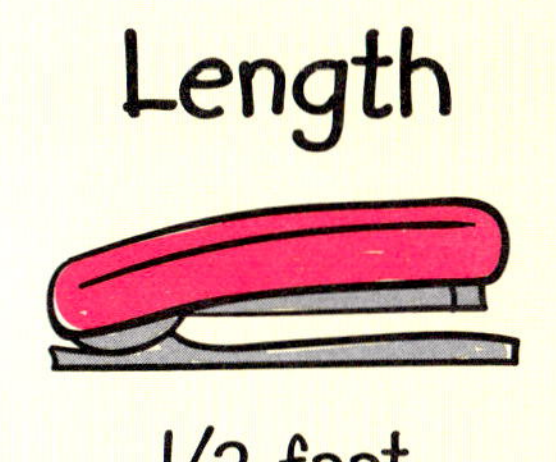

- On a poster board, they should display the pictures or drawings of the objects they chose for the units. Display the poster boards around the classroom for students to use as benchmark references when estimating measurements.

RtI Response to Intervention

Reteach Tier 1

Visual / Kinesthetic
Whole Class / Small Group

Materials ruler, yardstick, ruler (meter), classroom objects

- Have each group choose two classroom objects to estimate in length. Have them name the unit and the tool for each object.
- Ask groups to estimate each length and describe why they choose the unit and tool. Possible answer: the stapler was about 8 inches. Since the fish tank is about double the length of the stapler, the length is about double 8 inches. So, we could measure the fish tank in inches or feet.

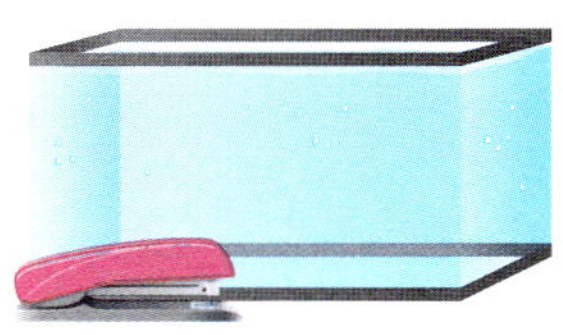

- Groups should do this with several objects or lengths.

Tier 2

Visual / Kinesthetic
Small Group

Materials ruler, notebook paper

- Show students the ruler. **How long is this?** 1 foot
- Have students measure the length of a sheet of notebook paper. 11 inches
- **Is the paper's length near 1 foot?** yes
- Have students find other objects in the classroom that are close to the same length as the paper. Then have them find objects that are about twice the length of the paper.
- Discuss how using the sheet of paper makes it easier to determine the length of an object without actually measuring.

COMMON CORE **CC.4.MD.1** Know relative sizes of measurement units within one system of units including km, m, cm; kg, g; lb, oz.; l, ml; hr, min, sec. Within a single system of measurement, express measurements in a larger unit in terms of a smaller unit. Record measurement equivalents in a two-column table.

1 ENGAGE

Draw a long horizontal line segment on the board. While students sit at their desks, have them discuss different ways to estimate the length of the segment. For example, a student says, "I think that the door to our classroom is about 7 feet tall, and the segment doesn't seem to be quite that long, so I estimate its length to be 6 feet."

2 TEACH and TALK

▶ Unlock the Problem

Is 4 yards a reasonable estimate for the length of a bicycle? Read and solve the problem to learn the answer.

Have students consider the *Customary Units of Length* chart. Make sure students understand that the baseball bat is being used as a benchmark. Point out that benchmarks aren't designed to give us precise measurements; instead, we use them in a general way to compare.

▶ Example 1

Discuss the problems and possible solutions. Then give students an opportunity to suggest other real-world examples of benchmarks and how they can be used for length, liquid volume, and weight.

Use **Math Talk** to focus on students' understanding of the relative sizes of customary units of weight.

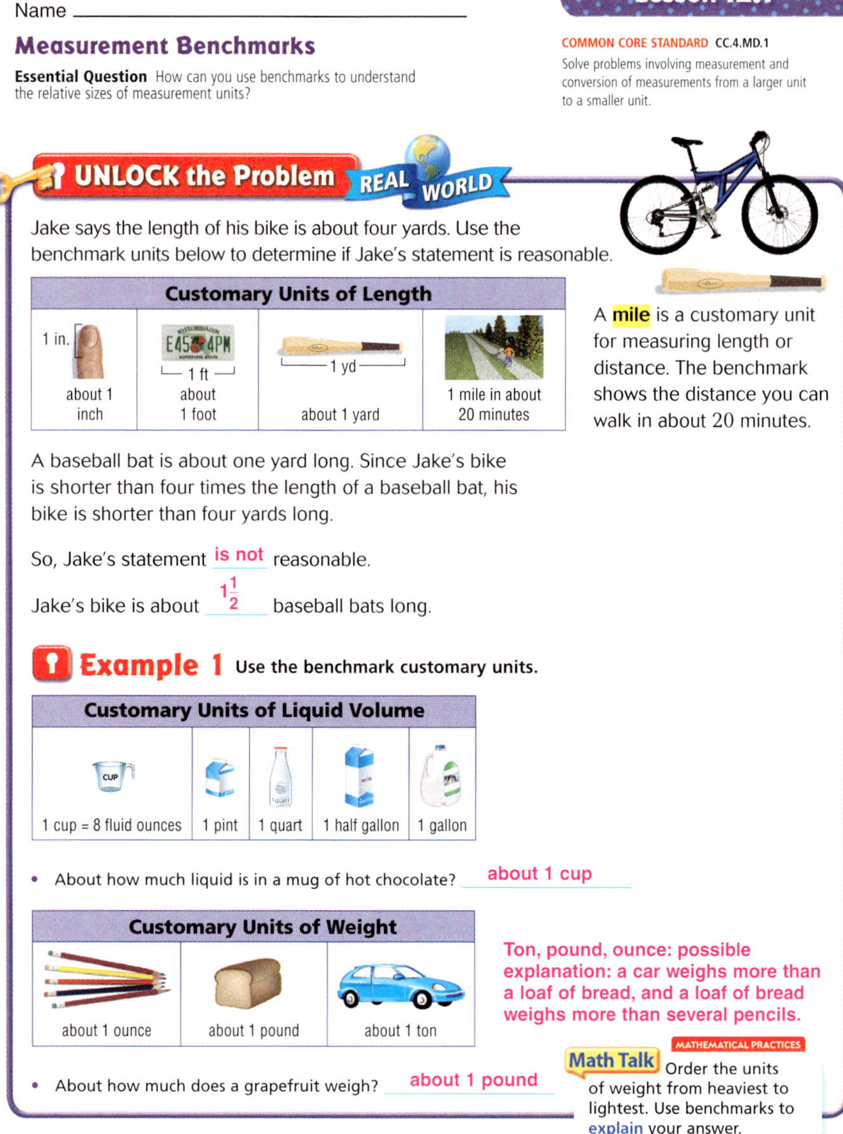

Lesson 12.1

Name ____________

Measurement Benchmarks

Essential Question How can you use benchmarks to understand the relative sizes of measurement units?

COMMON CORE STANDARD CC.4.MD.1
Solve problems involving measurement and conversion of measurements from a larger unit to a smaller unit.

UNLOCK the Problem REAL WORLD

Jake says the length of his bike is about four yards. Use the benchmark units below to determine if Jake's statement is reasonable.

Customary Units of Length			
1 in. about 1 inch	1 ft about 1 foot	1 yd about 1 yard	1 mile in about 20 minutes

A **mile** is a customary unit for measuring length or distance. The benchmark shows the distance you can walk in about 20 minutes.

A baseball bat is about one yard long. Since Jake's bike is shorter than four times the length of a baseball bat, his bike is shorter than four yards long.

So, Jake's statement is not reasonable.

Jake's bike is about $1\frac{1}{2}$ baseball bats long.

Example 1 Use the benchmark customary units.

Customary Units of Liquid Volume				
1 cup = 8 fluid ounces	1 pint	1 quart	1 half gallon	1 gallon

- About how much liquid is in a mug of hot chocolate? about 1 cup

Customary Units of Weight		
about 1 ounce	about 1 pound	about 1 ton

Ton, pound, ounce: possible explanation: a car weighs more than a loaf of bread, and a loaf of bread weighs more than several pencils.

- About how much does a grapefruit weigh? about 1 pound

Math Talk MATHEMATICAL PRACTICES Order the units of weight from heaviest to lightest. Use benchmarks to **explain** your answer.

© Houghton Mifflin Harcourt Publishing Company

Chapter 12 445

Standards Practice 12.1

Lesson 12.1

Name ____________

Measurement Benchmarks

COMMON CORE STANDARD CC.4.MD.1
Solve problems involving measurement and conversion of measurements from a larger unit to a smaller unit.

Use benchmarks to choose the customary unit you would use to measure each.

1. height of a computer foot
2. weight of a table pound
3. length of a semi-truck yard
4. the amount of liquid a bathtub holds gallon

Customary Units	
ounce	yard
pound	mile
inch	gallon
foot	cup

Use benchmarks to choose the metric unit you would use to measure each.

5. mass of a grasshopper gram
6. the amount of liquid a water bottle holds liter
7. length of a soccer field meter
8. length of a pencil centimeter

Metric Units	
milliliter	centimeter
liter	meter
gram	kilometer
kilogram	

Circle the better estimate.

9. mass of a chicken egg (50 grams) 50 kilograms
10. length of a car 12 miles (12 feet)
11. amount of liquid a drinking glass holds (8 ounces) 8 quarts

Complete the sentence. Write *more* or *less*.

12. A camera has a length of more than one centimeter.
13. A bowling ball weighs more than one pound.

Problem Solving REAL WORLD

14. What is the better estimate for the mass of a textbook, 1 gram or 1 kilogram? 1 kilogram
15. What is the better estimate for the height of a desk, 1 meter or 1 kilometer? 1 meter

© Houghton Mifflin Harcourt Publishing Company

Chapter 12 P221

Common Core SPIRAL REVIEW

TEST PREP

Lesson Check (CC.4.MD.1)

1. Which is the best estimate for the weight of a stapler?
   - Ⓐ 4 ounces
   - Ⓑ 4 pounds
   - Ⓒ 4 inches
   - Ⓓ 4 feet
2. Which is the best estimate for the length of a car?
   - Ⓐ 4 kilometers
   - Ⓑ 4 tons
   - Ⓒ 4 kilograms
   - Ⓓ 4 meters

Spiral Review (CC.4.NF.4c, CC.4.NF.6, CC.4.MD.5a, CC.4.MD.5b, CC.4.G.2)

3. Bart practices his trumpet $1\frac{1}{4}$ hours each day. How many hours will he practice in 6 days? (Lesson 8.4)
   - Ⓐ $8\frac{2}{4}$ hours
   - Ⓑ $7\frac{2}{4}$ hours
   - Ⓒ 7 hours
   - Ⓓ $6\frac{2}{4}$ hours
4. Millie collected 100 stamps from different countries. Thirty-two of the stamps are from countries in Africa. What is $\frac{32}{100}$ written as a decimal? (Lesson 9.2)
   - Ⓐ 32
   - Ⓑ 3.2
   - Ⓒ 0.32
   - Ⓓ 0.032
5. Diedre drew a quadrilateral with 4 right angles and 4 sides of the same length. What kind of polygon did Diedre draw? (Lesson 10.4)
   - Ⓐ square
   - Ⓑ trapezoid
   - Ⓒ hexagon
   - Ⓓ pentagon
6. How many degrees are in an angle that turns through $\frac{1}{2}$ of a circle? (Lesson 11.2)
   - Ⓐ 60°
   - Ⓑ 90°
   - Ⓒ 120°
   - Ⓓ 180°

© Houghton Mifflin Harcourt Publishing Company

P222

Benchmarks for Metric Units The metric system is based on place value. Each unit is 10 times as large as the next smaller unit. Below are some common metric benchmarks.

Example 2 Use the benchmark metric units.

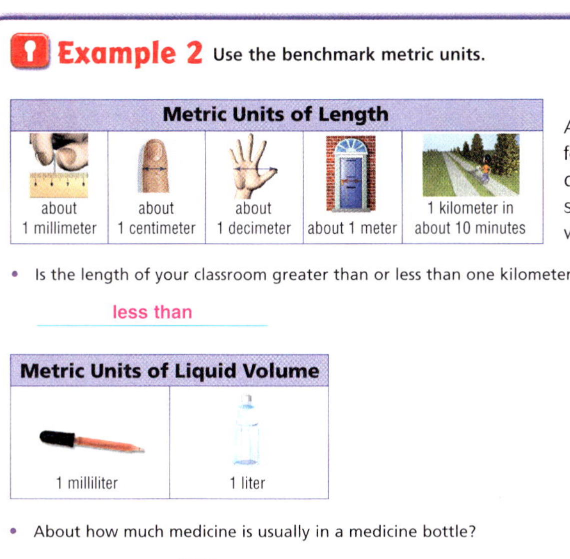

Metric Units of Length				
about 1 millimeter	about 1 centimeter	about 1 decimeter	about 1 meter	1 kilometer in about 10 minutes

A **kilometer** is a metric unit for measuring length or distance. The benchmark shows the distance you can walk in about 10 minutes.

- Is the length of your classroom greater than or less than one kilometer?

  less than

Metric Units of Liquid Volume	
1 milliliter	1 liter

- About how much medicine is usually in a medicine bottle?

  about 120 milliliters

Metric Units of Mass	
about 1 gram	about 1 kilogram

- About how much is the mass of a paper clip?

  about a gram

Possible explanation: I can compare different benchmarks with what I am measuring to see which one would be the best to use. Then I can choose the unit that is closest to that benchmark.

MATHEMATICAL PRACTICES

Math Talk **Explain** how benchmark measurements can help you decide which unit to use when measuring.

© Houghton Mifflin Harcourt Publishing Company

Benchmarks for Metric Units

Point out that the metric system is the primary measurement system in most countries of the world.

▶ Example 2

Have students review the *Metric Units of Length* chart.

- **How do the units of length compare as we move from left to right in the chart?** The units become greater, or longer.
- **How does a centimeter compare to a millimeter? How does it compare to a meter?** A centimeter is greater (longer) than a millimeter and less (shorter) than a meter.

Discuss the charts for *Metric Units of Liquid Volume* and *Metric Units of Mass*.

- **How does a liter compare to a milliliter?** A liter is greater than a milliliter.
- **To determine the mass of an envelope, would grams or kilograms be better to use? Why?** Possible answer: grams; a dollar bill is about 1 gram, and an envelope will have about the same mass as a dollar bill. The mass of a baseball bat is much greater than the mass of an envelope. So, it wouldn't make sense to use kilograms.

Use **Math Talk** to focus on students' understanding of choosing appropriate units for measurement. Ask students to include an example to support their answers.

Reteach 12.1

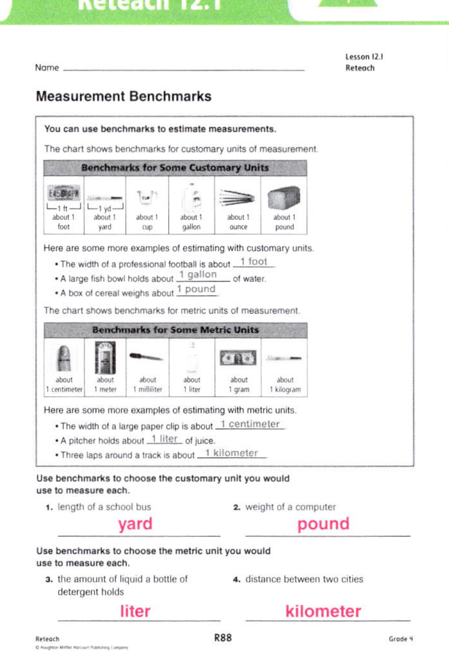

Name ______________________ Lesson 12.1 Reteach

Measurement Benchmarks

You can use benchmarks to estimate measurements.

The chart shows benchmarks for customary units of measurement.

Benchmarks for Some Customary Units					
1 ft about 1 foot	1 yd about 1 yard	about 1 cup	about 1 gallon	about 1 ounce	about 1 pound

Here are some more examples of estimating with customary units.

- The width of a professional football is about 1 foot.
- A large fish bowl holds about 1 gallon of water.
- A box of cereal weighs about 1 pound.

The chart shows benchmarks for metric units of measurement.

Benchmarks for Some Metric Units					
about 1 centimeter	about 1 meter	about 1 milliliter	about 1 liter	about 1 gram	about 1 kilogram

Here are some more examples of estimating with metric units.

- The width of a large paper clip is about 1 centimeter.
- A pitcher holds about 1 liter of juice.
- Three laps around a track is about 1 kilometer.

Use benchmarks to choose the customary unit you would use to measure each.

1. length of a school bus yard
2. weight of a computer pound

Use benchmarks to choose the metric unit you would use to measure each.

3. the amount of liquid a bottle of detergent holds liter
4. distance between two cities kilometer

Reteach R88 Grade 4
© Houghton Mifflin Harcourt Publishing Company

Enrich 12.1

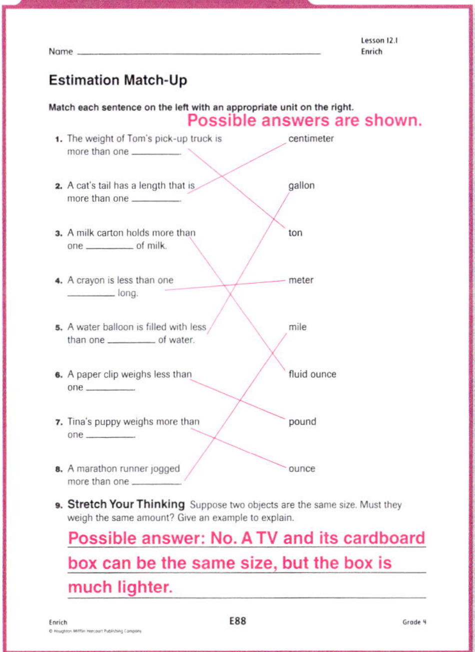

Name ______________________ Lesson 12.1 Enrich

Estimation Match-Up

Match each sentence on the left with an appropriate unit on the right.

Possible answers are shown.

1. The weight of Tom's pick-up truck is more than one ________. — centimeter
2. A cat's tail has a length that is more than one ________. — gallon
3. A milk carton holds more than one ________ of milk. — ton
4. A crayon is less than one ________ long. — meter
5. A water balloon is filled with less than one ________ of water. — mile
6. A paper clip weighs less than one ________. — fluid ounce
7. Tina's puppy weighs more than one ________. — pound
8. A marathon runner jogged more than one ________. — ounce
9. **Stretch Your Thinking** Suppose two objects are the same size. Must they weigh the same amount? Give an example to explain.

   Possible answer: No. A TV and its cardboard box can be the same size, but the box is much lighter.

Enrich E88 Grade 4
© Houghton Mifflin Harcourt Publishing Company

COMMON ERRORS

Error To estimate, students choose a benchmark that is too small.

Example A finger is the benchmark chosen to estimate the width of a desk.

Springboard to Learning Remind students that benchmarks are used to estimate, and not find actual measures—point out that we use tools such as rulers and scales for those measurements. Lead students to understand that if it takes a great deal of time to use a benchmark, a larger benchmark should be chosen.

3 PRACTICE 

▶ Share and Show • Guided Practice

The first problem connects to the learning model. Have students use the MathBoard to explain their thinking.

Use Exercises 2 and 5 for Quick Check. Students should use their MathBoards to show their solutions.

Use Math Talk to focus on students' understanding of choosing reasonable units of length.

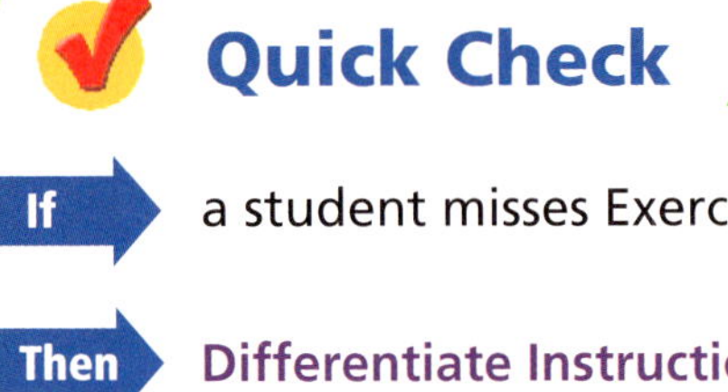

If a student misses Exercises 2 and 5

Then Differentiate Instruction with
- Reteach Activity p. 445B
- Reteach 12.1
- Soar to Success 42.09, 42.10, 43.11, 43.12

▶ On Your Own • Independent Practice

Invite volunteers to share their answers with the class. To offer more benchmark practice, have students choose appropriate customary benchmarks for Exercises 1 and 2, and appropriate metric benchmarks for Exercises 6 and 7. Remind students that mass is a metric measure and weight is a customary measure.

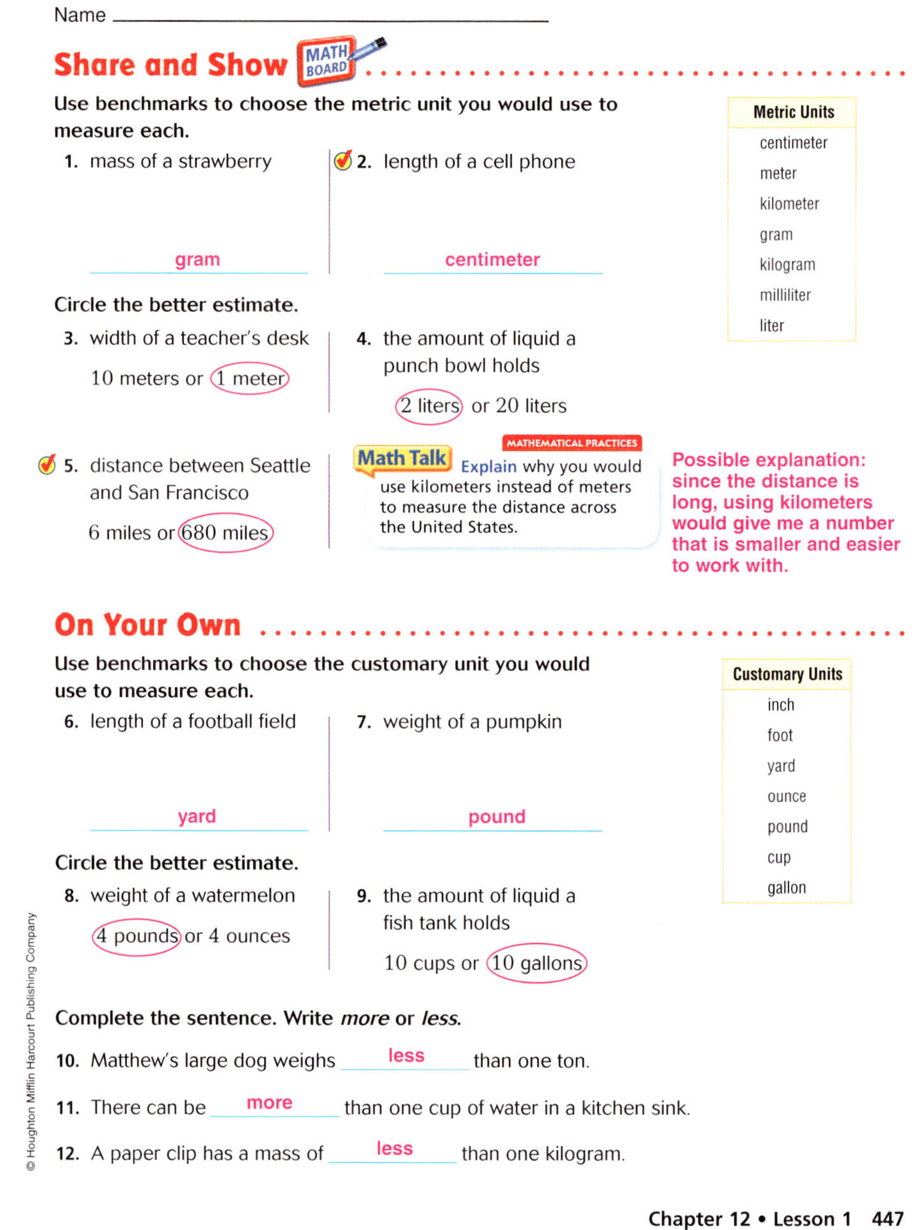

Name ____________

Share and Show MATH BOARD

Use benchmarks to choose the metric unit you would use to measure each.

Metric Units
centimeter
meter
kilometer
gram
kilogram
milliliter
liter

1. mass of a strawberry gram
2. length of a cell phone centimeter

Circle the better estimate.

3. width of a teacher's desk
   10 meters or (1 meter)
4. the amount of liquid a punch bowl holds
   (2 liters) or 20 liters
5. distance between Seattle and San Francisco
   6 miles or (680 miles)

Math Talk MATHEMATICAL PRACTICES Explain why you would use kilometers instead of meters to measure the distance across the United States.

Possible explanation: since the distance is long, using kilometers would give me a number that is smaller and easier to work with.

On Your Own

Use benchmarks to choose the customary unit you would use to measure each.

Customary Units
inch
foot
yard
ounce
pound
cup
gallon

6. length of a football field yard
7. weight of a pumpkin pound

Circle the better estimate.

8. weight of a watermelon
   (4 pounds) or 4 ounces
9. the amount of liquid a fish tank holds
   10 cups or (10 gallons)

Complete the sentence. Write *more* or *less*.

10. Matthew's large dog weighs less than one ton.
11. There can be more than one cup of water in a kitchen sink.
12. A paper clip has a mass of less than one kilogram.

© Houghton Mifflin Harcourt Publishing Company

Chapter 12 • Lesson 1 447

Extend the Math Activity

Check Your Benchmarks

Materials pan balance, nickels, small classroom objects

Investigate Students have learned to use benchmarks to measure items. In this activity, they will use a benchmark to estimate measurements and then check to see how close their estimates are to the actual measurements.

- Explain that a nickel has a mass of 5 grams.
- Have students estimate the mass of several classroom objects using the nickel as a benchmark. For example, have students estimate the mass of a small box of crayons.
- Have them place the object on one side of the pan balance and add nickels until the sides are balanced. Students should count the nickels to determine the object's mass using the benchmark. Then have students multiply by 5 to find the mass of the box of crayons in grams.

Summarize Discuss with students how their estimates compared to the actual mass of each object. Point out that a benchmark is not expected to provide exact measurements, but that it provides a good way to get a close measurement without actually measuring the object.

Model • Reason • Make Sense

Problem Solving REAL WORLD

Solve. For 13–15, use benchmarks to explain your answer.

13. Cristina is making macaroni and cheese for her family. Would Cristina use 1 pound of macaroni or 1 ounce of macaroni?

    1 pound; Cristina would need more pasta than 5 pencils worth.

14. Which is the better estimate for the length of a kitchen table, 200 centimeters or 200 meters?

    200 centimeters; a kitchen table is less than the width of 200 doors.

15. Amy thinks her dog weighs about 15 tons. Is this a reasonable estimate?

    No. 15 tons is too much. A dog weighs less than a car.

16. H.O.T. Write Math Dalton used benchmarks to estimate that there are more cups than quarts in one gallon. Is Dalton's estimate reasonable? Explain.

    Yes. Possible explanation: cups are smaller than quarts, so there would be more cups in a gallon.

17. Test Prep Which is the best estimate for a dose of medicine?

    (A) 2 milliliters (C) 2 millimeters
    (B) 2 liters (D) 2 meters

SHOW YOUR WORK

© Houghton Mifflin Harcourt Publishing Company

FOR MORE PRACTICE: Standards Practice Book, pp. P221–P222

FOR EXTRA PRACTICE: Standards Practice Book, p. P243

Problem Solving

Discuss and complete Exercises 13–16.

Go Deeper

Challenge students to explain how to change Exercises 13–15 so that the opposite answer is true. For Exercise 15, change "her dog" to "a dump truck" and the answer becomes "yes."

Test Prep Coach

Test Prep Coach helps teachers to identify common errors that students can make.

In Exercise 17, if students selected:

B They used the wrong size benchmark.
C or **D** They used the wrong type of measurement.

Essential Question

How can you use benchmarks to understand the relative sizes of measurement units?

Possible answer: when I know the size of one object, I can use it as a benchmark to find the sizes of other objects. For example, if I know that a baseball bat is 1 yard long, I can tell that the length of a car is about 5 baseball bats long, or 5 yards long.

Math Journal

Use benchmarks to determine the customary and metric units you would use to measure the height of your house. Explain your answer.

Differentiated Instruction

INDEPENDENT ACTIVITIES

Grab-and-Go!™

Differentiated Centers Kit

Activities

Measure Up

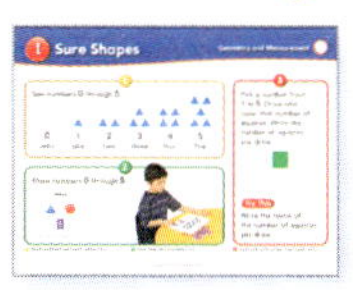

Students complete blue Activity Card 1 by comparing lengths.

Literature

Measuring the Mississippi

Students read about the different measurements that can be observed on a paddleboat trip down the Mississippi river.

LESSON 12.2

Customary Units of Length

LESSON AT A GLANCE

Common Core Standard

Solve problems involving measurement and conversion of measurements from a larger unit to a smaller unit.

CC.4.MD.1 Know relative sizes of measurement units within one system of units including km, m, cm; kg, g; lb, oz.; l, ml; hr, min, sec. Within a single system of measurement, express measurements in a larger unit in terms of a smaller unit. Record measurement equivalents in a two-column table.

Also CC.4.MD.2

Lesson Objective

Use models to compare customary units of length.

Essential Question

How can you use models to compare customary units of length?

Materials MathBoard, 1-Inch Grid Paper (see *eTeacher Resources*), scissors, tape

Digital Path

- Animated Math Models
- *i*Tools: Measurement
- HMH Mega Math
- eStudent Edition

About the Math

Why Teach This The customary system of measurement is used throughout the United States. It is important for students to understand the relationship between units in a system of units they use in daily life.

In this lesson, students use models to learn the relationship between inches, feet, and yards. They use 1-inch tiles to build 1 foot and then compare 1 foot to 1 inch. Students find that 1 foot is 12 times the size of 1 inch.

Students then use a table to relate feet and inches. Then students use fraction tiles to understand that 1 inch is $\frac{1}{12}$ of a foot.

Professional Development Video Podcasts

Daily Routines

Common Core

SPIRAL REVIEW

Problem of the Day

eTransparency 12.2

Test Prep Diane estimates the width of the classroom door. Which is the best estimate of the door's width?

Ⓐ 30 inches Ⓒ 30 yards
Ⓑ 30 feet Ⓓ 30 miles

Fluency Builder

Division Facts Write the following division facts on the board and have students find the answers as quickly as possible. Students can check their answers with a partner.

100 ÷ 10 = 10	56 ÷ 8 = 7
36 ÷ 4 = 9	42 ÷ 7 = 6
24 ÷ 8 = 3	60 ÷ 6 = 10
81 ÷ 9 = 9	49 ÷ 7 = 7
20 ÷ 4 = 5	40 ÷ 8 = 5
72 ÷ 9 = 8	48 ÷ 6 = 8
63 ÷ 7 = 9	36 ÷ 6 = 6
28 ÷ 4 = 7	18 ÷ 3 = 6

Differentiated Instruction Activities

ELL Language Support

Auditory / Visual
Small Group

Strategy: **Explore Concepts**

Materials 12-inch ruler, yardstick

- The terms *foot* and *yard* can be confusing to English language learners because of their multiple meanings.
- Tell students that *foot* and *yard* have different meanings in math. Point to your foot and show a foot-long ruler. Ask students to identify the foot used in math. Have students describe how each foot is different.
- Draw a picture of a house with a yard, and show a yardstick. Ask students to identify the yard used in math and discuss differences.

See ELL Activity Guide for leveled activities.

Enrich

Logical / Mathematical
Individual

- Have students research other units of length, such as a hand (4 inches), a fathom (6 feet), and a furlong (220 yards).
- Students can describe in what situations the unit is used and show its relationship to inches, feet, and/or yards using a model.

1 hand			
1 inch	1 inch	1 inch	1 inch

RtI Response to Intervention

Reteach Tier 1

Visual / Kinesthetic
Whole Class / Partner

Materials 1-Inch Grid Paper (see *eTeacher Resources*), scissors, tape

- **Edwin has 2 feet of ribbon. He needs 18 inches to decorate a flag. Does Edwin have enough ribbon?**
- Have partners cut out 18 one-inch tiles from grid paper and tape them end to end. **What does this represent?** 18 inches, the amount of ribbon Edwin needs
- Now have each partner cut out and tape 12 one-inch tiles so each student builds 1 foot. Have partners tape the two 1-foot lengths together. **What does this represent?** 2 feet, the amount of ribbon Edwin has
- **Does Edwin have enough ribbon? Explain.** Yes. Possible explanation: 2 feet is 24 inches. Edwin needs 18 inches. Since 24 inches > 18 inches, Edwin has enough.

Tier 2

Visual / Kinesthetic
Small Group

Materials Number Lines (see *eTeacher Resources*), color pencils

- Have students compare the size of a foot to the size an inch using a number line.
- Have students divide a number line into 12 equal parts and mark 0 to 12 below the number line for inches. Have students mark 0 to 1 above the number line for feet.
- Have students shade 1 foot using a color pencil. Then using a different color, have them shade 1 inch.

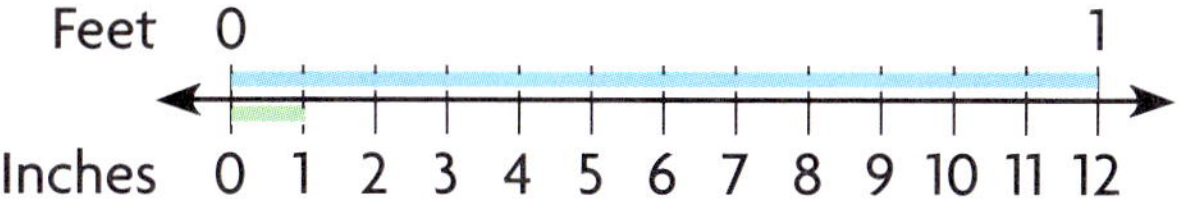

LESSON 12.2

CC.4.MD.1 Know relative sizes of measurement units within one system of units including km, m, cm; kg, g; lb, oz.; l, ml; hr, min, sec. Within a single system of measurement, express measurements in a larger unit in terms of a smaller unit. Record measurement equivalents in a two-column table.

1 ENGAGE

Materials inch rulers

Access Prior Knowledge Have students use an inch ruler to measure the lengths of several objects in the classroom to the nearest half inch.

- **How do you use a ruler to measure a length to the nearest half-inch?** Possible answer: line up the end of the ruler with the end of the length to be measured. Then find where the length of the object ends on the ruler. Read the measure to the nearest $\frac{1}{2}$-inch.

2 TEACH and TALK

▶ Unlock the Problem

Discuss the customary units of length: inch, foot, and yard.

- **How many inches are in 1 foot?** 12 inches
- **How many feet are in 1 yard?** 3 feet

▶ Activity

Discuss the activity with the class.

- **In Step 2, why do you use 12 one-inch tiles?** Possible answer: we are building 1 foot, and there are 12 inches in 1 foot.
- **Why is it important to place the tiles end-to-end with no space in between or no overlap?** Possible answer: if there was more space in between the tiles or if the tiles overlapped, then we would not measure accurately.
- **In Step 3, how does the size of 1 foot compare to the size of 1 inch?** Possible answer: 1 foot is 12 times the size of 1 inch because 12 one-inch tiles build 1 foot.

Use **Math Talk** to focus on students' understanding of how many inches would be needed to make 1 yard.

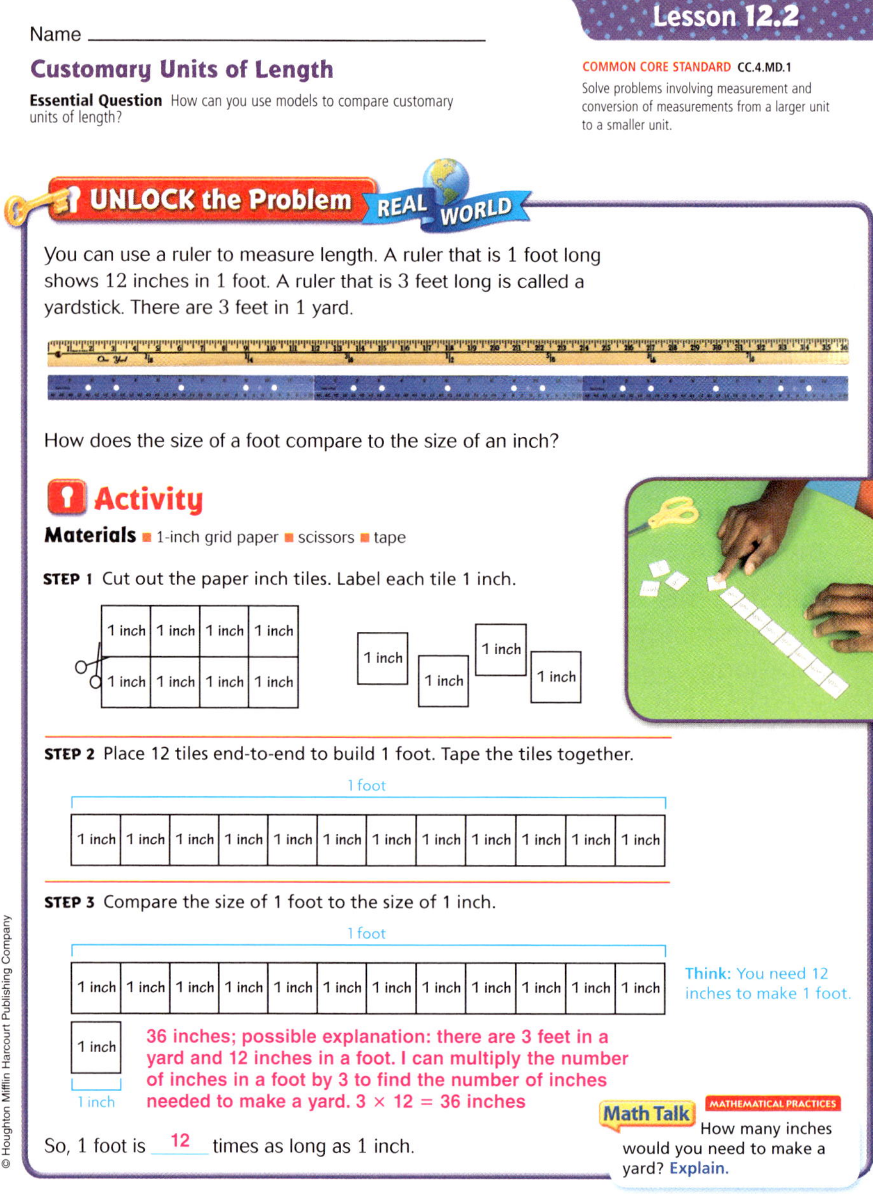

Lesson 12.2

Name ____________

Customary Units of Length

Essential Question How can you use models to compare customary units of length?

COMMON CORE STANDARD CC.4.MD.1
Solve problems involving measurement and conversion of measurements from a larger unit to a smaller unit.

UNLOCK the Problem REAL WORLD

You can use a ruler to measure length. A ruler that is 1 foot long shows 12 inches in 1 foot. A ruler that is 3 feet long is called a yardstick. There are 3 feet in 1 yard.

How does the size of a foot compare to the size of an inch?

Activity

Materials ■ 1-inch grid paper ■ scissors ■ tape

STEP 1 Cut out the paper inch tiles. Label each tile 1 inch.

STEP 2 Place 12 tiles end-to-end to build 1 foot. Tape the tiles together.

STEP 3 Compare the size of 1 foot to the size of 1 inch.

Think: You need 12 inches to make 1 foot.

36 inches; possible explanation: there are 3 feet in a yard and 12 inches in a foot. I can multiply the number of inches in a foot by 3 to find the number of inches needed to make a yard. $3 \times 12 = 36$ inches

So, 1 foot is __12__ times as long as 1 inch.

Math Talk MATHEMATICAL PRACTICES How many inches would you need to make a yard? **Explain.**

© Houghton Mifflin Harcourt Publishing Company

Chapter 12 449

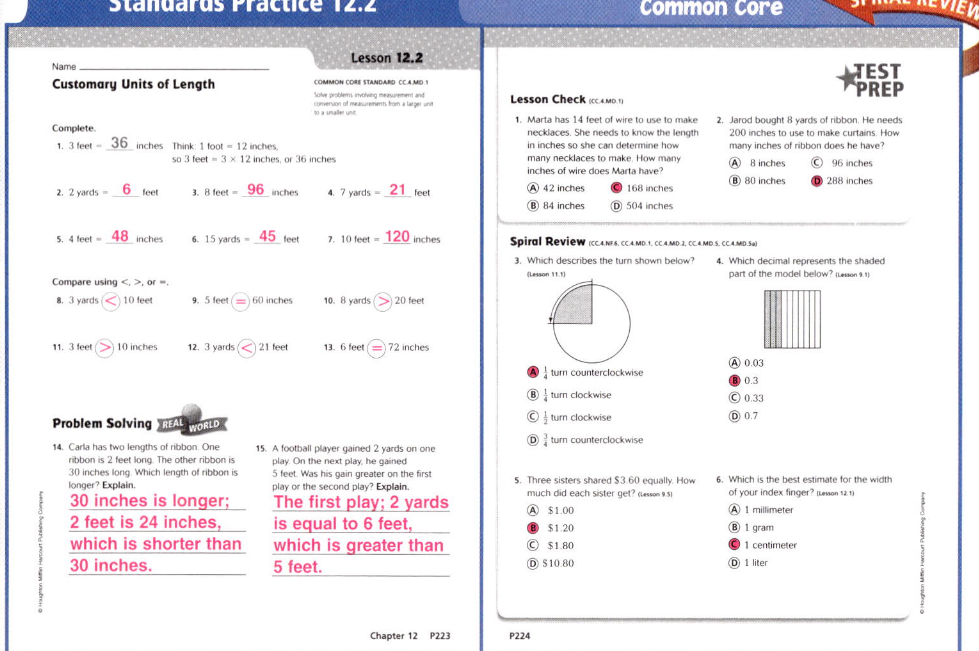

Standards Practice 12.2

Lesson 12.2

Name ____________

Customary Units of Length

COMMON CORE STANDARD CC.4.MD.1
Solve problems involving measurement and conversion of measurements from a larger unit to a smaller unit.

Complete.

1. 3 feet = __36__ inches Think: 1 foot = 12 inches, so 3 feet = 3 × 12 inches, or 36 inches
2. 2 yards = __6__ feet
3. 8 feet = __96__ inches
4. 7 yards = __21__ feet
5. 4 feet = __48__ inches
6. 15 yards = __45__ feet
7. 10 feet = __120__ inches

Compare using <, >, or =.

8. 3 yards (<) 10 feet
9. 5 feet (=) 60 inches
10. 8 yards (>) 20 feet
11. 3 feet (>) 10 inches
12. 3 yards (<) 21 feet
13. 6 feet (=) 72 inches

Problem Solving REAL WORLD

14. Carla has two lengths of ribbon. One ribbon is 2 feet long. The other ribbon is 30 inches long. Which length of ribbon is longer? **Explain.**
30 inches is longer; 2 feet is 24 inches, which is shorter than 30 inches.

15. A football player gained 2 yards on one play. On the next play, he gained 5 feet. Was his gain greater on the first play or the second play? **Explain.**
The first play; 2 yards is equal to 6 feet, which is greater than 5 feet.

© Houghton Mifflin Harcourt Publishing Company

Chapter 12 P223

Common Core SPIRAL REVIEW

TEST PREP

Lesson Check (CC.4.MD.1)

1. Marta has 14 feet of wire to use to make necklaces. She needs to know the length in inches so she can determine how many necklaces to make. How many inches of wire does Marta have?
Ⓐ 42 inches Ⓑ 84 inches Ⓒ 168 inches Ⓓ 504 inches

2. Jarod bought 8 yards of ribbon. He needs 200 inches to use to make curtains. How many inches of ribbon does he have?
Ⓐ 8 inches Ⓑ 80 inches Ⓒ 96 inches Ⓓ 288 inches

Spiral Review (CC.4.NF.6, CC.4.MD.1, CC.4.MD.2, CC.4.MD.5, CC.4.MD.5a)

3. Which describes the turn shown below? (Lesson 11.1)
Ⓐ $\frac{1}{4}$ turn counterclockwise
Ⓑ $\frac{1}{4}$ turn clockwise
Ⓒ $\frac{1}{2}$ turn clockwise
Ⓓ $\frac{3}{4}$ turn counterclockwise

4. Which decimal represents the shaded part of the model below? (Lesson 9.1)
Ⓐ 0.03
Ⓑ 0.3
Ⓒ 0.33
Ⓓ 0.7

5. Three sisters shared \$3.60 equally. How much did each sister get? (Lesson 9.5)
Ⓐ \$1.00
Ⓑ \$1.20
Ⓒ \$1.80
Ⓓ \$10.80

6. Which is the best estimate for the width of your index finger? (Lesson 12.1)
Ⓐ 1 millimeter
Ⓑ 1 gram
Ⓒ 1 centimeter
Ⓓ 1 liter

© Houghton Mifflin Harcourt Publishing Company

P224

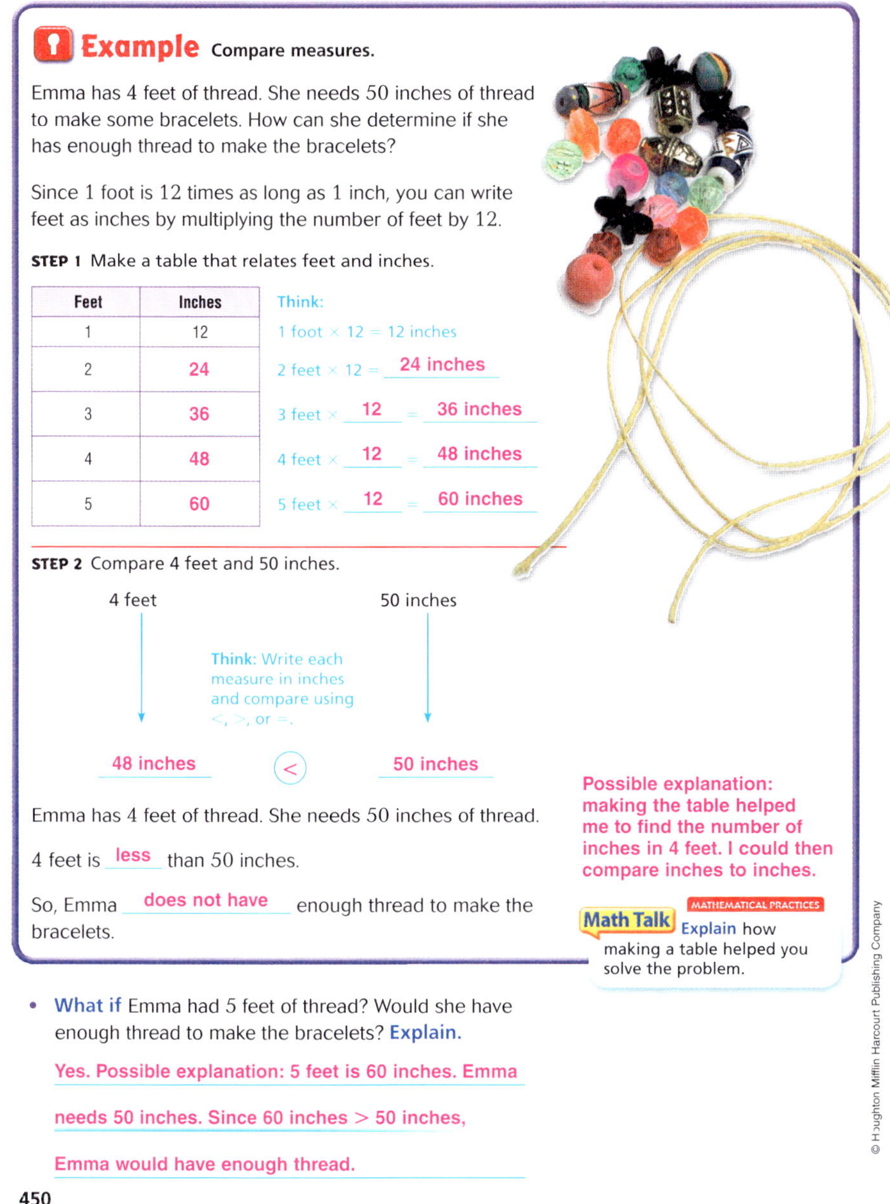

Example Compare measures.

Emma has 4 feet of thread. She needs 50 inches of thread to make some bracelets. How can she determine if she has enough thread to make the bracelets?

Since 1 foot is 12 times as long as 1 inch, you can write feet as inches by multiplying the number of feet by 12.

STEP 1 Make a table that relates feet and inches.

Feet	Inches	Think:
1	12	1 foot × 12 = 12 inches
2	**24**	2 feet × 12 = **24 inches**
3	**36**	3 feet × **12** = **36 inches**
4	**48**	4 feet × **12** = **48 inches**
5	**60**	5 feet × **12** = **60 inches**

STEP 2 Compare 4 feet and 50 inches.

4 feet → **48 inches** | 50 inches → **50 inches**

Think: Write each measure in inches and compare using <, >, or =.

48 inches < **50 inches**

Emma has 4 feet of thread. She needs 50 inches of thread.

4 feet is **less** than 50 inches.

So, Emma **does not have** enough thread to make the bracelets.

Math Talk MATHEMATICAL PRACTICES **Explain** how making a table helped you solve the problem.

Possible explanation: making the table helped me to find the number of inches in 4 feet. I could then compare inches to inches.

- **What if** Emma had 5 feet of thread? Would she have enough thread to make the bracelets? **Explain.**

Yes. Possible explanation: 5 feet is 60 inches. Emma needs 50 inches. Since 60 inches > 50 inches, Emma would have enough thread.

450

© Houghton Mifflin Harcourt Publishing Company

▶ Example

Read and discuss the problem with the class.

- **What information do you know?** Emma has 4 feet of thread. She needs 50 inches of thread to make some bracelets.
- **What are you trying to find out?** if Emma has enough thread to make the bracelets
- **How can you solve the problem?** Possible answer: I can compare 4 feet and 50 inches by writing 4 feet as inches.
- **Why do you change the larger unit, feet, to a smaller unit, inches?** Possible answer: I need to compare the measurements using the same measurement unit. I know 1 foot is 12 times as long as 1 inch, so I can write feet as inches by multiplying the number of feet by 12. Then I can compare inches to inches.

Use **Math Talk** to focus on students' understanding of how making a table helped them solve the problem.

Go Deeper

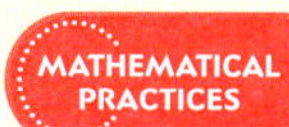

Tell students that there are 1,760 yards in 1 mile.

- **How can you use a model to find how many yards are in 3 miles?** Possible answer: I can make a table that relates miles and yards. I can think that 1 mile × 1,760 = 1,760 yards; 2 miles × 1,760 = 3,520 yards; 3 miles × 1,760 = 5,280 yards.

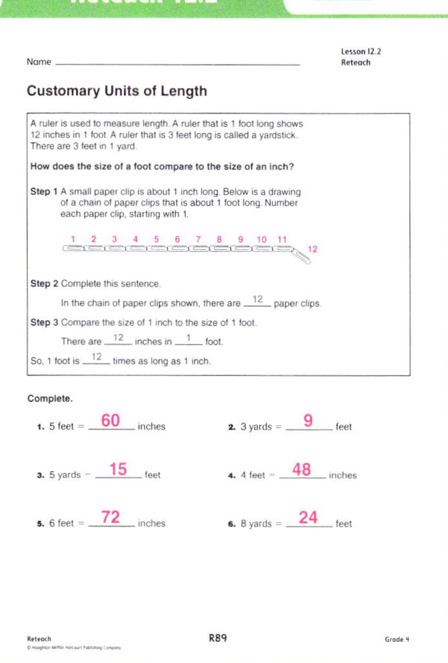

Reteach 12.2

Name ______ Lesson 12.2 Reteach

Customary Units of Length

A ruler is used to measure length. A ruler that is 1 foot long shows 12 inches in 1 foot. A ruler that is 3 feet long is called a yardstick. There are 3 feet in 1 yard.

How does the size of a foot compare to the size of an inch?

Step 1 A small paper clip is about 1 inch long. Below is a drawing of a chain of paper clips that is about 1 foot long. Number each paper clip, starting with 1.

1 2 3 4 5 6 7 8 9 10 11 12

Step 2 Complete this sentence.

In the chain of paper clips shown, there are 12 paper clips.

Step 3 Compare the size of 1 inch to the size of 1 foot.

There are 12 inches in 1 foot.

So, 1 foot is 12 times as long as 1 inch.

Complete.

1. 5 feet = **60** inches
2. 3 yards = **9** feet
3. 5 yards = **15** feet
4. 4 feet = **48** inches
5. 6 feet = **72** inches
6. 8 yards = **24** feet

Reteach R89 Grade 4

© Houghton Mifflin Harcourt Publishing Company

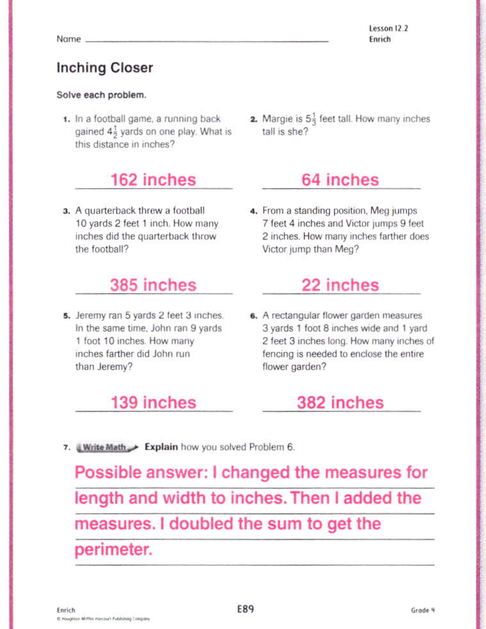

Enrich 12.2

Name ______ Lesson 12.2 Enrich

Inching Closer

Solve each problem.

1. In a football game, a running back gained $4\frac{1}{2}$ yards on one play. What is this distance in inches? **162 inches**
2. Margie is $5\frac{1}{3}$ feet tall. How many inches tall is she? **64 inches**
3. A quarterback threw a football 10 yards 2 feet 1 inch. How many inches did the quarterback throw the football? **385 inches**
4. From a standing position, Meg jumps 7 feet 4 inches and Victor jumps 9 feet 2 inches. How many inches farther does Victor jump than Meg? **22 inches**
5. Jeremy ran 5 yards 2 feet 3 inches. In the same time, John ran 9 yards 1 foot 10 inches. How many inches farther did John run than Jeremy? **139 inches**
6. A rectangular flower garden measures 3 yards 1 foot 8 inches wide and 1 yard 2 feet 3 inches long. How many inches of fencing is needed to enclose the entire flower garden? **382 inches**
7. Write Math **Explain** how you solved Problem 6.
Possible answer: I changed the measures for length and width to inches. Then I added the measures. I doubled the sum to get the perimeter.

Enrich E89 Grade 4

© Houghton Mifflin Harcourt Publishing Company

COMMON ERRORS

Error Students may multiply by the wrong number when comparing units of length.

Example 2 yards > 6 feet because 2 yards × 12 = 24 feet and 24 feet > 6 feet.

Springboard to Learning Remind students that there are 12 inches in 1 foot and 3 feet in 1 yard. So, to compare inches and feet, multiply the number of feet by 12. To compare feet and yards, multiply the number of yards by 3.

3 PRACTICE

Share and Show • Guided Practice

Use Exercises 2 and 4 for Quick Check.

Use Math Talk to focus on how the size of the unit affects the number of units for a given measurement.

Quick Check

If a student misses Exercises 2 and 4

Then Differentiate Instruction with

- RtI Tier 1 Activity, p. 449B
- Reteach 12.2
- Soar to Success Math 41.09, 44.36

On Your Own • Independent Practice

If students complete Exercises 2 and 4 correctly, they may continue with Independent Practice.

Problem Solving

Test Prep Coach

In Exercise 12, if students selected:

A They divided the number of yards by 3.

B They added the number of feet in 1 yard to the number of yards.

D They found the number of inches of carpet Jim has.

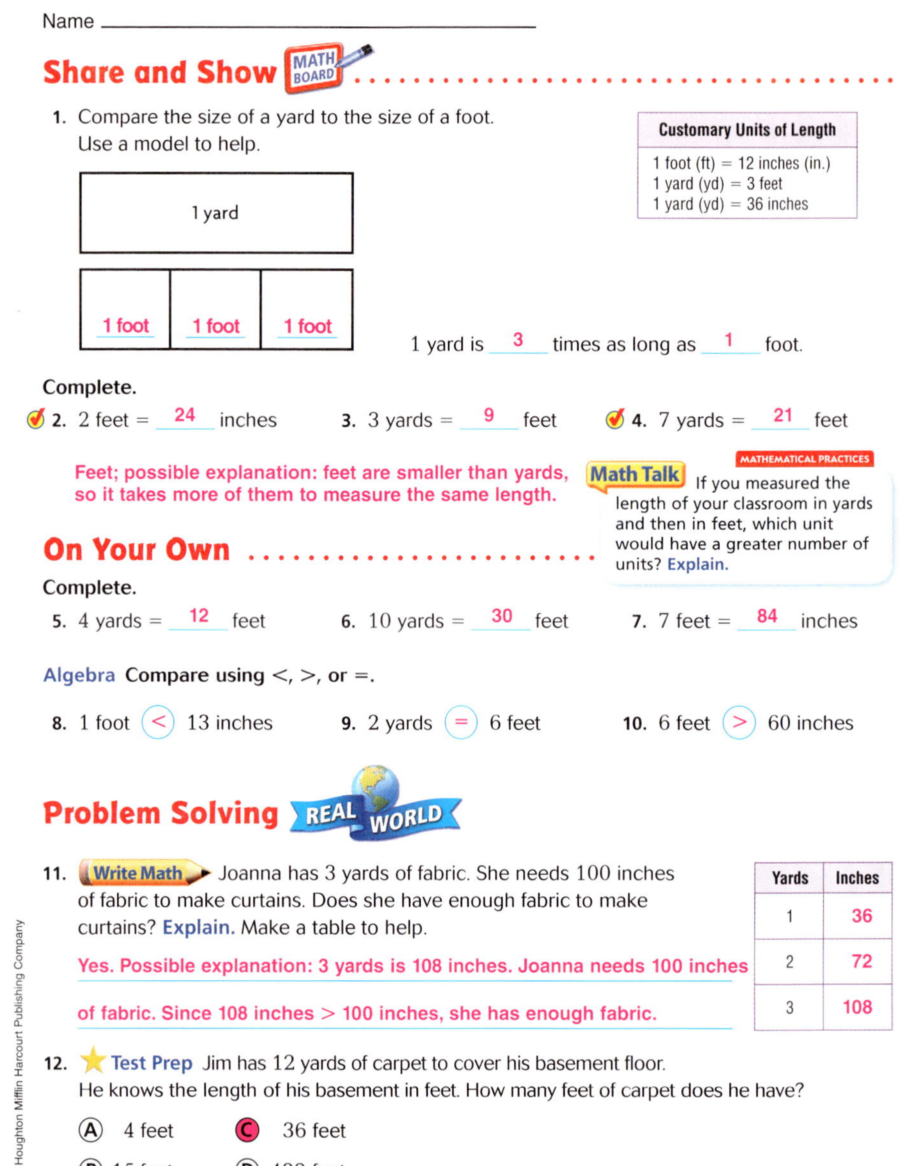

Name ______________________

Share and Show MATH BOARD

1. Compare the size of a yard to the size of a foot. Use a model to help.

Customary Units of Length
1 foot (ft) = 12 inches (in.)
1 yard (yd) = 3 feet
1 yard (yd) = 36 inches

1 yard is __3__ times as long as __1__ foot.

Complete.

2. 2 feet = __24__ inches
3. 3 yards = __9__ feet
4. 7 yards = __21__ feet

Feet; possible explanation: feet are smaller than yards, so it takes more of them to measure the same length.

Math Talk MATHEMATICAL PRACTICES If you measured the length of your classroom in yards and then in feet, which unit would have a greater number of units? **Explain.**

On Your Own

Complete.

5. 4 yards = __12__ feet
6. 10 yards = __30__ feet
7. 7 feet = __84__ inches

Algebra Compare using <, >, or =.

8. 1 foot (<) 13 inches
9. 2 yards (=) 6 feet
10. 6 feet (>) 60 inches

Problem Solving REAL WORLD

11. **Write Math** Joanna has 3 yards of fabric. She needs 100 inches of fabric to make curtains. Does she have enough fabric to make curtains? **Explain.** Make a table to help.

Yes. Possible explanation: 3 yards is 108 inches. Joanna needs 100 inches of fabric. Since 108 inches > 100 inches, she has enough fabric.

Yards	Inches
1	36
2	72
3	108

12. **Test Prep** Jim has 12 yards of carpet to cover his basement floor. He knows the length of his basement in feet. How many feet of carpet does he have?

Ⓐ 4 feet　Ⓑ 15 feet　**Ⓒ 36 feet**　Ⓓ 432 feet

© Houghton Mifflin Harcourt Publishing Company

Chapter 12 • Lesson 2 451

COMMON CORE PROFESSIONAL DEVELOPMENT

Mathematical Practices in Your Classroom

CC.K–12.MP.4 Model with mathematics.

In this lesson, students build an understanding of the relative sizes of an inch, a foot, and a yard by using three different models: 1-inch tiles, a two-column table, and a fraction-strip model. First, students explore the relative sizes of an inch and a foot by building 1 foot using 1-inch tiles. Then, students use a table and multiplication to explore the relationship between feet and inches. Finally, students use fraction strips to compare units of length.

Ask questions such as the following to help students see how each model can help them compare customary units of length:

- Suppose you have 3 feet of rope. You need 38 inches to build a rope swing. How can you use a table to compare the lengths? Possible answer: make a table that relates feet and inches. List the feet in one column, from 1 to 3, and then multiply the number of feet by 12 to find the number of inches: 1 foot × 12 = 12 inches, 2 feet × 12 = 24 inches, 3 feet × 12 = 36 inches. So, 3 feet < 38 inches because 36 inches < 38 inches.
- How can you use fraction tiles to compare the lengths? Possible answer: I know 12 inches, or 12 one-twelfth tiles, is the same as 1 foot, or 1 whole. I can use 38 one-twelfth tiles and compare the length to the length of 3 wholes.

MATHEMATICAL PRACTICES **Model • Reason • Make Sense**

H.O.T. Sense or Nonsense?

13. Jasmine and Luke used fraction strips to compare the size of a foot to the size of an inch using fractions. They drew models to show their answers. Whose answer makes sense? Whose answer is nonsense? **Explain** your reasoning.

Jasmine's Work

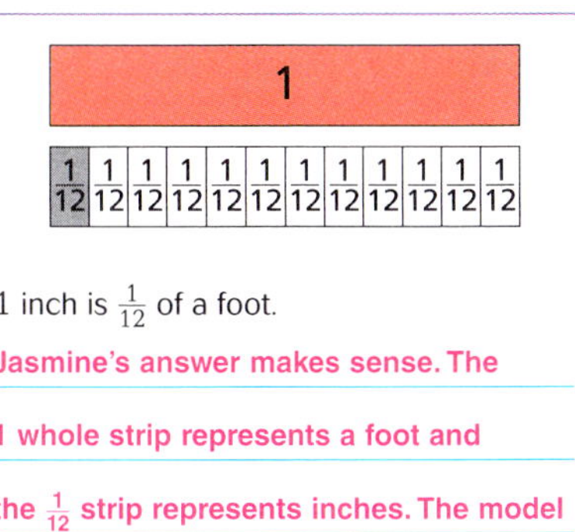

1 inch is $\frac{1}{12}$ of a foot.

Jasmine's answer makes sense. The 1 whole strip represents a foot and the $\frac{1}{12}$ strip represents inches. The model shows that 1 inch is $\frac{1}{12}$ of a foot.

Luke's Work

1		
$\frac{1}{3}$	$\frac{1}{3}$	$\frac{1}{3}$

1 inch is $\frac{1}{3}$ of a foot.

Luke's answer is nonsense. His model is not correct. There are 12 inches, not 3 inches, in a foot.

a. For the answer that is nonsense, write an answer that makes sense.

Possible answer: Luke's model should show 1 foot as the whole and 1 inch as $\frac{1}{12}$ of the whole.

b. Look back at Luke's model. Which two units could you compare using his model? **Explain.**

Yards and feet; possible explanation: the 1 whole strip could represent 1 yard and the $\frac{1}{3}$ strip could represent feet; there are 3 feet in 1 yard; 1 foot is $\frac{1}{3}$ as long as a yard.

© Houghton Mifflin Harcourt Publishing Company

FOR MORE PRACTICE:
Standards Practice Book, pp. P223–P224

H.O.T. Problem Exercise 13 requires students to analyze two answers to determine which one makes sense and which one doesn't and explain why. Point out that the fraction strip models show a relationship, not the actual size of the units.

4 SUMMARIZE

Essential Question

How can you use models to compare customary units of length? Possible answer: I can use models, such as inch tiles, a table, or fraction strips, to show the relationship between the units being compared.

Math Journal

Write a problem that can be solved by comparing feet and inches using a model. Include a solution. Explain why you are changing from a larger unit to a smaller unit.

Differentiated Instruction

INDEPENDENT ACTIVITIES

Differentiated Centers Kit

Activities

Measure Up

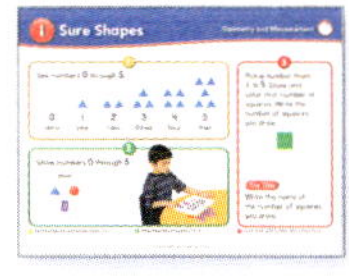

Students complete blue Activity Card 1 by comparing lengths.

Literature

Measuring the Mississippi

Students read about the different measurements that can be observed on a paddleboat trip down the Mississippi river.

Digital Path

- Animated Math Models
- *i*Tools
- HMH Mega Math
- Soar to Success Math
- *e*Student Edition

LESSON 12.3

Customary Units of Weight

LESSON AT A GLANCE

Common Core Standard

Solve problems involving measurement and conversion of measurements from a larger unit to a smaller unit.

CC.4.MD.1 Know relative sizes of measurement units within one system of units including km, m, cm; kg, g; lb, oz.; l, ml; hr, min, sec. Within a single system of measurement, express measurements in a larger unit in terms of a smaller unit. Record measurement equivalents in a two-column table.

Also CC.4.MD.2

Lesson Objective

Use models to compare customary units of weight.

Essential Question

How can you use models to compare customary units of weight?

Vocabulary

ounce, **pound**, **ton**

Materials

MathBoard, color pencils

Digital Path

- Animated Math Models
- *i*Tools: Measurement
- HMH Mega Math
- eStudent Edition

Daily Routines

Common Core

SPIRAL REVIEW

Problem of the Day

eTransparency 12.3

Test Prep Marvin estimates the weight of a watermelon he grew in his backyard. Which is the best estimate of the watermelon's weight?

Ⓐ 7 ounces Ⓒ 70 pounds

Ⓑ 7 pounds Ⓓ 700 pounds

Vocabulary Builder

Materials index cards

Definitions Have students make vocabulary cards for the customary units of weight introduced in the lesson: ounce, pound, and ton. Students can show the relationship between units on the card using one of the models in the lesson. Have students include the abbreviation for each unit: ounce (oz), pound (lb), and ton (T). Remind students that the abbreviations do not include a period.

COMMON CORE PROFESSIONAL DEVELOPMENT

About the Math

Why Teach This The customary units of weight form a system of units that students need to understand in order to interact in daily life in the United States.

In this lesson, students use models to learn the relationship between ounces, pounds, and tons. They use a number line and a table to understand the relationship between pounds and ounces. They will extend the table to also relate tons and pounds.

Professional Development Video Podcasts

Differentiated Instruction Activities

ELL Language Support

Auditory
Small Group

Strategy: Model Language

- Students can learn correct pronunciation and sentence structure by repeating words and sentences modeled by the teacher.
- In the lesson, when you are comparing two units of measure, have students state the comparison as well. Model each sentence before having students repeat it.

You need 16 ounces to make 1 pound.	**So, 1 pound is 16 times as heavy as 1 ounce.**

See ELL Activity Guide for leveled activities.

Enrich

Logical / Mathematical
Partners

Materials index cards

- Have students write comparison problems involving units of customary weight. Students can write the problem on an index card and its solution on the back:

Inga's puppy weighs 34 ounces. Bradley's puppy weighs 2 pounds. Whose puppy weighs more?

Inga's puppy; 34 ounces > 32 ounces, or 2 pounds

- Have students exchange and solve each other's problems, checking their answers on the back of the index card.

RtI Response to Intervention

Reteach Tier 1

Visual / Kinesthetic
Whole Class / Partner

Materials 1-Centimeter Grid Paper (see *eTeacher Resources*), scissors, tape

- **Jubin has 2 pounds of apples. He needs 20 ounces for a recipe. Does he have enough apples?**
- **Let each square on the grid paper represent 1 ounce. A row of 16 squares represents 1 pound. How many pounds do 2 rows represent?** 2 pounds Have students cut out 2 rows of 16 squares and tape them together end to end.
- Have students cut out and form a row of 20 squares to represent the 20 ounces Jubin needs.
- Have students compare the lengths of the strips. **Does Jubin have enough apples? Explain.** Yes. Possible explanation: 2 pounds is 32 ounces. He needs 20 ounces. Since 32 ounces > 20 ounces, he has enough.

Tier 2

Visual / Kinesthetic
Small Group

Materials 1-Centimeter Grid Paper (see *eTeacher Resources*), color pencils

- Students will compare the size of 1 pound to the size of 1 ounce using grid paper.
- Have students color a row of 16 squares and label it 1 pound. Have students color 1 square beneath the first square of the 1 pound row and label it 1 ounce.
- Point to 1 pound and then to 1 ounce. **How many ounces do you need to make 1 pound?** 16 ounces **So, 1 pound is how many times as heavy as 1 ounce?** 16 times as heavy

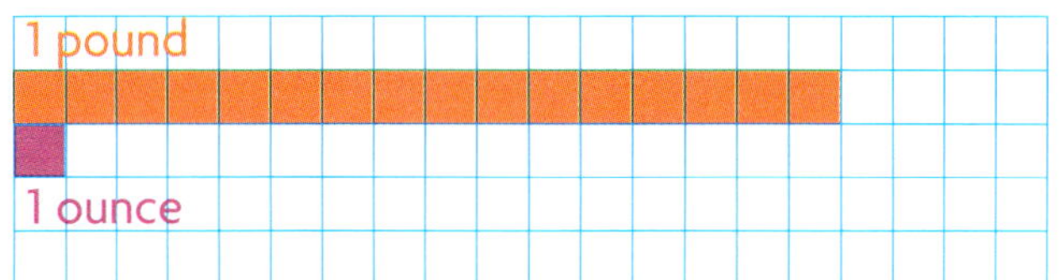

LESSON 12.3

CC.4.MD.1 Know relative sizes of measurement units within one system of units including km, m, cm; kg, g; lb, oz.; l, ml; hr, min, sec. Within a single system of measurement, express measurements in a larger unit in terms of a smaller unit. Record measurement equivalents in a two-column table.

1 ENGAGE

Materials *i*Tools: Measurement

Access Prior Knowledge Select two objects and ask:

- **Which object do you think is heavier?** Answers will vary.
- **How can we find out which object weighs more?** Possible answer: place each object on a scale and weigh it, and then compare the weights.

Continue selecting other objects and having volunteers determine which object weighs more.

2 TEACH and TALK

Unlock the Problem

Introduce the customary units of weight. Explain that in the customary system of measurement, two units that can be used to measure weight are ounces and pounds.

Activity

Work through the activity with the class.

- **In Step 1, what do you shade to represent 1 pound on the number line?** from 0 to 1 on the top portion of the number line
- **In Step 2, what do you shade to represent 1 ounce on the number line?** from 0 to 1 on the bottom portion of the number line
- **In Step 3, how many ounces make 1 pound? Explain how you know.** 16 ounces; possible explanation: the number line shows 16 ounces is the same as 1 pound.
- **If you know 1 pound is 16 times as heavy as 1 ounce, how can you compare the size of 2 pounds to the size of 1 ounce?** Possible answer: since a pound is 16 times as heavy as an ounce, 2 pounds would be 2 × 16 times, or 32 times, as heavy as an ounce.

Use **Math Talk** to help students recognize how to compare customary units of weight.

Name ______

Lesson 12.3

Customary Units of Weight

Essential Question How can you use models to compare customary units of weight?

COMMON CORE STANDARD CC.4.MD.1
Solve problems involving measurement and conversion of measurements from a larger unit to a smaller unit.

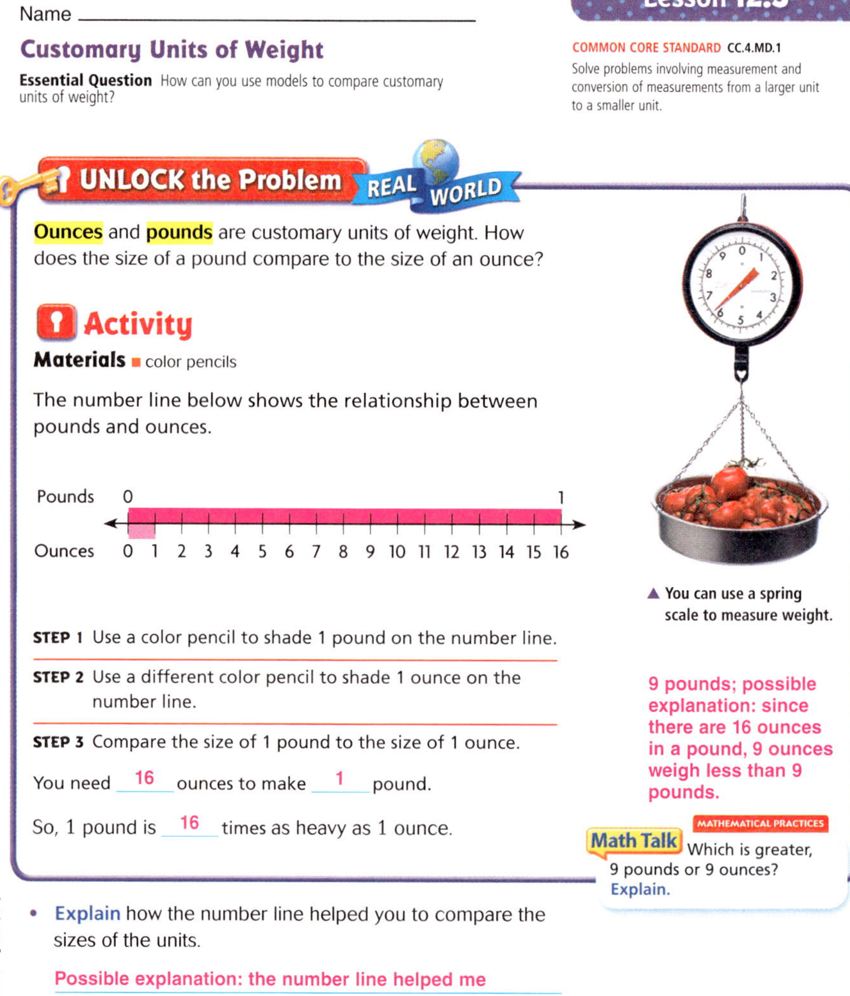

UNLOCK the Problem REAL WORLD

Ounces and **pounds** are customary units of weight. How does the size of a pound compare to the size of an ounce?

Activity

Materials ■ color pencils

The number line below shows the relationship between pounds and ounces.

▲ You can use a spring scale to measure weight.

STEP 1 Use a color pencil to shade 1 pound on the number line.

STEP 2 Use a different color pencil to shade 1 ounce on the number line.

STEP 3 Compare the size of 1 pound to the size of 1 ounce.

You need __16__ ounces to make __1__ pound.

So, 1 pound is __16__ times as heavy as 1 ounce.

MATHEMATICAL PRACTICES

Math Talk Which is greater, 9 pounds or 9 ounces? Explain.

9 pounds; possible explanation: since there are 16 ounces in a pound, 9 ounces weigh less than 9 pounds.

- **Explain** how the number line helped you to compare the sizes of the units.

Possible explanation: the number line helped me compare the size of a pound to the size of an ounce. It makes it easy to see that there are 16 ounces in a pound, so 1 pound weighs 16 times as much as 1 ounce.

© Houghton Mifflin Harcourt Publishing Company

Chapter 12 453

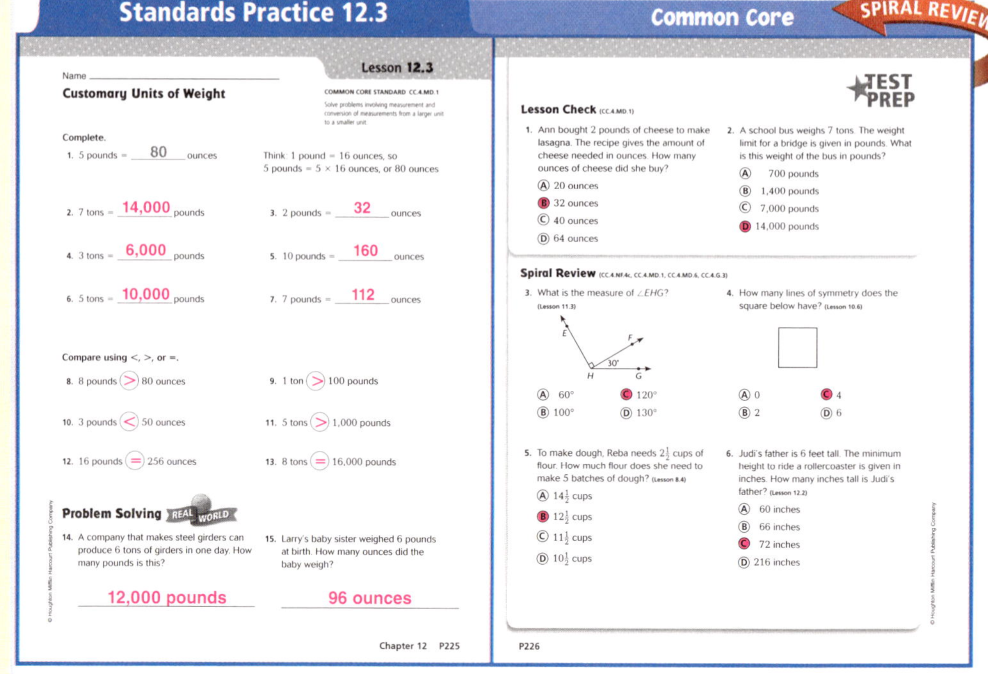

Standards Practice 12.3

Name ______

Lesson 12.3

Customary Units of Weight

COMMON CORE STANDARD CC.4.MD.1
Solve problems involving measurement and conversion of measurements from a larger unit to a smaller unit.

Complete.

1. 5 pounds = __80__ ounces

   Think: 1 pound = 16 ounces, so 5 pounds = 5 × 16 ounces, or 80 ounces

2. 7 tons = __14,000__ pounds
3. 2 pounds = __32__ ounces
4. 3 tons = __6,000__ pounds
5. 10 pounds = __160__ ounces
6. 5 tons = __10,000__ pounds
7. 7 pounds = __112__ ounces

Compare using <, >, or =.

8. 8 pounds (>) 80 ounces
9. 1 ton (>) 100 pounds
10. 3 pounds (<) 50 ounces
11. 5 tons (>) 1,000 pounds
12. 16 pounds (=) 256 ounces
13. 8 tons (=) 16,000 pounds

Problem Solving REAL WORLD

14. A company that makes steel girders can produce 6 tons of girders in one day. How many pounds is this?

    12,000 pounds

15. Larry's baby sister weighed 6 pounds at birth. How many ounces did the baby weigh?

    96 ounces

© Houghton Mifflin Harcourt Publishing Company

Chapter 12 P225

Common Core

SPIRAL REVIEW

TEST PREP

Lesson Check (CC.4.MD.1)

1. Ann bought 2 pounds of cheese to make lasagna. The recipe gives the amount of cheese needed in ounces. How many ounces of cheese did she buy?
   - Ⓐ 20 ounces
   - Ⓑ 32 ounces
   - Ⓒ 40 ounces
   - Ⓓ 64 ounces
2. A school bus weighs 7 tons. The weight limit for a bridge is given in pounds. What is this weight of the bus in pounds?
   - Ⓐ 700 pounds
   - Ⓑ 1,400 pounds
   - Ⓒ 7,000 pounds
   - Ⓓ 14,000 pounds

Spiral Review (CC.4.NF.4c, CC.4.MD.1, CC.4.MD.6, CC.4.G.3)

3. What is the measure of $\angle EHG$? (Lesson 11.3)

   E F 30° H G

   - Ⓐ 60°
   - Ⓑ 100°
   - Ⓒ 120°
   - Ⓓ 130°
4. How many lines of symmetry does the square below have? (Lesson 10.6)
   - Ⓐ 0
   - Ⓑ 2
   - Ⓒ 4
   - Ⓓ 6
5. To make dough, Reba needs $2\frac{1}{2}$ cups of flour. How much flour does she need to make 5 batches of dough? (Lesson 8.4)
   - Ⓐ $14\frac{1}{2}$ cups
   - Ⓑ $12\frac{1}{2}$ cups
   - Ⓒ $11\frac{1}{2}$ cups
   - Ⓓ $10\frac{1}{2}$ cups
6. Judi's father is 6 feet tall. The minimum height to ride a rollercoaster is given in inches. How many inches tall is Judi's father? (Lesson 12.2)
   - Ⓐ 60 inches
   - Ⓑ 66 inches
   - Ⓒ 72 inches
   - Ⓓ 216 inches

© Houghton Mifflin Harcourt Publishing Company

P226

Example Compare measures.

Nancy needs 5 pounds of flour to bake pies for a festival. She has 90 ounces of flour. How can she determine if she has enough flour to bake the pies?

STEP 1 Make a table that relates pounds and ounces.

Pounds	Ounces
1	16
2	32
3	48
4	64
5	80

Think:
1 pound × 16 = 16 ounces
2 pounds × 16 = 32 ounces
3 pounds × 16 = 48 ounces
4 pounds × 16 = 64 ounces
5 pounds × 16 = 80 ounces

STEP 2 Compare 90 ounces and 5 pounds.

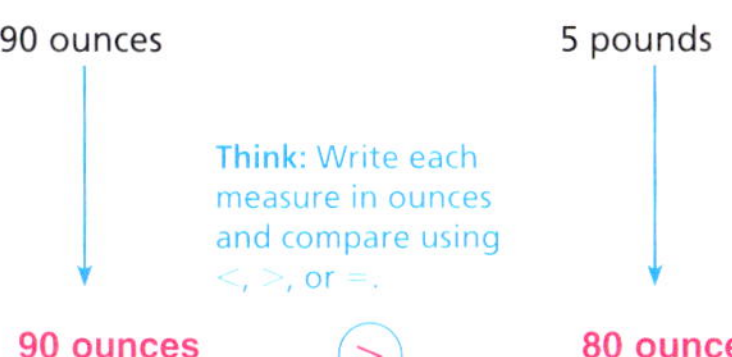

Nancy has 90 ounces of flour. She needs 5 pounds of flour.

90 ounces is greater than 5 pounds.

So, Nancy has enough flour to make the pies.

Try This! There are 2,000 pounds in 1 ton.
Make a table that relates tons and pounds.

Tons	Pounds
1	2,000
2	4,000
3	6,000

1 ton is 2,000 times as heavy as 1 pound.

© Houghton Mifflin Harcourt Publishing Company

454

▶ Example

Read and discuss the problem with the class.

- **What information do you know?** Nancy needs 5 pounds of flour to bake pies. She has 90 ounces of flour.
- **What are you trying to find?** if Nancy has enough flour to bake the pies
- **How can you solve the problem?** Possible answer: I can compare 5 pounds and 90 ounces by writing 5 pounds as ounces.
- **Why do you change the larger unit, pounds, to a smaller unit, ounces?** Possible answer: I need to compare the measurements using the same measurement unit. I know 1 pound is 16 times as heavy as 1 ounce, so I can write pounds as ounces by multiplying the number of pounds by 16. Then I can compare ounces to ounces.
- **Suppose Nancy needed 6 pounds of flour to bake the pies. Would she have enough flour? Explain.** No; possible explanation: 6 pounds × 16 = 96 ounces; 90 ounces < 96 ounces, so she would not have enough flour.

Try This!

Introduce the customary unit of weight, a ton. Explain that a ton is used to measure the weight of very heavy objects.

- **What are some objects that might weigh 1 ton or more?** Answers will vary. Possible answers: an elephant, a school bus, a ship
- **How can you use the table to relate tons and pounds?** Possible answer: since 2,000 pounds make 1 ton, multiply the number of tons by 2,000 to find the number of pounds.

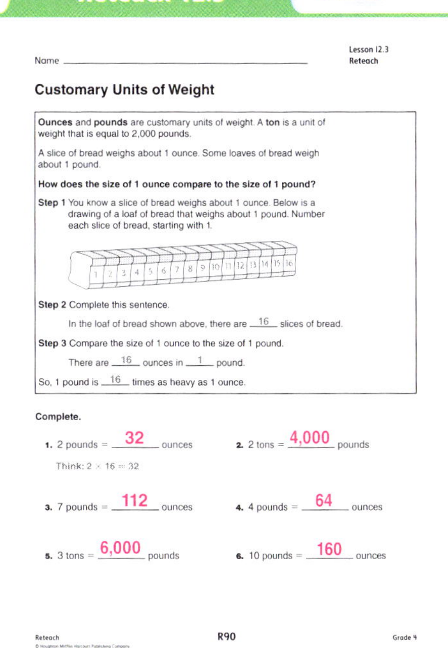

Reteach 12.3 RtI

Name ______ Lesson 12.3 Reteach

Customary Units of Weight

Ounces and **pounds** are customary units of weight. A **ton** is a unit of weight that is equal to 2,000 pounds.

A slice of bread weighs about 1 ounce. Some loaves of bread weigh about 1 pound.

How does the size of 1 ounce compare to the size of 1 pound?

Step 1 You know a slice of bread weighs about 1 ounce. Below is a drawing of a loaf of bread that weighs about 1 pound. Number each slice of bread, starting with 1.

1 2 3 4 5 6 7 8 9 10 11 12 13 14 15 16

Step 2 Complete this sentence.

In the loaf of bread shown above, there are 16 slices of bread.

Step 3 Compare the size of 1 ounce to the size of 1 pound.

There are 16 ounces in 1 pound.

So, 1 pound is 16 times as heavy as 1 ounce.

Complete.

1. 2 pounds = 32 ounces
   Think: 2 × 16 = 32
2. 2 tons = 4,000 pounds
3. 7 pounds = 112 ounces
4. 4 pounds = 64 ounces
5. 3 tons = 6,000 pounds
6. 10 pounds = 160 ounces

Reteach R90 Grade 4
© Houghton Mifflin Harcourt Publishing Company

Enrich 12.3

Name ______ Lesson 12.3 Enrich

Weighty Matters

Solve each problem.

1. A truck weighs 1 ton 1,350 pounds. The weight limit for a bridge is given in pounds. How many pounds does the truck weigh?
   3,350 pounds
2. Jasmine's new kitten weighs 2 pounds 6 ounces. Feeding instructions are given for weights in ounces. How many ounces does the kitten weigh?
   38 ounces
3. At the zoo, one elephant weighs 7 tons 400 pounds. Another elephant weighs 4 tons 1,800 pounds. How many more pounds does the first elephant weigh?
   4,600 pounds
4. Jim's dog weighs 18 pounds 10 ounces. His cat weighs 6 pounds 3 ounces. How many more ounces does Jim's dog weigh than his cat?
   199 ounces
5. Owen's math book weighs 2 pounds 13 ounces. His science book weighs 1 pound 15 ounces. His backpack weighs 1 pound 1 ounce. What is the total weight in ounces of the backpack and the two books?
   93 ounces
6. A truck is transporting 6 cars to a dealership. Each car weighs 1 ton 1,400 pounds. What is the total weight in pounds of the cars the truck is transporting?
   20,400 pounds
7. Write Math **Explain** how you solved Problem 3.
   Possible answer: I changed 7 tons 400 pounds to 14,400 pounds and 4 tons 1,800 pounds to 9,800 pounds. Then I subtracted 14,400 − 9,800.

Enrich E90 Grade 4
© Houghton Mifflin Harcourt Publishing Company

COMMON ERRORS

Error Students may multiply by the wrong unit when comparing units of weight.

Example Students might multiply 5 tons × 16 to change tons to pounds, then conclude that 5 tons, or 80 pounds < 500 pounds.

Springboard to Learning Remind students that there are 16 ounces in 1 pound and 2,000 pounds in 1 ton. So, to compare ounces and pounds, multiply the number of pounds by 16. To compare pounds and tons, multiply the number of tons by 2,000.

3 PRACTICE

Share and Show • Guided Practice

Use Exercises 2 and 4 for Quick Check.

Use Math Talk to focus on using an equation to change from one unit to another.

Quick Check

If a student misses Exercises 2 and 4

Then Differentiate Instruction with

- RtI Tier 1 Activity, p. 453B
- Reteach 12.3
- Soar to Success Math 42.05, 45.30

On Your Own • Independent Practice

If students complete Exercises 2 and 4 correctly, they may continue with Independent Practice.

Problem Solving

Test Prep Coach

In Exercise 10, if students selected:

A They chose the same number of ounces as pounds.

B They chose the number of ounces in 1 pound.

C They doubled the number of pounds.

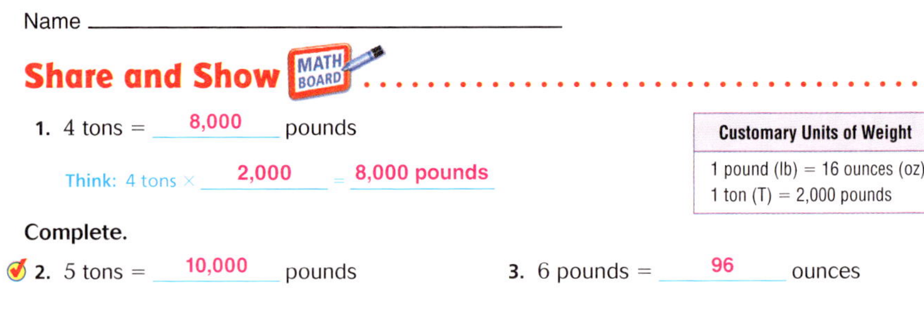

Name ____________

Share and Show

1. 4 tons = 8,000 pounds

Think: 4 tons × 2,000 = 8,000 pounds

Customary Units of Weight
1 pound (lb) = 16 ounces (oz)
1 ton (T) = 2,000 pounds

Complete.

2. 5 tons = 10,000 pounds
3. 6 pounds = 96 ounces

Math Talk (MATHEMATICAL PRACTICES): What equation can you use to solve Exercise 4? Explain.

On Your Own

Complete.

4. 7 pounds = 112 ounces
5. 6 tons = 12,000 pounds

Algebra Compare using >, <, or =.

6. 1 pound (>) 15 ounces
7. 2 tons (>) 2 pounds

Problem Solving

8. A landscaping company ordered 8 tons of gravel. They sell the gravel in 50 pound bags. How many pounds of gravel did the company order?

16,000 pounds

9. H.O.T. Write Math If you could draw a number line that shows the relationship between tons and pounds, what would it look like? Explain.

Possible answer: since 1 ton = 2,000 pounds, the number line would show tick marks for every whole number from 0 to 2,000. Each tick mark from 0 to 2,000 would represent 1 pound. The tick mark at 2,000 would represent 1 ton.

10. Test Prep Kwadir is recording his baby sister's weight in pounds and in ounces each week. This week she weighs 10 pounds. How many ounces does she weigh?

Ⓐ 10 ounces
Ⓑ 16 ounces
Ⓒ 20 ounces
Ⓓ 160 ounces (marked)

Math Talk: 7 × 16 = ■; possible explanation: you can multiply the number of pounds, 7, by the number of ounces in a pound, 16, to find how many ounces are in 7 pounds.

© Houghton Mifflin Harcourt Publishing Company

Cross-Curricular

SCIENCE

- Many animals use camouflage as a means of protection. Their enemies cannot see them because they blend in with their environment.
- The Arctic fox is one such animal. It changes the color of its fur based on the season.
- In the warm months, the fur is a gray-brown to blend in with the plants and rocks of the tundra. In the cold months, the fur turns white to blend in with the snow.
- The Arctic fox is about 10 to 16 inches long and weighs about 6 to 12 pounds. How many ounces is 6 pounds? 96 ounces

SOCIAL STUDIES

- In 1803, Thomas Jefferson commissioned Meriwether Lewis and William Clark to lead an expedition to find a route to the West. They were to record information about the land, animals, and people along the way.
- Lewis and Clark and their men traveled west by river using a keelboat and two other smaller boats called pirogues.
- Their keelboat was 55 feet long and had a ridge, or keel, down the center of the bottom to help it go straight. The boat could be rowed, sailed, poled, or towed from the shore.
- The keelboat weighed 7 tons when empty. How many pounds did it weigh when empty? 14,000 pounds

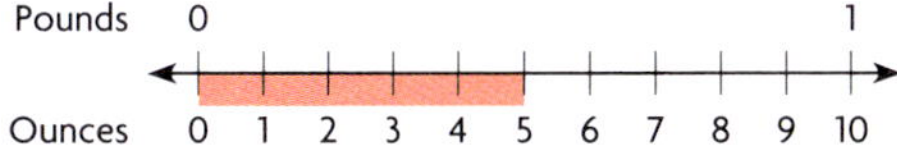

What's the Error?

11. Alexis bought $\frac{1}{2}$ pound of grapes. How many ounces of grapes did she buy?

Dan drew the number line below to solve the problem. He says his model shows that there are 5 ounces in $\frac{1}{2}$ pound. What is his error?

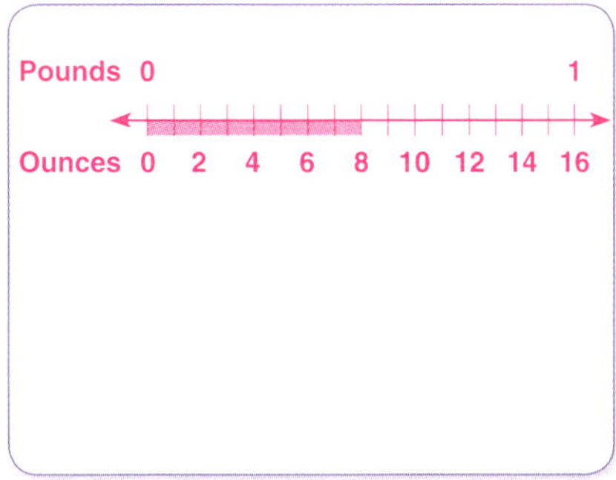

Look at the way Dan solved the problem. Find and describe his error.

Possible answer: Dan's number line does not correctly show the number of ounces in a pound. There are 16 ounces in a pound. Half of 16 is 8, so there are 8 ounces in $\frac{1}{2}$ pound.

Draw a correct number line and solve the problem.

Pounds 0 1

Ounces 0 2 4 6 8 10 12 14 16

So, Alexis bought 8 ounces of grapes.

- Look back at the number line you drew. How many ounces are in $\frac{1}{4}$ pound? Explain.

4 ounces; possible explanation: there are 16 ounces in a pound. Each jump of 4 represents $\frac{1}{4}$ of the number line. So, $\frac{1}{4}$ of the 16 ounces is 4 ounces. There are 4 ounces in $\frac{1}{4}$ pound.

© Houghton Mifflin Harcourt Publishing Company

 FOR MORE PRACTICE: Standards Practice Book, pp. P225–P226

H.O.T. Problem Exercise 11 requires students to identify an error in a solution involving a fraction of a pound.

- **How can you use a number line to find the number of ounces in a fraction of a pound?** Possible answer: use the number line to show the relationship between pounds and ounces. Shade to show the fraction of the pound. Find the number of ounces in the fraction of the pound.

4 SUMMARIZE

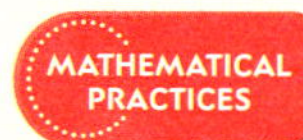

Essential Question

How can you use models to compare customary units of weight? Possible answer: I can use models, such as a number line or a table, to show the relationship between the units being compared.

Math Journal

Write a problem that can be solved by comparing pounds and ounces using a model. Include a solution. Explain why you are changing from a larger unit to a smaller unit.

Differentiated Instruction

INDEPENDENT ACTIVITIES

Differentiated Centers Kit

Activities
Balancing Act

Students complete blue Activity Card 14 by measuring mass and weight.

Activities
Challenging Changes

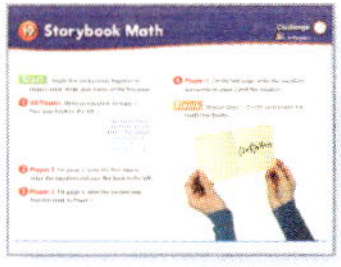

Students complete purple Activity Card 14 by performing simple conversions between different units of weight within the customary measurement system.

Digital Path

- Animated Math Models
- *i*Tools
- HMH Mega Math
- Soar to Success Math
- *e*Student Edition

LESSON 12.4

Customary Units of Liquid Volume

LESSON AT A GLANCE

Common Core Standard

Solve problems involving measurement and conversion of measurements from a larger unit to a smaller unit.

CC.4.MD.1 Know relative sizes of measurement units within one system of units including km, m, cm; kg, g; lb, oz.; l, ml; hr, min, sec. Within a single system of measurement, express measurements in a larger unit in terms of a smaller unit. Record measurement equivalents in a two-column table.

Also CC.4.MD.2

Lesson Objective

Use models to compare customary units of liquid volume.

Essential Question

How can you use models to compare customary units of liquid volume?

Vocabulary

cup, **fluid ounce**, **gallon**, **half gallon**, **liquid volume**, **pint**, **quart**

Materials

MathBoard

Digital Path

- Animated Math Models
- HMH Mega Math
- *i*Tools: Measurement
- eStudent Edition

COMMON CORE PROFESSIONAL DEVELOPMENT

About the Math

Why Teach This In this lesson, students learn the relationships among the customary units of liquid volume (fluid ounces, cups, pints, quarts, half gallons, and gallons). Liquid volume is the measure of the space a liquid occupies. It is often confused with capacity, which is the amount a container can hold when filled.

Students review that an ounce is a customary unit of weight, while a fluid ounce is a customary unit of liquid volume.

Students use models—bars and tables—to show the relative sizes of units.

Professional Development Video Podcasts

Daily Routines

Common Core

SPIRAL REVIEW

Problem of the Day

eTransparency 12.4

Test Prep Mrs. Lin's car has a full tank of gas. Which is the best estimate of how much gas is in Mrs. Lin's car?

Ⓐ 5 cups Ⓒ 5 gallons
Ⓑ 15 cups Ⓓ 15 gallons

Fluency Builder

Materials large paper, color pencils

Visualizing Relationships Have students make a poster showing the relationships among the units introduced in the lesson: fluid ounces, cups, pints, quarts, half gallons, and gallons. Have students include the abbreviation for each unit: fluid ounce (fl oz), cup (c), pint (pt), quart (qt), and gallon (gal). Remind students that the abbreviations do not include a period. Students can title their poster Units of Liquid Volume and include a brief definition for *liquid volume* below the title.

Differentiated Instruction Activities

ELL Language Support

Visual
Small Group

Strategy: Draw

Materials index cards, color pencils

- Students can acquire new vocabulary by making and studying drawings that illustrate new concepts and unfamiliar words.
- Have students draw examples of the relationships between the units of liquid volume on index cards.

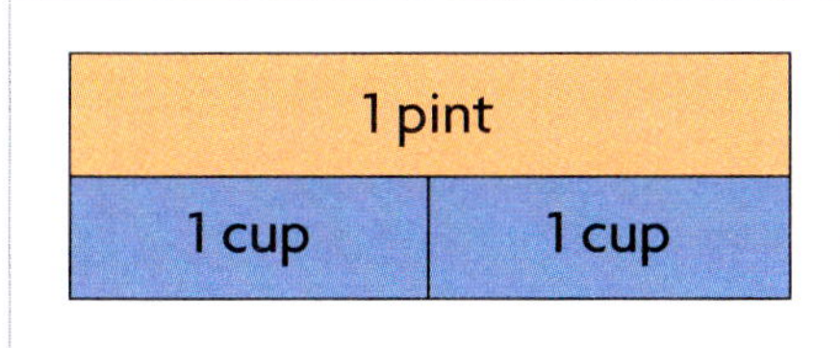

- Then students can study the cards to help them understand the new concepts and terms.

See ELL Activity Guide for leveled activities.

Enrich

Logical / Mathematical
Partners / Small Groups

Materials index cards, Spinner (8-section), Digit Cards (1–8) (see *eTeacher Resources*)

- Have students label a spinner from 1 to 8. Then ask students to write each unit of liquid volume on a separate index card: fluid ounces, cups, pints, quarts, half gallons, and gallons.
- Students, as partners or in small groups, shuffle their index cards and place them facedown.
- Each player turns over a card and spins the spinner, placing the digit card for the number spun next to the unit card.
- Then players compare the amounts. The player with the greatest amount wins 1 point.

- Play continues until one player reaches 8 points.

RtI Response to Intervention

Reteach Tier 1

Visual / Kinesthetic
Whole Class / Partner

Materials Fraction Strips (see *eTeacher Resources*)

- **Rita has 1 quart of punch. She wants to serve 6 cups of punch. Does she have enough punch?**
- Guide students to model 1 quart with a fraction strip. One one-fourth strip is 1 cup.
- **How many cups are in 1 quart?** 4 cups **How can you show 1 quart with $\frac{1}{4}$-strips?** four $\frac{1}{4}$-strips
- **How can we represent the 6 cups that Rita wants to serve?** Put down six $\frac{1}{4}$-strips.
- **Does Rita have enough punch? Explain.** No. 1 quart is 4 cups. She needs 6 cups. Since 4 cups $<$ 6 cups, she doesn't have enough punch.

Tier 2

Visual
Small Group

Materials different-sized containers that represent 1 fluid ounce, 1 cup, 1 pint, 1 quart, 1 half gallon, and 1 gallon

- If possible, have students use real containers to see the relationship among the units of liquid volume.
- Fill a 1-fluid ounce container with water and pour it into a 1-cup container until it is full. **How many fluid ounces make 1 cup?** 8 fluid ounces
- Fill a 1-cup container with water and pour it into a 1-pint container until it is full. **How many cups make 1 pint?** 2 cups
- Continue in a similar manner with the remaining containers and units of liquid volume.

LESSON 12.4

COMMON CORE CC.4.MD.1 Know relative sizes of measurement units within one system of units including km, m, cm; kg, g; lb, oz.; l, ml; hr, min, sec. Within a single system of measurement, express measurements in a larger unit in terms of a smaller unit. Record measurement equivalents in a two-column table.

1 ENGAGE

Materials supermarket flyers

Access Prior Knowledge Use supermarket flyers to show students different items that can be measured using units of liquid volume. Encourage students to come up with examples of their own.

2 TEACH and TALK

Animated Math Models

▶ Unlock the Problem

Define liquid volume as the amount of space a liquid occupies. Discuss the model and how it shows the relationships among gallons, half gallons, quarts, pints, cups, and fluid ounces.

- **How are fluid ounces different from ounces?** Possible answer: an ounce is a customary unit used to measure weight; a fluid ounce is a customary unit used to measure liquid volume.

▶ Example

Work through the Example with the class.

- **In Step 1, why do you draw two bars the same length?** Possible answer: because you need to show the relationship between the two units
- **How do you know how to show the number of quarts in the bar?** Possible answer: 4 quarts are in 1 gallon, so divide the bar for quarts into 4 equal parts. Each part represents 1 quart.
- **How can you compare the size of a half gallon to the size of 1 quart?** Possible answer: if I mark the halfway point on the bar for 1 gallon, I can see that a half gallon is 2 times as much as 1 quart.

Use **Math Talk** to help students recognize a pattern in the units of liquid volume.

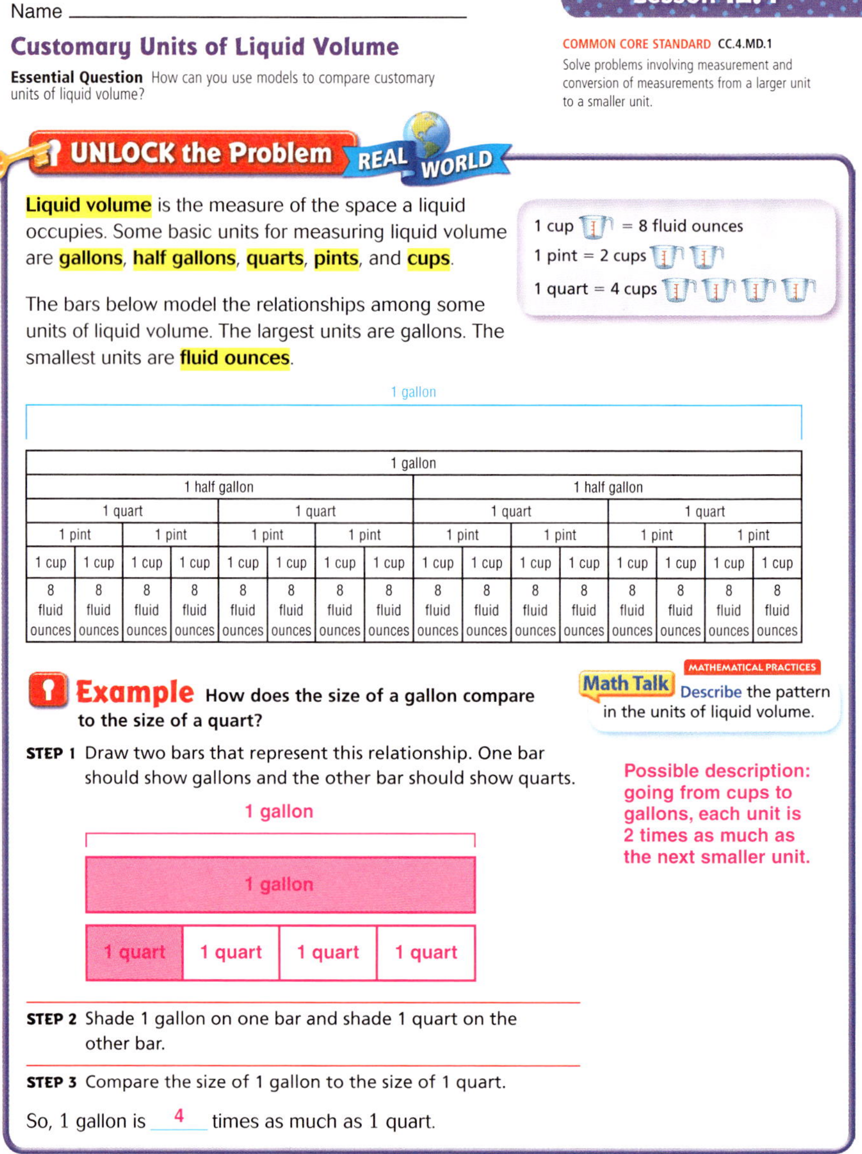

Name ________________

Lesson 12.4

Customary Units of Liquid Volume

Essential Question How can you use models to compare customary units of liquid volume?

COMMON CORE STANDARD CC.4.MD.1
Solve problems involving measurement and conversion of measurements from a larger unit to a smaller unit.

UNLOCK the Problem REAL WORLD

Liquid volume is the measure of the space a liquid occupies. Some basic units for measuring liquid volume are **gallons**, **half gallons**, **quarts**, **pints**, and **cups**.

1 cup = 8 fluid ounces
1 pint = 2 cups
1 quart = 4 cups

The bars below model the relationships among some units of liquid volume. The largest units are gallons. The smallest units are **fluid ounces**.

1 gallon

1 gallon															
1 half gallon								1 half gallon							
1 quart				1 quart				1 quart				1 quart			
1 pint		1 pint		1 pint		1 pint		1 pint		1 pint		1 pint		1 pint	
1 cup	1 cup	1 cup	1 cup	1 cup	1 cup	1 cup	1 cup	1 cup	1 cup	1 cup	1 cup	1 cup	1 cup	1 cup	1 cup
8 fluid ounces	8 fluid ounces	8 fluid ounces	8 fluid ounces	8 fluid ounces	8 fluid ounces	8 fluid ounces	8 fluid ounces	8 fluid ounces	8 fluid ounces	8 fluid ounces	8 fluid ounces	8 fluid ounces	8 fluid ounces	8 fluid ounces	8 fluid ounces

Example How does the size of a gallon compare to the size of a quart?

STEP 1 Draw two bars that represent this relationship. One bar should show gallons and the other bar should show quarts.

1 gallon

1 gallon			
1 quart	1 quart	1 quart	1 quart

STEP 2 Shade 1 gallon on one bar and shade 1 quart on the other bar.

STEP 3 Compare the size of 1 gallon to the size of 1 quart.

So, 1 gallon is __4__ times as much as 1 quart.

MATHEMATICAL PRACTICES **Math Talk** Describe the pattern in the units of liquid volume.

Possible description: going from cups to gallons, each unit is 2 times as much as the next smaller unit.

© Houghton Mifflin Harcourt Publishing Company

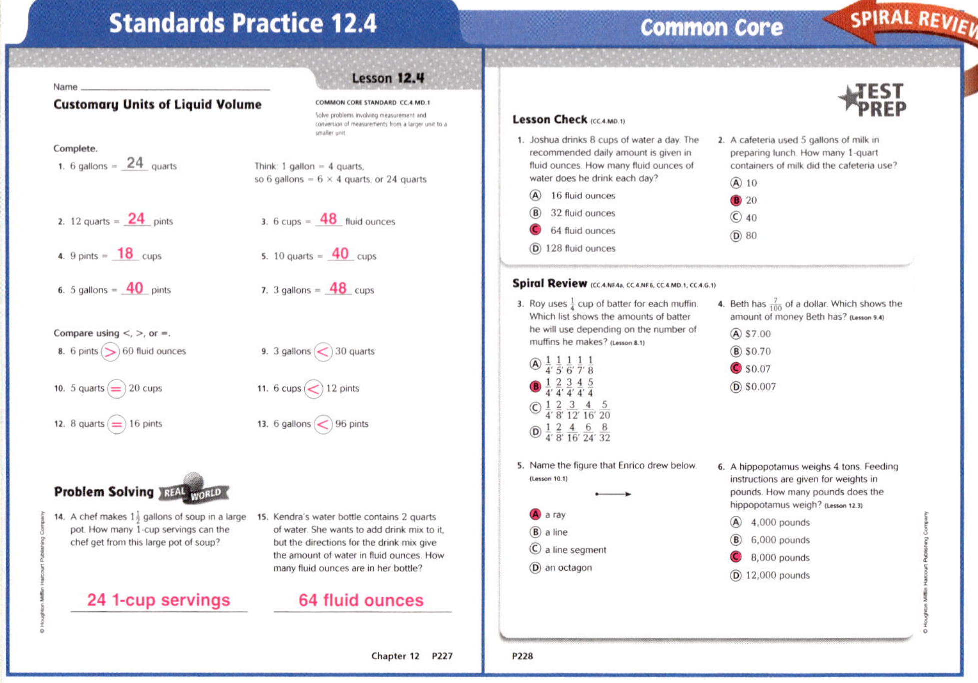

Standards Practice 12.4

Name ________________

Lesson 12.4

Customary Units of Liquid Volume

COMMON CORE STANDARD CC.4.MD.1
Solve problems involving measurement and conversion of measurements from a larger unit to a smaller unit.

Complete.

1. 6 gallons = __24__ quarts
   Think: 1 gallon = 4 quarts, so 6 gallons = 6 × 4 quarts, or 24 quarts
2. 12 quarts = __24__ pints
3. 6 cups = __48__ fluid ounces
4. 9 pints = __18__ cups
5. 10 quarts = __40__ cups
6. 5 gallons = __40__ pints
7. 3 gallons = __48__ cups

Compare using <, >, or =.

8. 6 pints (>) 60 fluid ounces
9. 3 gallons (<) 30 quarts
10. 5 quarts (=) 20 cups
11. 6 cups (<) 12 pints
12. 8 quarts (=) 16 pints
13. 6 gallons (<) 96 pints

Problem Solving REAL WORLD

14. A chef makes $1\frac{1}{2}$ gallons of soup in a large pot. How many 1-cup servings can the chef get from this large pot of soup?
    __24 1-cup servings__
15. Kendra's water bottle contains 2 quarts of water. She wants to add drink mix to it, but the directions for the drink mix give the amount of water in fluid ounces. How many fluid ounces are in her bottle?
    __64 fluid ounces__

© Houghton Mifflin Harcourt Publishing Company

Common Core SPIRAL REVIEW

TEST PREP

Lesson Check (CC.4.MD.1)

1. Joshua drinks 8 cups of water a day. The recommended daily amount is given in fluid ounces. How many fluid ounces of water does he drink each day?
   Ⓐ 16 fluid ounces
   Ⓑ 32 fluid ounces
   Ⓒ 64 fluid ounces (marked)
   Ⓓ 128 fluid ounces
2. A cafeteria used 5 gallons of milk in preparing lunch. How many 1-quart containers of milk did the cafeteria use?
   Ⓐ 10
   Ⓑ 20 (marked)
   Ⓒ 40
   Ⓓ 80

Spiral Review (CC.4.NF.4a, CC.4.NF.6, CC.4.MD.1, CC.4.G.1)

3. Roy uses $\frac{1}{4}$ cup of batter for each muffin. Which list shows the amounts of batter he will use depending on the number of muffins he makes? (Lesson 8.1)
   Ⓐ $\frac{1}{4}, \frac{1}{5}, \frac{1}{6}, \frac{1}{7}, \frac{1}{8}$
   Ⓑ $\frac{1}{4}, \frac{2}{4}, \frac{3}{4}, \frac{4}{4}, \frac{5}{4}$ (marked)
   Ⓒ $\frac{1}{4}, \frac{2}{8}, \frac{3}{12}, \frac{4}{16}, \frac{5}{20}$
   Ⓓ $\frac{1}{4}, \frac{2}{8}, \frac{4}{16}, \frac{6}{24}, \frac{8}{32}$
4. Beth has $\frac{7}{100}$ of a dollar. Which shows the amount of money Beth has? (Lesson 9.4)
   Ⓐ $7.00
   Ⓑ $0.70
   Ⓒ $0.07 (marked)
   Ⓓ $0.007
5. Name the figure that Enrico drew below. (Lesson 10.1)
   Ⓐ a ray (marked)
   Ⓑ a line
   Ⓒ a line segment
   Ⓓ an octagon
6. A hippopotamus weighs 4 tons. Feeding instructions are given for weights in pounds. How many pounds does the hippopotamus weigh? (Lesson 12.3)
   Ⓐ 4,000 pounds
   Ⓑ 6,000 pounds
   Ⓒ 8,000 pounds (marked)
   Ⓓ 12,000 pounds

© Houghton Mifflin Harcourt Publishing Company

Serena needs to make 3 gallons of lemonade for the lemonade sale. She has a powder mix that makes 350 fluid ounces of lemonade. How can she decide if she has enough powder mix?

STEP 1 Use the model on page 457. Find the relationship between gallons and fluid ounces.

1 gallon = __16__ cups

1 cup = __8__ fluid ounces

1 gallon = __16__ cups × __8__ fluid ounces

1 gallon = __128__ fluid ounces

STEP 2 Make a table that relates gallons and fluid ounces.

Gallons	Fluid Ounces
1	128
2	256
3	384

Think:

1 gallon = 128 fluid ounces

2 gallons × 128 = __256__ fluid ounces

3 gallons × 128 = __384__ fluid ounces

STEP 3 Compare 350 fluid ounces and 3 gallons.

350 fluid ounces — 3 gallons

Think: Write each measure in fluid ounces and compare using <, >, or =.

__350 fluid ounces__  __384 fluid ounces__

Serena has enough mix to make 350 fluid ounces. She needs to make 3 gallons of lemonade.

350 fluid ounces is __less__ than 3 gallons.

So, Serena __does not have__ enough mix to make 3 gallons of lemonade.

© Houghton Mifflin Harcourt Publishing Company

Reteach 12.4

Name ____________ Lesson 12.4 Reteach

Customary Units of Liquid Volume

Liquid volume is the measure of the space a liquid occupies. Some basic units for measuring liquid volume are **gallons, half gallons, quarts, pints, cups,** and **fluid ounces**. The table at the right shows the relationships among some units of liquid volume.

1 cup = 8 fluid ounces
1 pint = 2 cups
1 quart = 2 pints
1 half gallon = 2 quarts
1 gallon = 4 quarts

How does the size of a gallon compare to the size of a pint?

Step 1 Use the information in the table. Draw a bar to represent 1 gallon.

1 gallon

Step 2 The table shows that 1 gallon is equal to 4 quarts. Draw a bar to show 4 quarts.

1 quart	1 quart	1 quart	1 quart

Step 3 The table shows that 1 quart is equal to 2 pints. Draw a bar to show 2 pints for each of the 4 quarts.

1 pint	1 pint	1 pint	1 pint	1 pint	1 pint	1 pint	1 pint

Step 4 Compare the size of 1 gallon to the size of 1 pint.

There are __8__ pints in __1__ gallon.

So, 1 gallon is __8__ times as much as 1 pint.

Complete. Draw a model to help.

1. 2 quarts = __4__ pints
2. 1 gallon = __16__ cups
3. 1 pint = __16__ fluid ounces
4. 3 pints = __6__ cups
5. 3 quarts = __12__ cups
6. 1 half gallon = __4__ pints

Reteach R91 Grade 4

Enrich 12.4

Name ____________ Lesson 12.4 Enrich

Using Measures of Liquid Volume

Solve each problem.

1. At his lemonade stand, Ishmael has enough lemonade mix to make 3 gallons 2 quarts 1 pint of lemonade. How many 1-cup servings of lemonade can he make?

   __58 servings__

2. Irene has 1 gallon of milk. She uses 4 fluid ounces of milk in each bowl of cereal. How many bowls of cereal can she fill before she has used all the milk?

   __32 bowls of cereal__

3. One day at lunch, the cafeteria sold thirty-four 1-pint containers of milk. The cafeteria also sold forty-eight 12-fl-oz bottles of water. Did the cafeteria sell more fluid ounces of water or milk? How many more?

   __water; 32 fluid ounces__

4. Mrs. Nelson bought a 2-gallon container of ice cream. How many 2-fl-oz scoops of ice cream can be served from this container?

   __128 scoops__

5. Write Math **Explain** how you solved Problem 3.

   Possible answer: I multiplied 34 by 16 to find the number of fluid ounces of milk. I multiplied 48 by 12 to find the number of fluid ounces of water. Then I compared and subtracted.

Enrich E91 Grade 4

▶ Example

Read and discuss the problem with the class.

- **What information do you know?** Serena needs to make 3 gallons of lemonade. She has a powder mix that makes 350 fluid ounces of lemonade.
- **What are you trying to find?** if Serena has enough powder mix
- **How can you solve the problem?** Possible answer: I can compare 3 gallons and 350 fluid ounces by writing 3 gallons as fluid ounces.
- **Why do you change the larger unit, gallons, to a smaller unit, fluid ounces?** Possible answer: I need to compare the measurements using the same measurement unit. From the model, I know 1 gallon is 16 times as much as 1 cup and there are 8 fluid ounces in 1 cup. I can find how many fluid ounces are in 1 gallon by multiplying 16 cups × 8 fluid ounces, which is 128 fluid ounces. Then I can relate gallons to fluid ounces using a table, so I can compare ounces to ounces.

Go Deeper

- **Suppose Serena needed to make $2\frac{1}{2}$ gallons of lemonade. Would she have enough powder mix? Explain.** Yes; possible explanation: 1 gallon is 128 fluid ounces, so 2 gallons is 256 fluid ounces. $\frac{1}{2}$ gallon = 128 ÷ 2, or 64 fluid ounces. 256 fluid ounces + 64 fluid ounces = 320 fluid ounces. 350 fluid ounces > 320 fluid ounces, so she has enough powder mix.

COMMON ERRORS

Error Students may not use the correct relationship between units of liquid volume.

Example 4 gallons = 16 pints

Springboard to Learning Encourage students to use a model to identify the relationship between the units.

▶ Share and Show • Guided Practice

Use Exercises 2 and 4 for Quick Check.

Use Math Talk to help students recognize the relationship between the chart and bar model.

Quick Check

If a student misses Exercises 2 and 4

Then Differentiate Instruction with

- RtI Tier 1 Activity, p. 457B
- Reteach 12.4
- Soar to Success Math 43.07, 46.37

▶ On Your Own • Independent Practice

If students complete Exercises 2 and 4 correctly, they may continue with Independent Practice.

▶ Problem Solving

Test Prep Coach

In Exercise 11, if students selected:

A They chose the number of cups in 1 quart.
B They doubled the number of quarts.
D They multiplied the number of quarts by 8 instead of 4.

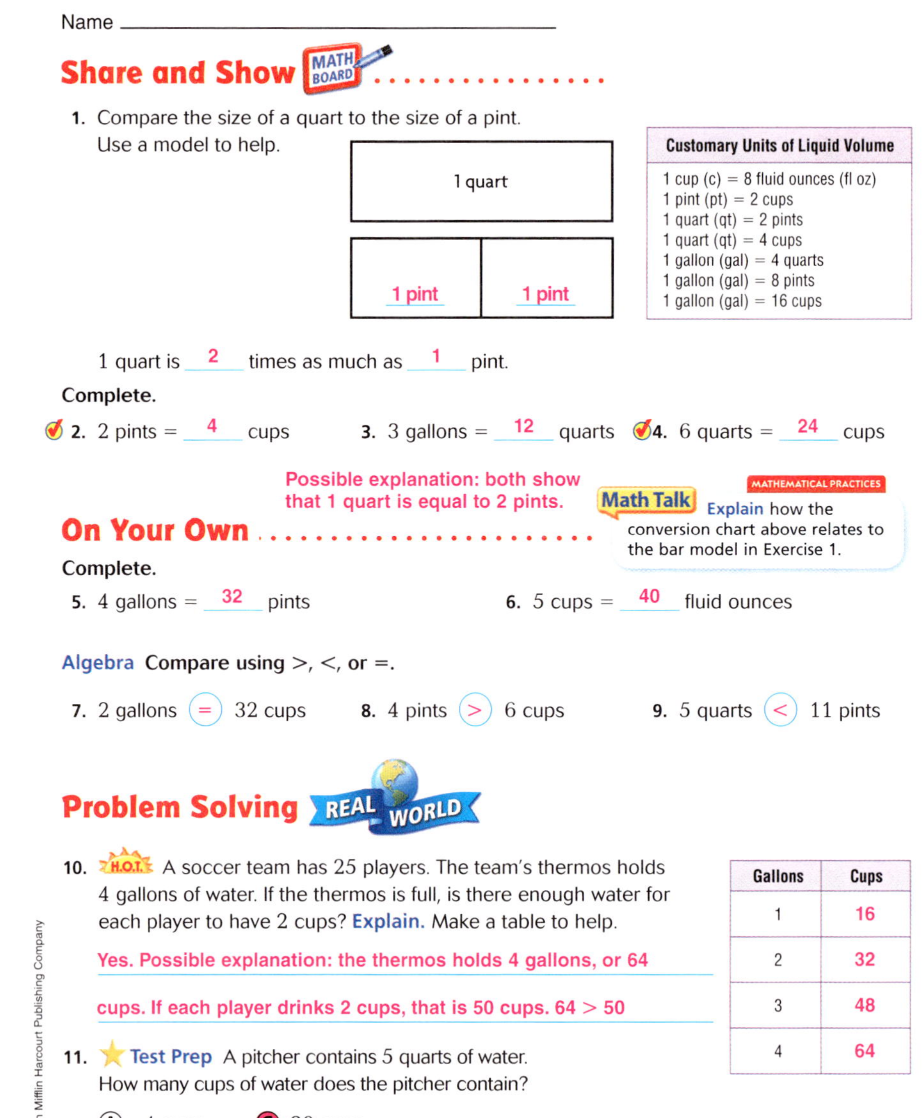

Name ______________________

Share and Show

1. Compare the size of a quart to the size of a pint. Use a model to help.

1 quart	
1 pint	1 pint

Customary Units of Liquid Volume
1 cup (c) = 8 fluid ounces (fl oz)
1 pint (pt) = 2 cups
1 quart (qt) = 2 pints
1 quart (qt) = 4 cups
1 gallon (gal) = 4 quarts
1 gallon (gal) = 8 pints
1 gallon (gal) = 16 cups

1 quart is __2__ times as much as __1__ pint.

Complete.

2. 2 pints = __4__ cups
3. 3 gallons = __12__ quarts
4. 6 quarts = __24__ cups

Possible explanation: both show that 1 quart is equal to 2 pints.

MATHEMATICAL PRACTICES **Math Talk** Explain how the conversion chart above relates to the bar model in Exercise 1.

On Your Own

Complete.

5. 4 gallons = __32__ pints
6. 5 cups = __40__ fluid ounces

Algebra Compare using >, <, or =.

7. 2 gallons (=) 32 cups
8. 4 pints (>) 6 cups
9. 5 quarts (<) 11 pints

Problem Solving REAL WORLD

10. H.O.T. A soccer team has 25 players. The team's thermos holds 4 gallons of water. If the thermos is full, is there enough water for each player to have 2 cups? **Explain.** Make a table to help.

Yes. Possible explanation: the thermos holds 4 gallons, or 64 cups. If each player drinks 2 cups, that is 50 cups. 64 > 50

Gallons	Cups
1	16
2	32
3	48
4	64

11. Test Prep A pitcher contains 5 quarts of water. How many cups of water does the pitcher contain?

Ⓐ 4 cups
Ⓑ 10 cups
Ⓒ 20 cups
Ⓓ 40 cups

© Houghton Mifflin Harcourt Publishing Company

Problem Solving REAL WORLD

H.O.T. Sense or Nonsense?

12. Whose statement makes sense? Whose statement is nonsense? Explain your reasoning.

Zach's Statement	Angela's Statement
Zach's statement is nonsense. There are 8 pints in a gallon, not 4, so a pint cannot be $\frac{1}{4}$ of a gallon.	Angela's statement makes sense. A gallon is 8 times as much as a pint, so 1 pint is $\frac{1}{8}$ of a gallon.

a. For the statement that is nonsense, write a statement that makes sense.
Possible answer: since there are 4 pints in a half gallon, 1 pint is $\frac{1}{4}$ of a half gallon.

b. Describe the size of a pint as it relates to a quart using fractions.
Possible answer: since there are 2 pints in a quart, 1 pint is $\frac{1}{2}$ of a quart.

© Houghton Mifflin Harcourt Publishing Company

FOR MORE PRACTICE: Standards Practice Book, pp. P227–P228

FOR EXTRA PRACTICE: Standards Practice Book, p. P243

Problem Solving

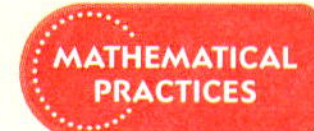

H.O.T. Problem Exercise 12 requires students to explain which statement makes sense and which one is nonsense.

- **How can you use a bar model to find the number of pints in a fraction of a gallon?** Possible answer: use the bar model to show the relationship between 1 gallon and pints. Shade to show the fraction of the gallon. Find the number of pints in the fraction of the gallon.

4 SUMMARIZE

Essential Question

How can you use models to compare customary units of liquid volume? Possible answer: I can use models, such as bars or a table, to show the relationship between the units being compared.

Math Journal

Write a problem that can be solved by comparing quarts and cups using a model. Include a solution. Explain why you are changing from a larger unit to a smaller unit.

Differentiated Instruction

INDEPENDENT ACTIVITIES

Differentiated Centers Kit

Activities
Capacity Overload!

Students complete orange Activity Card 16 by estimating liquid volume of real-world containers.

Activities
Capacity Challenge

Students complete purple Activity Card 16 by changing customary units of liquid volume.

LESSON 12.5

Line Plots

LESSON AT A GLANCE

Common Core Standard

Represent and interpret data.

CC.4.MD.4 Make a line plot to display a data set of measurements in fractions of a unit (1/2, 1/4, 1/8). Solve problems involving addition and subtraction of fractions by using information presented in line plots.

Also CC.4.MD.2

Lesson Objective

Make and interpret line plots with fractional data.

Essential Question

How can you make and interpret line plots with fractional data?

Vocabulary line plot

Materials MathBoard

Digital Path

*i*Tools: Graphs

HMH Mega Math

eStudent Edition

About the Math

Teaching for Depth Proper organization of data is critical when solving problems. Students have used number lines extensively in the past, and learning to use line plots provides a logical way for them to extend the use of number lines to organize problem-solving data.

Using line plots to order and count the frequency of data helps prepare students for later studies of mean, median, and mode. Reinforce how using line plots does not change any data; instead, a line plot simply shows all the data that are involved, and the number of times each number is found in the data set.

Professional Development Video Podcasts

Daily Routines

Common Core

SPIRAL REVIEW

Problem of the Day

eTransparency 12.5

Test Prep Amy has 3 sets of stamps. Each set has 20 stamps. How many stamps does she have?

Ⓐ 66 Ⓒ 23
Ⓑ 60 Ⓓ 17

Fluency Builder

Counting Tape

Materials Counting Tape

Continue to have students identify and mark multiples of 2, 3, 4, 5, 6, 7, and 8 with Multiple Markers. Begin marking multiples of 9 with Dotted Square Multiple Markers.

As students call out the multiples of 9, point out that 9 is one less than 10, so the 2nd multiple of 9 is 2 less than 20, or 18.

- **On what number will we hang our 7th Dotted Square? Our 9th Dotted Square?**
- **How can we use 10 groups of any number to find 9 groups of the same number?** Multiply the number by ten, then subtract that number from the product.

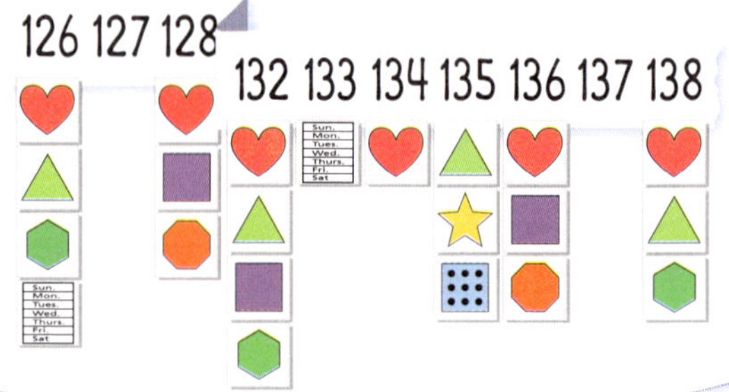

Differentiated Instruction Activities

ELL Language Support

Visual
Small Group

Strategy: **Draw**

Materials MathBoards

- Students will develop a better understanding of line plots by following step-by-step instructions to draw one. Draw a number line on the board. Have students copy the number line on their MathBoards.
- Write the following numbers on the board: $\frac{3}{5}$, $\frac{3}{5}$, $\frac{4}{5}$, $\frac{1}{5}$, $\frac{2}{5}$, $\frac{1}{5}$, $\frac{3}{5}$, $\frac{2}{5}$; $\frac{1}{5}$.
- Have students order the fractions from least to greatest, and then draw and label tick marks on the number line for the data: $\frac{1}{5}$, $\frac{2}{5}$, $\frac{3}{5}$, and so on.
- Ask students to describe the line plot. For example, "the data include the fractions $\frac{1}{5}$, $\frac{2}{5}$, $\frac{3}{5}$, and $\frac{4}{5}$. The fraction $\frac{1}{5}$ was found 3 times." Then have them plot the appropriate number of Xs above each value. Discuss the results.

Enrich

Visual
Partners

Materials index cards, poster board

- Have each student choose one of the following fractions to write on an index card: $\frac{1}{10}$, $\frac{1}{5}$, $\frac{3}{10}$, $\frac{2}{5}$, $\frac{1}{2}$, $\frac{3}{5}$, $\frac{7}{10}$, $\frac{4}{5}$, and $\frac{9}{10}$. Collect and show the cards.
- Have the group work together to order the values from least to greatest.
- Have pairs draw a number line on poster board and draw tick marks on their number lines for the data. Then have them count to determine the number of times each fraction was chosen.
- Have pairs complete their line plots by plotting the appropriate number of Xs for each value.

RtI Response to Intervention

Reteach Tier 1

Kinesthetic / Visual
Whole Class / Small Group

Materials MathBoards

- Have students draw a number line on their MathBoards. Then write the following numbers on the board: $\frac{1}{2}$, $\frac{1}{4}$, $\frac{3}{4}$, $\frac{1}{2}$, $\frac{3}{4}$, $\frac{3}{4}$, $\frac{1}{4}$, $\frac{3}{4}$, $\frac{3}{4}$.
- **What numbers should be used to label a line plot for these data?** $\frac{1}{2}$, $\frac{1}{4}$, $\frac{3}{4}$
- **How do you order these values from least to greatest?** $\frac{1}{4}$, $\frac{1}{2}$, $\frac{3}{4}$
- Have students add three tick marks to their number lines and label them.
- **How many times does $\frac{3}{4}$ appear in the data?** 5
- Have students plot 5 Xs above $\frac{3}{4}$. Then have them count and plot Xs for $\frac{1}{4}$ and $\frac{1}{2}$. Discuss the line plot.

Tier 2

Kinesthetic / Visual
Small Group

Materials index cards, sticky notes

- Draw a large number line on poster board with tick marks and labels from 0 through $\frac{5}{8}$.
- Prepare 8 index cards with the following fractions, one to a card: $\frac{1}{8}$, $\frac{1}{8}$, $\frac{1}{8}$, $\frac{1}{8}$, $\frac{4}{8}$, $\frac{4}{8}$, $\frac{4}{8}$, $\frac{5}{8}$.
- Display the cards. **How can we show these numbers on a line plot?** Draw an X above each number for every time it appears.
- Have students draw an X on a sticky note and place it above the appropriate fraction for each time that fraction appears in the data set.
- Have them count the cards to check the line plot. Discuss how they know the results were accurate.

CC.4.MD.4 Make a line plot to display a data set of measurements in fractions of a unit (1/2, 1/4, 1/8). Solve problems involving addition and subtraction of fractions by using information presented in line plots.

1 ENGAGE

Access Prior Knowledge Draw a number line with 3 tick marks on the board. Label the first tick mark 0 and the last tick mark 1. Ask students to suggest the number that the middle tick mark represents. Since it is in the middle of 0 and 1, the mark represents $\frac{1}{2}$.

2 TEACH and TALK

Unlock the Problem

Have students predict how they think the line plot will help them solve the problem. Revisit their predictions after finding the solution.

Example 1

Explain that it is important to organize the information available before making a line plot. In this case, students should list the numbers in order from the least value to the greatest value.

Make sure students include $\frac{2}{4}$ on the number line.

- **Why is there no X above $\frac{2}{4}$?** Possible answer: there is no data for that number.
- **What do the 2 Xs above $\frac{4}{4}$ represent?** Possible answer: the 2 Xs above $\frac{4}{4}$ represent the 2 buttons that are $\frac{4}{4}$ or 1 inch long.

Use **Math Talk** to focus on students' understanding of how to identify and label information shown in line plots.

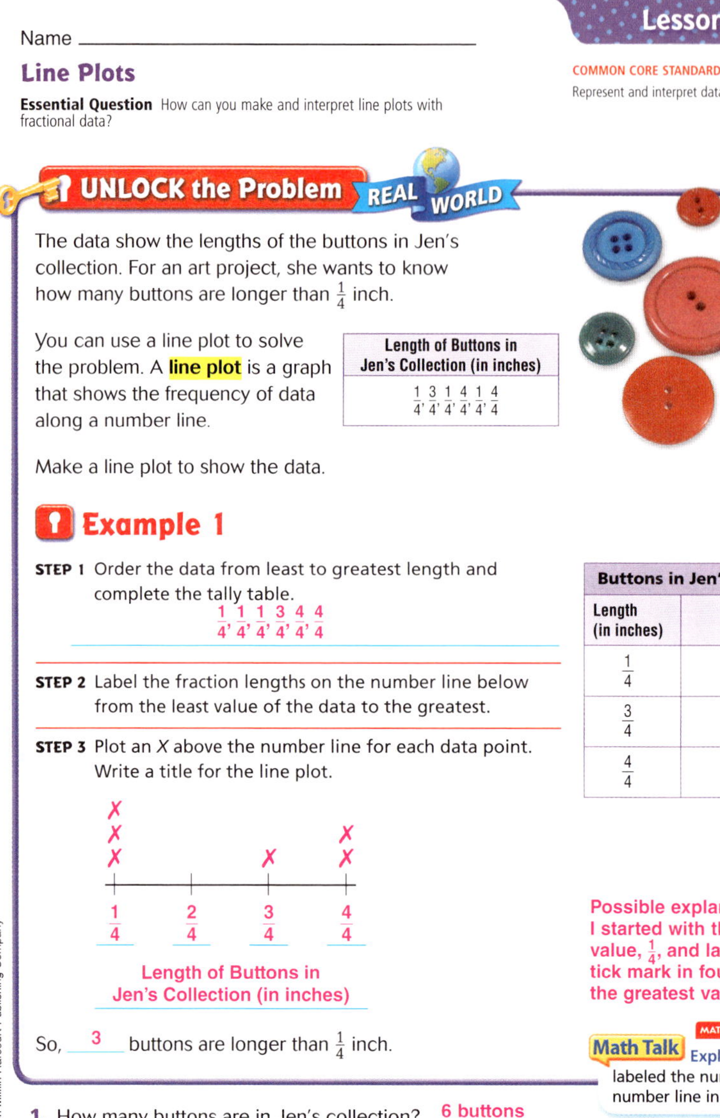

Lesson 12.5

Name ______

Line Plots

COMMON CORE STANDARD CC.4.MD.4
Represent and interpret data.

Essential Question How can you make and interpret line plots with fractional data?

UNLOCK the Problem REAL WORLD

The data show the lengths of the buttons in Jen's collection. For an art project, she wants to know how many buttons are longer than $\frac{1}{4}$ inch.

You can use a line plot to solve the problem. A **line plot** is a graph that shows the frequency of data along a number line.

Length of Buttons in Jen's Collection (in inches)
$\frac{1}{4}$, $\frac{3}{4}$, $\frac{1}{4}$, $\frac{4}{4}$, $\frac{1}{4}$, $\frac{4}{4}$

Make a line plot to show the data.

Example 1

STEP 1 Order the data from least to greatest length and complete the tally table.
$\frac{1}{4}$, $\frac{1}{4}$, $\frac{1}{4}$, $\frac{3}{4}$, $\frac{4}{4}$, $\frac{4}{4}$

Buttons in Jen's Collection	
Length (in inches)	Tally
$\frac{1}{4}$	|||
$\frac{3}{4}$		
$\frac{4}{4}$	||

STEP 2 Label the fraction lengths on the number line below from the least value of the data to the greatest.

STEP 3 Plot an X above the number line for each data point. Write a title for the line plot.

Possible explanation: I started with the least value, $\frac{1}{4}$, and labeled each tick mark in fourths until the greatest value, $\frac{4}{4}$.

So, 3 buttons are longer than $\frac{1}{4}$ inch.

MATHEMATICAL PRACTICES **Math Talk** Explain how you labeled the numbers on the number line in Step 2.

1. How many buttons are in Jen's collection? 6 buttons
2. What is the difference in length between the longest button and the shortest button in Jen's collection? $\frac{3}{4}$ inch

Think: To find the difference, subtract the numerators. The denominators stay the same.

© Houghton Mifflin Harcourt Publishing Company

Chapter 12 461

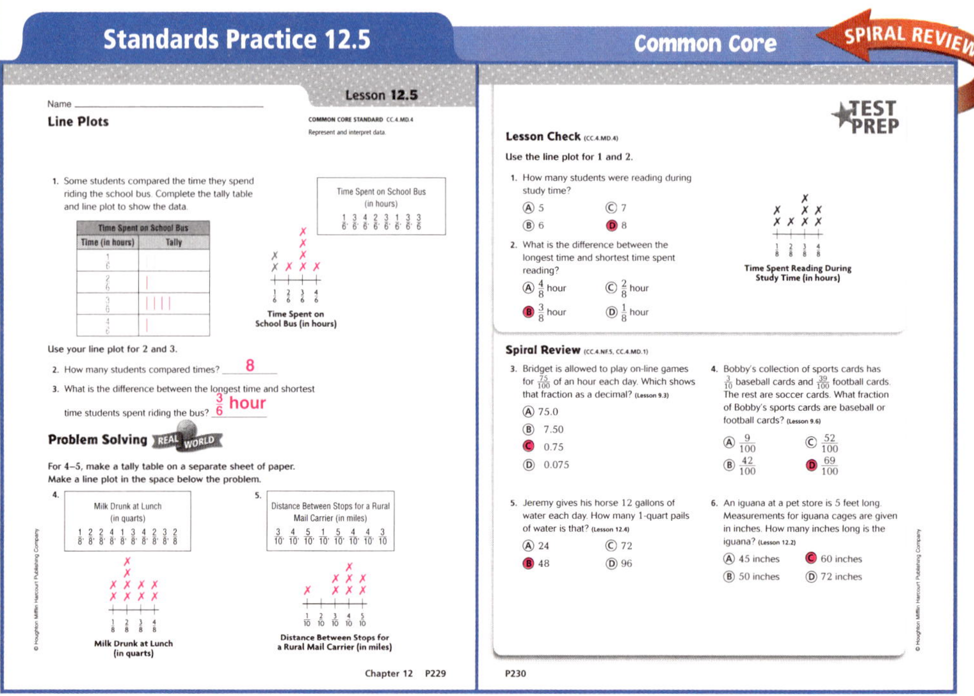

Standards Practice 12.5

Lesson 12.5

Name ______

Line Plots

COMMON CORE STANDARD CC.4.MD.4
Represent and interpret data.

1. Some students compared the time they spend riding the school bus. Complete the tally table and line plot to show the data.

Time Spent on School Bus (in hours)
$\frac{1}{6}$, $\frac{3}{6}$, $\frac{4}{6}$, $\frac{2}{6}$, $\frac{3}{6}$, $\frac{1}{6}$, $\frac{3}{6}$, $\frac{3}{6}$

Time Spent on School Bus	
Time (in hours)	Tally
$\frac{1}{6}$	||
$\frac{2}{6}$		
$\frac{3}{6}$	||||
$\frac{4}{6}$		

Use your line plot for 2 and 3.

2. How many students compared times? 8
3. What is the difference between the longest time and shortest time students spent riding the bus? $\frac{3}{6}$ hour

Problem Solving REAL WORLD

For 4–5, make a tally table on a separate sheet of paper. Make a line plot in the space below the problem.

4.

Milk Drunk at Lunch (in quarts)
$\frac{1}{8}$, $\frac{2}{8}$, $\frac{2}{8}$, $\frac{4}{8}$, $\frac{1}{8}$, $\frac{3}{8}$, $\frac{4}{8}$, $\frac{2}{8}$, $\frac{3}{8}$, $\frac{2}{8}$

5.

Distance Between Stops for a Rural Mail Carrier (in miles)
$\frac{3}{10}$, $\frac{4}{10}$, $\frac{5}{10}$, $\frac{1}{10}$, $\frac{5}{10}$, $\frac{4}{10}$, $\frac{4}{10}$, $\frac{3}{10}$

© Houghton Mifflin Harcourt Publishing Company

Chapter 12 P229

Common Core SPIRAL REVIEW

TEST PREP

Lesson Check (CC.4.MD.4)

Use the line plot for 1 and 2.

1. How many students were reading during study time?
   (A) 5 (B) 6 (C) 7 (D) 8
2. What is the difference between the longest time and shortest time spent reading?
   (A) $\frac{4}{8}$ hour (B) $\frac{3}{8}$ hour (C) $\frac{2}{8}$ hour (D) $\frac{1}{8}$ hour

Spiral Review (CC.4.NF.5, CC.4.MD.1)

3. Bridget is allowed to play on-line games for $\frac{75}{100}$ of an hour each day. Which shows that fraction as a decimal? (Lesson 9.3)
   (A) 75.0 (B) 7.50 (C) 0.75 (D) 0.075
4. Bobby's collection of sports cards has $\frac{3}{10}$ baseball cards and $\frac{39}{100}$ football cards. The rest are soccer cards. What fraction of Bobby's sports cards are baseball or football cards? (Lesson 9.6)
   (A) $\frac{9}{100}$ (B) $\frac{42}{100}$ (C) $\frac{52}{100}$ (D) $\frac{69}{100}$
5. Jeremy gives his horse 12 gallons of water each day. How many 1-quart pails of water is that? (Lesson 12.4)
   (A) 24 (B) 48 (C) 72 (D) 96
6. An iguana at a pet store is 5 feet long. Measurements for iguana cages are given in inches. How many inches long is the iguana? (Lesson 12.2)
   (A) 45 inches (B) 50 inches (C) 60 inches (D) 72 inches

© Houghton Mifflin Harcourt Publishing Company

P230

Example 2

Some of the students in Ms. Lee's class walk to school. The data show the distances these students walk. What distance do most students walk?

Distance Students Walk to School (in miles)
$\frac{1}{2}, \frac{1}{2}, \frac{1}{4}, \frac{3}{4}, \frac{1}{4}, \frac{1}{2}, \frac{1}{2}$

Make a line plot to show the data.

STEP 1 Order the data from least to greatest distance and complete the tally table.

$\frac{1}{4}, \frac{1}{4}, \frac{1}{2}, \frac{1}{2}, \frac{1}{2}, \frac{1}{2}, \frac{3}{4}$

STEP 2 Label the fraction lengths on the number line below from the least value of the data to the greatest.

STEP 3 Plot an *X* above the number line for each data point. Write a title for the line plot.

Distance Students Walk to School	
Distance (in miles)	Tally
$\frac{1}{4}$	||
$\frac{1}{2}$	||||
$\frac{3}{4}$	|

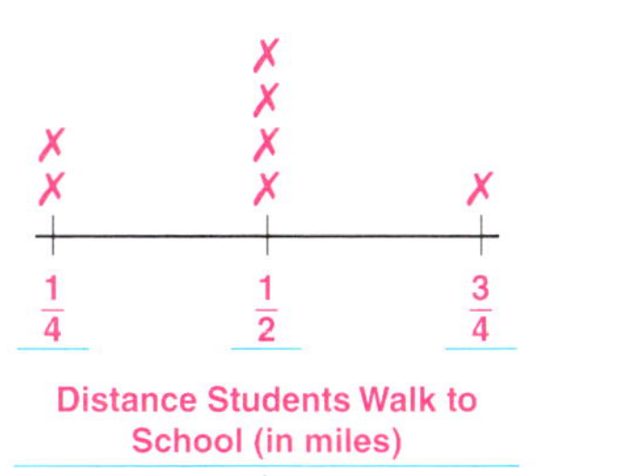

Distance Students Walk to School (in miles)

So, most students walk $\frac{1}{2}$ mile.

3. How many more students walk $\frac{1}{2}$ mile than $\frac{1}{4}$ mile to school?

   2 more students

4. What is the difference between the longest distance and the shortest distance that students walk?

   $\frac{2}{4}$ or $\frac{1}{2}$ mile

5. **What if** a new student joins Ms. Lee's class who walks $\frac{3}{4}$ mile to school? How would the line plot change? **Explain.**

   Possible explanation: there would be an additional *X* above $\frac{3}{4}$.

© Houghton Mifflin Harcourt Publishing Company

Reteach 12.5

Name ______ Lesson 12.5 Reteach

Line Plots

Howard gave a piece of paper with several survey questions to his friends. Then he made a list to show how long it took for his friends to answer the survey. Howard wants to know how many surveys took longer than $\frac{2}{12}$ hour.

Time for Survey Answers (in hours)
$\frac{1}{12}$ $\frac{3}{12}$ $\frac{1}{12}$ $\frac{2}{12}$ $\frac{6}{12}$ $\frac{3}{12}$ $\frac{5}{12}$

Make a line plot to show the data.

Step 1 Order the data from least to greatest.

$\frac{1}{12}, \frac{1}{12}, \frac{2}{12}, \frac{3}{12}, \frac{3}{12}, \frac{5}{12}, \frac{6}{12}$

Step 2 Make a tally table of the data.

Step 3 Label the fractions of an hour on the number line from least to greatest. Notice that $\frac{4}{12}$ is included even though it is not in the data.

Step 4 Plot an *X* above the number line for each piece of data. Write a title for the line plot.

Step 5 Count the number of *X*s that represent data points greater than $\frac{2}{12}$ hour.

There are 4 data points greater than $\frac{2}{12}$ hour.

So, 4 surveys took more than $\frac{2}{12}$ hour.

Survey	
Time (in hours)	Tally
$\frac{1}{12}$	||
$\frac{2}{12}$	|
$\frac{3}{12}$	||
$\frac{5}{12}$	|
$\frac{6}{12}$	|

Time for Survey Answers (in hours)

Use the line plot above for 1 and 2.

1. How many of the surveys that Howard gave to his friends were answered? 7

2. What is the difference in hours between the longest time and the shortest time that it took Howard's friends to answer the survey?

   $\frac{5}{12}$ hour

Reteach R92 Grade 4

© Houghton Mifflin Harcourt Publishing Company

Enrich 12.5

Name ______ Lesson 12.5 Enrich

Discover the Line Plot

The students in Richie's class were asked how much juice they drink at breakfast. Use the clues to make a line plot. Draw your line plot in the space below. Remember to include a title.

1. The most any student drinks is $1\frac{1}{2}$ cups of juice.
2. The response given most often was $\frac{3}{4}$ cup. The number of responses was 1 more than the next greatest amount.
3. Two students said that they don't drink any juice in the morning.
4. The students drink a total of $8\frac{1}{4}$ cups of juice.
5. Three students drink 1 cup of juice each.
6. Together, only three students gave a response of $\frac{1}{4}, \frac{1}{2}, 1\frac{1}{4}$, or $1\frac{1}{2}$, and none of these had more than 1 response.

0, $\frac{1}{4}$, $\frac{2}{4}$ ($\frac{1}{2}$), $\frac{3}{4}$, $\frac{4}{4}$ (1), $\frac{5}{4}$ ($1\frac{1}{4}$), $\frac{6}{4}$ ($1\frac{1}{2}$)

Amount of Juice Students Drink at Breakfast (in cups)

7. **Stretch Your Thinking** What fraction of the students drank more than $\frac{1}{2}$ cup of juice? **Explain.**

   $\frac{2}{3}$; Possible explanation: From the clues and the line plot, 8 students out of the 12 drink more than $\frac{1}{2}$ cup, and $\frac{8}{12} = \frac{2}{3}$.

Enrich E92 Grade 4

© Houghton Mifflin Harcourt Publishing Company

Example 2

Have students read the problem. Work together through the steps and draw the line plot on the board as students make the line plot on their paper.

Step 1 Remind students that ordering the data is an important step in making a line plot.

Step 2 Draw a number line on the board and have students call out the labels that should be used. Remind them that they label the number line in equal intervals from the least to the greatest data value. Discuss how the denominators of the fractions are not all the same, but the intervals on the number line are equal.

Step 3 Have volunteers plot the values on the line plot drawn on the board.

- **Which fraction has the most Xs?** $\frac{1}{2}$
- **Which fraction has the fewest Xs?** $\frac{3}{4}$

Reinforce to students that a line plot is simply a number line used to organize information.

Go Deeper

Ask students how they would add a new student who walked $1\frac{1}{4}$ miles to school to the line plot. Discuss that the distance could be shown as $\frac{5}{4}$ and added as the greatest value on the line.

COMMON ERRORS

Error Students may not include all data in a line plot.

Example In Example 2, students plot only 3 Xs above $\frac{1}{2}$.

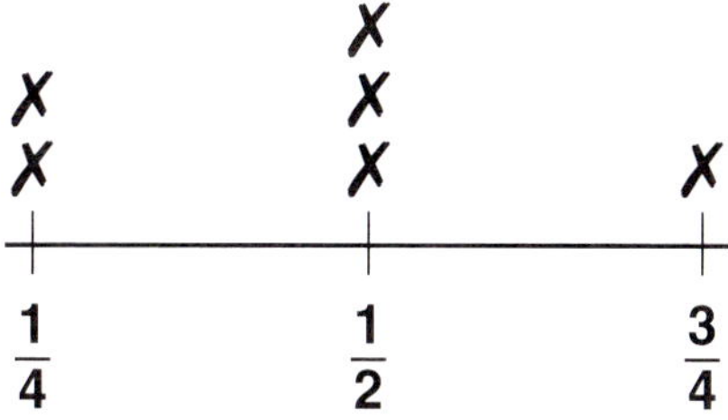

Springboard to Learning Have students list the data they will use in the line plot in order, and mark each number as they plot it.

3 PRACTICE 

▶ Share and Show • Guided Practice

The first problem connects to the learning model. Have students use the MathBoard to explain their thinking. To help students understand the data, show them a clock and point out how each fraction relates to an hour, such as $\frac{1}{4}$ hour = 15 minutes.

Use Exercises 2 and 3 for Quick Check.

Use Math Talk to focus on students' understanding of how to interpret the data in a line plot.

 **Quick Check** 

If a student misses Exercises 2 and 3

Then Differentiate Instruction with
- RtI Tier 1 Activity, p. 461B
- Reteach 12.5
- Soar to Success Math 54.17

▶ On Your Own • Independent Practice

If students complete Exercises 2 and 3 correctly, they may continue with Independent Practice.

Name ____________________

Share and Show 

1. A food critic collected data on the lengths of time customers waited for their food. Order the data from least to greatest time. Make a tally table and a line plot to show the data.

Time Customers Waited for Food (in hours)
$\frac{1}{2}$, $\frac{1}{4}$, $\frac{1}{4}$, $\frac{3}{4}$, $\frac{1}{4}$, $\frac{1}{2}$, 1

Time Customers Waited for Food	
Time (in hours)	Tally
$\frac{1}{4}$	|||
$\frac{1}{2}$	||
$\frac{3}{4}$	|
1	|

$\frac{1}{4}$	$\frac{1}{2}$	$\frac{3}{4}$	1
X X X	X X	X	X

Time Customers Waited for Food (in hours)

Possible explanation: I counted all the Xs that represent the collected data.

MATHEMATICAL PRACTICES **Math Talk** Explain how the line plot helped you answer the question for Exercise 2.

Use your line plot for 2 and 3.

2. On how many customers did the food critic collect data? 7 customers

3. What is the difference between the longest time and the shortest time that customers waited? $\frac{3}{4}$ hour

On Your Own

4. The data show the lengths of the ribbons Mia used to wrap packages. Make a tally table and a line plot to show the data.

Ribbon Length Used to Wrap Packages (in yards)
$\frac{1}{6}$, $\frac{2}{6}$, $\frac{5}{6}$, $\frac{3}{6}$, $\frac{2}{6}$, $\frac{6}{6}$, $\frac{3}{6}$, $\frac{2}{6}$

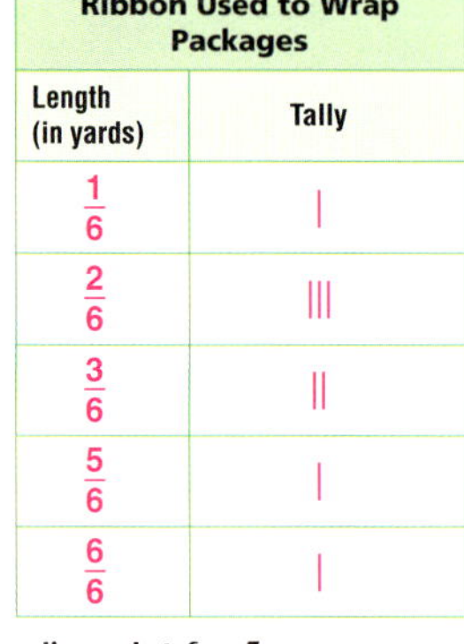

Ribbon Used to Wrap Packages	
Length (in yards)	Tally
$\frac{1}{6}$	|
$\frac{2}{6}$	|||
$\frac{3}{6}$	||
$\frac{5}{6}$	|
$\frac{6}{6}$	|

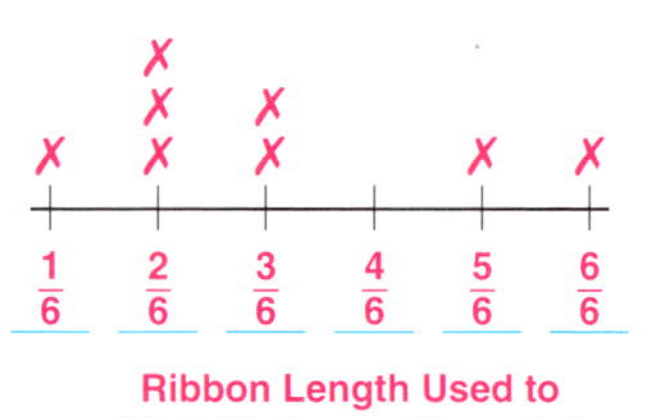

$\frac{1}{6}$	$\frac{2}{6}$	$\frac{3}{6}$	$\frac{4}{6}$	$\frac{5}{6}$	$\frac{6}{6}$
X	X X X	X X		X	X

Ribbon Length Used to Wrap Packages (in yards)

Use your line plot for 5.

5. What is the difference in length between the longest ribbon and the shortest ribbon Mia used? $\frac{5}{6}$ yard

© Houghton Mifflin Harcourt Publishing Company

Extend the Math Activity

Collecting Data

Materials rulers

Investigate Students have learned how to create line plots. In this activity, they will collect their own fractional data to display using a line plot.

- Have pairs use rulers to find classroom objects with the following measurements: $\frac{1}{4}$ inch, $\frac{1}{2}$ inch, $\frac{3}{4}$ inch.
- Have students list the objects and their measurements. Pairs should make a line plot to display the data they collect.

Summarize Allow students to share their line plots. Discuss the number of objects each pair found for the given measurements, and compare the line plots in relation to on the objects found. Ask students to suggest how the line plots might have been different if another fractional measurement had been included.

6. The line plot shows the distances the students in Mr. Boren's class ran at the track in miles. Altogether, did the students run more or less than 5 miles?

X X X X X X X X

$\frac{1}{5}$ $\frac{2}{5}$ $\frac{3}{5}$ $\frac{4}{5}$ $\frac{5}{5}$

Distance Students Ran at the Track (in miles)

a. What are you asked to find? if the students ran more or less than 5 miles altogether

b. What information do you need to use? the distance each student ran

c. How will the line plot help you solve the problem? The line plot tells me how far each student ran.

d. What operation will you use to solve the problem? addition

e. Show the steps to solve the problem.

$\frac{1}{5}+\frac{1}{5}+\frac{2}{5}+\frac{2}{5}+\frac{3}{5}+\frac{4}{5}+\frac{4}{5}+\frac{5}{5}=\frac{22}{5}$

$=4\frac{2}{5}$

f. Complete the sentences.

The students ran a total of $4\frac{2}{5}$ miles.

$4\frac{2}{5}$ miles $<$ 5 miles; so, altogether the students ran less than 5 miles.

7. H.O.T. Write Math Lena collects antique spoons. The line plot shows the lengths of the spoons in her collection. If she lines up all of her spoons in order of size, what is the size of the middle spoon? Explain.

$\frac{4}{4}$ or 1 foot; possible explanation: I ordered the data from the least to greatest value and found the middle value.

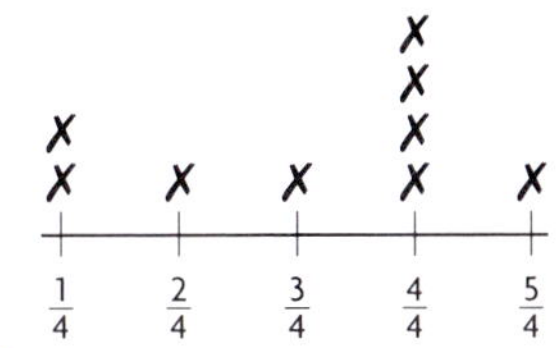

Length of Spoons (in feet)

8. Test Prep The line plot shows the distances some students hiked. What is the difference between the longest distance and the shortest distance the students hiked?

Ⓐ $\frac{1}{8}$ mile

Ⓑ $\frac{3}{8}$ mile

Ⓒ $\frac{7}{8}$ mile

Ⓓ $\frac{11}{8}$ mile

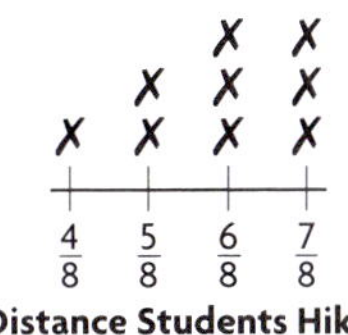

Distance Students Hiked (in miles)

© Houghton Mifflin Harcourt Publishing Company

FOR MORE PRACTICE: Standards Practice Book, pp. P229–P230

FOR EXTRA PRACTICE: Standards Practice Book, p. P243

▶ Unlock the Problem

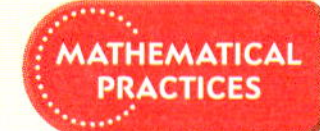

H.O.T. Problem Exercise 7 requires students to organize the given information by size before identifying the middle value. Make sure students order the values and not the number of Xs shown for each.

Test Prep Coach

In Exercise 8, if students selected:

A They chose the difference between the longest distance and 1.

C They chose the longest distance.

D They added the longest distance and the shortest distance.

4 SUMMARIZE

Essential Question

How can you make and interpret line plots with fractional data? Possible answer: I order the fractions from least to greatest. Then I draw a number line and label it with those values. I draw an X over the value each time it is used, and then count the Xs to see which values were used most and least.

Math Journal

Write a problem that can be solved using a line plot. Draw and label the line plot and solve the problem.

Differentiated Instruction

INDEPENDENT ACTIVITIES

Differentiated Centers Kit

Activities

Measure Up

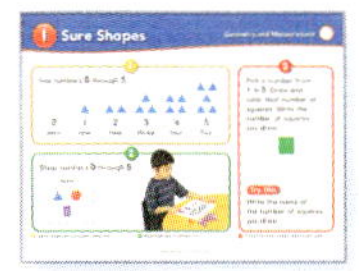

Students complete blue Activity Card 1 by comparing lengths.

Literature

A Trip to the Pond

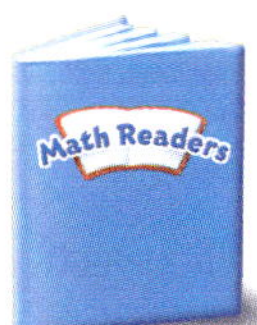

Students read about using metric units to measure and identify insects.

Mid-Chapter Checkpoint

LESSONS 12.1 TO 12.5

Formative Assessment

Use the **Mid-Chapter Checkpoint** to assess students' learning and progress in the first half of the chapter. The formative assessment provides the opportunity to adjust teaching methods for individual or whole class instruction.

Name ____________________

Mid-Chapter Checkpoint

Vocabulary

Choose the best term from the box to complete the sentence.

Vocabulary
pint
pound
yard

1. A **pound** is a customary unit used to measure weight. (p. 453)
2. The cup and the **pint** are both customary units for measuring liquid volume. (p. 457)

Concepts and Skills

Complete the sentence. Write *more* or *less*. (CC.4.MD.1)

3. A cat weighs **more** than one ounce.
4. Serena's shoe is **less** than one yard long.

Complete. (CC.4.MD.1)

5. 5 feet = **60** inches
6. 4 tons = **8,000** pounds
7. 4 cups = **2** pints

8. Mrs. Byrne's class went raspberry picking. The data show the weights of the cartons of raspberries the students picked. Make a tally table and a line plot to show the data. (CC.4.MD.4)

Weight of Cartons of Raspberries Picked (in pounds)
$\frac{3}{4}$, $\frac{1}{4}$, $\frac{2}{4}$, $\frac{4}{4}$, $\frac{1}{4}$, $\frac{1}{4}$, $\frac{2}{4}$, $\frac{3}{4}$, $\frac{3}{4}$

Cartons of Raspberries Picked	
Weight (in pounds)	Tally
$\frac{1}{4}$	III
$\frac{2}{4}$	II
$\frac{3}{4}$	III
$\frac{4}{4}$	I

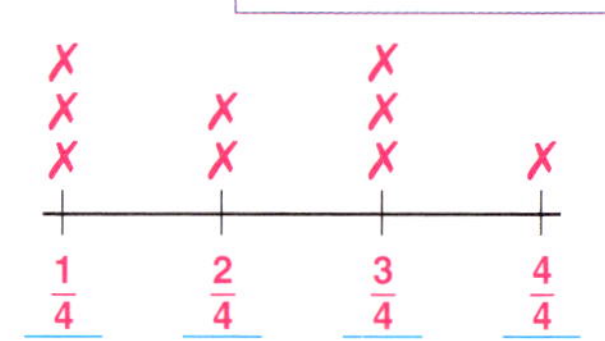

Weight of Cartons of Raspberries Picked (in pounds)

© Houghton Mifflin Harcourt Publishing Company

Use your line plot for 9 and 10. (CC.4.MD.4)

9. What is the difference in weight between the heaviest carton and lightest carton of raspberries? **$\frac{3}{4}$ pound**
10. How many pounds of raspberries did Mrs. Byrne's class pick in all? **5 pounds**

Data-Driven Decision Making

Based on the results of the Mid-Chapter Checkpoint, use the following resources to strengthen individual or whole class instruction.

Item	Lesson	*CCSS	Common Error	Intervene With	Soar to Success Math
3, 4	12.1	CC.4.MD.1	May confuse measurement benchmarks	**R**—12.1; **TE**—p. 445B	41.16, 41.17, 42.09, 42.10, 43.11, 43.12
5	12.2	CC.4.MD.1	May multiply units of length incorrectly	**R**—12.2; **TE**—p. 449B	41.09, 44.36
6	12.3	CC.4.MD.1	May multiply units of weight incorrectly	**R**—12.3; **TE**—p. 453B	42.05, 45.30
7	12.4	CC.4.MD.1	May multiply units of liquid volume incorrectly	**R**—12.4; **TE**—p. 457B	43.07, 46.37
8–10	12.5	CC.4.MD.4	May not correctly place all data in the line plot	**R**—12.5; **TE**—p. 461B	54.17

***CCSS**—Common Core State Standards **Key: R**—Reteach Book; **TE**—RtI Activities

Fill in the bubble completely to show your answer.

11. A jug contains 2 gallons of water. How many quarts of water does the jug contain? (CC.4.MD.1)

    Ⓐ 4 quarts

    Ⓑ 8 quarts

    Ⓒ 16 quarts

    Ⓓ 32 quarts

12. Serena bought 4 pounds of dough to make pizzas. The recipe gives the amount of dough needed for a pizza in ounces. How many ounces of dough did she buy? (CC.4.MD.1)

    Ⓐ 8 ounces

    Ⓑ 16 ounces

    Ⓒ 64 ounces

    Ⓓ 96 ounces

13. Vaughn threw the shot put 9 yards at a track meet. The official used a tape measure to measure the distance in feet. How many feet did he throw the shot put? (CC.4.MD.1)

    Ⓐ 27 feet

    Ⓑ 30 feet

    Ⓒ 108 feet

    Ⓓ 324 feet

14. What is the best estimate for the amount of liquid a watering can holds? (CC.4.MD.1)

    Ⓐ 5 ounces

    Ⓑ 5 cups

    Ⓒ 5 quarts

    Ⓓ 5 gallons

© Houghton Mifflin Harcourt Publishing Company

Data-Driven Decision Making

Item	Lesson	CCSS	Common Error	Intervene With	Soar to Success Math
11	12.4	CC.4.MD.1	May not multiply by the correct number of quarts	**R**—12.4; **TE**—p. 457B	43.07, 46.37
12	12.3	CC.4.MD.1	May not multiply by the correct number of ounces	**R**—12.3; **TE**—p. 453B	42.05, 45.30
13	12.2	CC.4.MD.1	May not multiply by the correct number of feet	**R**—12.2; **TE**—p. 449B	41.09, 44.36
14	12.1	CC.4.MD.1	May not choose a unit used for liquid volume	**R**—12.1; **TE**—p. 445B	41.16, 41.17, 42.09, 42.10, 43.11, 43.12

***CCSS**—Common Core State Standards **Key: R**—Reteach Book; **TE**—RtI Activities

LESSON 12.6

Investigate • Metric Units of Length

LESSON AT A GLANCE

Common Core Standard

Solve problems involving measurement and conversion of measurements from a larger unit to a smaller unit.

CC.4.MD.1 Know relative sizes of measurement units within one system of units including km, m, cm; kg, g; lb, oz.; l, ml; hr, min, sec. Within a single system of measurement, express measurements in a larger unit in terms of a smaller unit. Record measurement equivalents in a two-column table.

Lesson Objective

Use models to compare metric units of length.

Essential Question

How can you use models to compare metric units of length?

Vocabulary

decimeter, millimeter

Materials

MathBoard, Ruler (meter) (*see eTeacher Resources*), scissors, tape

Digital Path

Animated Math Models

eStudent Edition

HMH Mega Math

COMMON CORE PROFESSIONAL DEVELOPMENT

About the Math

Teaching for Depth The metric system of measurement is based on the powers of 10 (10, 100, 1,000, and so on). Tell students that metric measures of length, liquid volume, and mass are used throughout the world. Help them understand that working with powers of 10 makes it easy to change from a larger unit to a smaller unit.

Demonstrate to students how changing from a larger unit to a smaller unit in the metric system, such as from centimeters to millimeters, is much simpler than changing from a larger unit to a smaller unit in the customary system, such as feet to inches. Multiplication by powers of 10 is easier than multiplication by 12 or other unit conversion amounts.

Professional Development Video Podcasts

Daily Routines

Common Core

SPIRAL REVIEW

Problem of the Day

Test Prep The tiger at the local zoo eats 15 pounds of meat each day. How many pounds does the tiger eat in 7 days?

Ⓐ 95 pounds Ⓒ 115 pounds
Ⓑ 105 pounds Ⓓ 125 pounds

Vocabulary Builder

Measurement Units Have students make vocabulary cards for the metric units introduced in this lesson: millimeter, centimeter, decimeter, and meter. Students can show the relationships between units on the card. Have students include the abbreviation for each unit: millimeter (mm), centimeter (cm), decimeter (dm), and meter (m). Remind students that the abbreviations do not include a period.

Literature

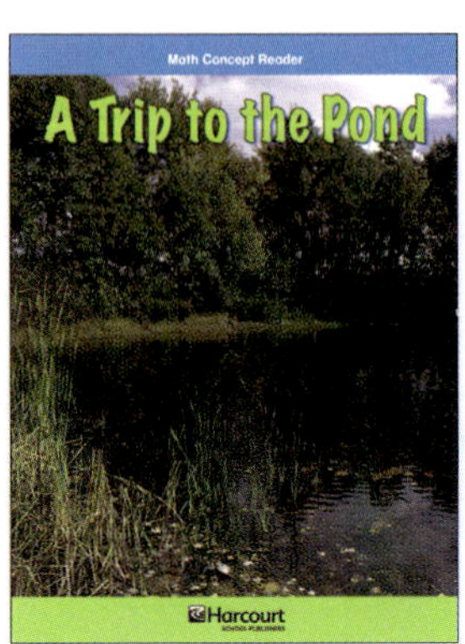

A Trip to the Pond

From the Grab-and-Go™ Differentiated Centers Kit

Students read about using metric units to measure and identify insects.

Differentiated Instruction Activities

ELL Language Support  Visual / Small Group

Strategy: Draw

Materials 1-Centimeter Grid Paper (see *eTeacher Resources*)

- Have them turn the grid paper lengthwise and draw a line the length of one square on the grid paper. Tell them that this line represents 1 centimeter, and have them label it.
- Ask students how many squares long they should make a line that represents 1 decimeter. 10 Have them draw a line that is 10 squares long and label it as 1 decimeter.
- Have students draw lines that have a total length of 100 centimeters. After students cut and tape the lines together, explain that the line represents one meter. Discuss the relative lengths of the lines.

See ELL Activity Guide for leveled activities.

Enrich  Visual / Individual / Small Group

Materials Ruler (meter) (see *eTeacher Resources*), index cards, poster board

- Have each student write a fraction with a denominator of 10 and a numerator less than 10, or a denominator of 100 and a numerator less than 100. Tell them to write *meters* as the unit for each fraction.
- Place the cards face down in a pile. Each student draws a card and then uses the meterstick to draw a line on the poster board the length of the fraction of a meter given.
- Have students label the lines with the lengths as fractions of a meter. Then have the group work together to rename each measurement using decimeters or centimeters. Tell them to label each line with the new units as well. Display the poster in the classroom.

Response to Intervention

Reteach Tier 1  Kinesthetic / Visual / Whole Class / Small Group

Materials Ruler (meter) (see *eTeacher Resources*)

- Provide students with measurements in centimeters or in decimeters of objects around the classroom. Write each item and its measurement on the board.
- **How many decimeters in a meter?** 10 **How many centimeters in a meter?** 100
- For each measurement in centimeters, have pairs write the length as a fraction of a meter. Remind them that since there are 100 centimeters in a meter, the denominator should be 100. For decimeters, remind students to use 10 as the denominator since there are 10 decimeters in a meter.

Tier 2  Kinesthetic / Visual / Small Group

Materials Ruler (meter) (see *eTeacher Resources*)

- Write the following on the board: 1 meter = 10 decimeters; 1 meter = 100 centimeters.
- Point to 1 decimeter on the meterstick. **What is this measurement?** 1 decimeter Repeat with 1 centimeter.
- Ask each student to find one of the following measurements: 8 decimeters, 17 centimeters, 3 decimeters, 53 centimeters, 9 decimeters.
- Write each measurement on the board. Then have students write each measurement as a fraction of a meter. Remind them to start with a denominator of 100 for centimeters and a denominator of 10 for decimeters.

CCC.4.MD.1 Know relative sizes of measurement units within one system of units including km, m, cm; kg, g; lb, oz.; l, ml; hr, min, sec. Within a single system of measurement, express measurements in a larger unit in terms of a smaller unit. Record measurement equivalents in a two-column table.

1 ENGAGE

Access Prior Knowledge Show students a yardstick. Ask them to describe it. Point out that a yardstick is used to measure length in yards and inches, which are customary units.

- **How many inches are in a foot? How many feet are in a yard?** 12; 3

2 TEACH and TALK

▶ Investigate

Guide students to explore the meterstick.

- **What do you notice about the units on the meterstick?** Possible answer: the meterstick has units that repeat, and it has large units divided into smaller units that are the same size.
- **What abbreviations do you see on the meterstick?** mm, cm, dm, and m
- **What unit is *mm* an abbreviation for?** millimeters
- **What unit is *cm* an abbreviation for?** centimeters
- **What unit is *dm* an abbreviation for?** decimeters
- **What unit is *m* an abbreviation for?** meters

Discuss these units on the meterstick.

- **Which unit on the meterstick is the smallest in length?** millimeters
- **Which unit is the largest in length?** meter

▶ Draw Conclusions

- **How many centimeters are in 1 meter?** 100

Remind students that metric measurements of length use powers of 10, and 100 is a power of 10.

Lesson 12.6

Name ____________________

Metric Units of Length

Essential Question How can you use models to compare metric units of length?

COMMON CORE STANDARD CC.4.MD.1
Solve problems involving measurement and conversion of measurements from a larger unit to a smaller unit.

Investigate

Materials ■ ruler (meter) ■ scissors ■ tape

Meters (m), **decimeters** (dm), centimeters (cm), and **millimeters** (mm) are all metric units of length.

Build a meterstick to show how these units are related.

A. Cut out the meterstick strips.

B. Place the strips end-to-end to build 1 meter. Tape the strips together.

C. Look at your meter strip. What patterns do you notice about the sizes of the units?

1 meter is __10__ times as long as 1 decimeter.

1 decimeter is __10__ times as long as 1 centimeter.

1 centimeter is __10__ times as long as 1 millimeter.

Describe the pattern you see.

Possible description: each metric unit is 10 times as long as the next smaller unit.

Math Idea
If you lined up 1,000 metersticks end-to-end, the length of the metersticks would be 1 kilometer.

Draw Conclusions

1. **Compare** the size of 1 meter to the size of 1 centimeter. Use your meterstick to help.

1 meter is 100 times as long as 1 centimeter.

© Houghton Mifflin Harcourt Publishing Company

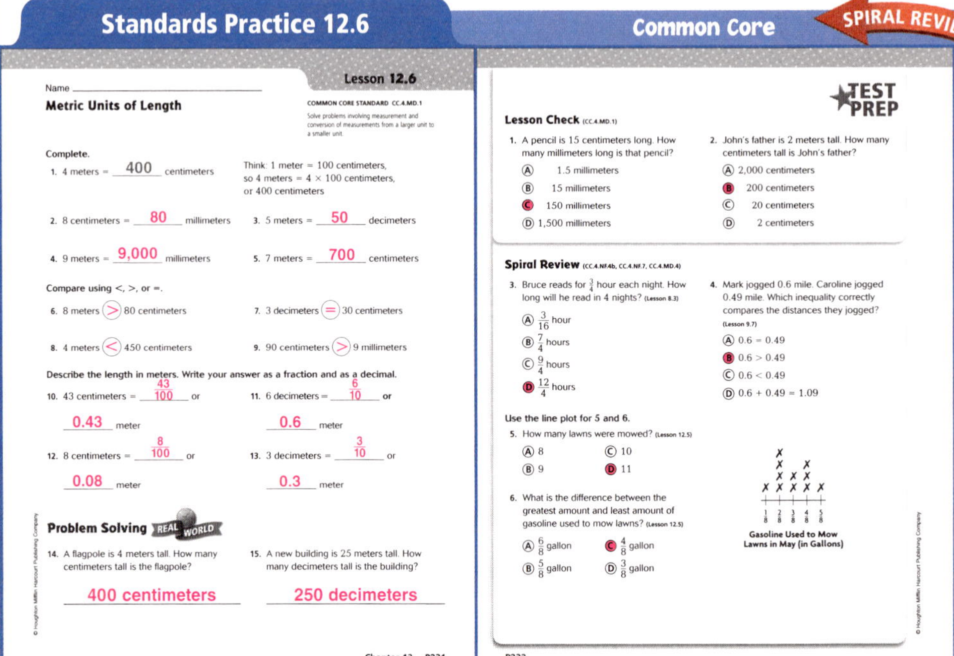

Standards Practice 12.6

Lesson 12.6

Name ____________________

Metric Units of Length

COMMON CORE STANDARD CC.4.MD.1
Solve problems involving measurement and conversion of measurements from a larger unit to a smaller unit.

Complete.

1. 4 meters = __400__ centimeters — Think: 1 meter = 100 centimeters, so 4 meters = 4 × 100 centimeters, or 400 centimeters
2. 8 centimeters = __80__ millimeters
3. 5 meters = __50__ decimeters
4. 9 meters = __9,000__ millimeters
5. 7 meters = __700__ centimeters

Compare using <, >, or =.

6. 8 meters (>) 80 centimeters
7. 3 decimeters (=) 30 centimeters
8. 4 meters (<) 450 centimeters
9. 90 centimeters (>) 9 millimeters

Describe the length in meters. Write your answer as a fraction and as a decimal.

10. 43 centimeters = __$\frac{43}{100}$__ or __0.43__ meter
11. 6 decimeters = __$\frac{6}{10}$__ or __0.6__ meter
12. 8 centimeters = __$\frac{8}{100}$__ or __0.08__ meter
13. 3 decimeters = __$\frac{3}{10}$__ or __0.3__ meter

Problem Solving REAL WORLD

14. A flagpole is 4 meters tall. How many centimeters tall is the flagpole?
__400 centimeters__
15. A new building is 25 meters tall. How many decimeters tall is the building?
__250 decimeters__

© Houghton Mifflin Harcourt Publishing Company

Chapter 12 P231

Common Core SPIRAL REVIEW

TEST PREP

Lesson Check (CC.4.MD.1)

1. A pencil is 15 centimeters long. How many millimeters long is that pencil?
   - Ⓐ 1.5 millimeters
   - Ⓑ 15 millimeters
   - Ⓒ 150 millimeters
   - Ⓓ 1,500 millimeters
2. John's father is 2 meters tall. How many centimeters tall is John's father?
   - Ⓐ 2,000 centimeters
   - Ⓑ 200 centimeters
   - Ⓒ 20 centimeters
   - Ⓓ 2 centimeters

Spiral Review (CC.4.NF.4b, CC.4.NF.7, CC.4.MD.4)

3. Bruce reads for $\frac{3}{4}$ hour each night. How long will he read in 4 nights? (Lesson 8.3)
   - Ⓐ $\frac{3}{16}$ hour
   - Ⓑ $\frac{7}{4}$ hours
   - Ⓒ $\frac{9}{4}$ hours
   - Ⓓ $\frac{12}{4}$ hours
4. Mark jogged 0.6 mile. Caroline jogged 0.49 mile. Which inequality correctly compares the distances they jogged? (Lesson 9.7)
   - Ⓐ 0.6 = 0.49
   - Ⓑ 0.6 > 0.49
   - Ⓒ 0.6 < 0.49
   - Ⓓ 0.6 + 0.49 = 1.09

Use the line plot for 5 and 6.

5. How many lawns were mowed? (Lesson 12.5)
   - Ⓐ 8
   - Ⓑ 9
   - Ⓒ 10
   - Ⓓ 11
6. What is the difference between the greatest amount and least amount of gasoline used to mow lawns? (Lesson 12.5)
   - Ⓐ $\frac{6}{8}$ gallon
   - Ⓑ $\frac{5}{8}$ gallon
   - Ⓒ $\frac{4}{8}$ gallon
   - Ⓓ $\frac{3}{8}$ gallon

$\frac{1}{8}$ $\frac{2}{8}$ $\frac{3}{8}$ $\frac{4}{8}$ $\frac{5}{8}$

Gasoline Used to Mow Lawns in May (in Gallons)

© Houghton Mifflin Harcourt Publishing Company

P232

2. Compare the size of 1 meter to the size of 1 millimeter. Use your meterstick to help.

1 meter is 1,000 times as long as 1 millimeter.

3.  Apply What operation could you use to find how many centimeters are in 3 meters? Explain.

Possible answer: multiplication; possible explanation: there are 100 centimeters in 1 meter. Multiply the number of meters, 3, by 100 to find the number of centimeters in 3 meters. $3 \times 100 = 300$ centimeters

Make Connections

You can use different metric units to describe the same metric length. For example, you can measure the length of a book as 3 decimeters or as 30 centimeters. Since the metric system is based on the number 10, decimals or fractions can be used to describe metric lengths as equivalent units.

Think of 1 meter as one whole. Use your meterstick to write equivalent units as fractions and decimals.

1 meter = 10 decimeters	1 meter = 100 centimeters
Each decimeter is $\frac{1}{10}$ or 0.1 of a meter.	Each centimeter is $\frac{1}{100}$ or 0.01 of a meter.

Complete the sentence.

- A length of 51 centimeters is $\frac{51}{100}$ or 0.51 of a meter.
- A length of 8 decimeters is $\frac{8}{10}$ or 0.8 of a meter.
- A length of 82 centimeters is $\frac{82}{100}$ or 0.82 of a meter.

Math Talk MATHEMATICAL PRACTICES Explain how you are able to locate and write decimeters and centimeters as parts of a meter on the meterstick.

Possible explanation: I can find and write decimeters as ten parts of a meter and centimeters as one hundred parts of a meter by first writing the length with a denominator of 10 or 100 and then as a decimal.

© Houghton Mifflin Harcourt Publishing Company

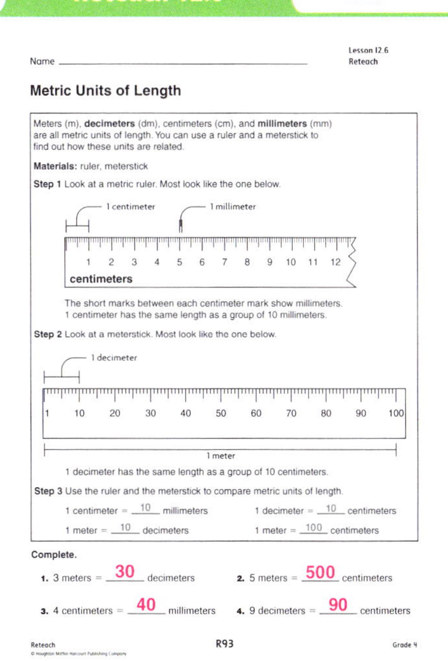

Reteach 12.6 RtI

Name ______ Lesson 12.6 Reteach

Metric Units of Length

Meters (m), **decimeters** (dm), centimeters (cm), and **millimeters** (mm) are all metric units of length. You can use a ruler and a meterstick to find out how these units are related.

Materials: ruler, meterstick

Step 1 Look at a metric ruler. Most look like the one below.

The short marks between each centimeter mark show millimeters. 1 centimeter has the same length as a group of 10 millimeters.

Step 2 Look at a meterstick. Most look like the one below.

1 decimeter has the same length as a group of 10 centimeters.

Step 3 Use the ruler and the meterstick to compare metric units of length.

1 centimeter = 10 millimeters 1 decimeter = 10 centimeters

1 meter = 10 decimeters 1 meter = 100 centimeters

Complete.

1. 3 meters = 30 decimeters
2. 5 meters = 500 centimeters
3. 4 centimeters = 40 millimeters
4. 9 decimeters = 90 centimeters

Reteach © Houghton Mifflin Harcourt Publishing Company R93 Grade 4

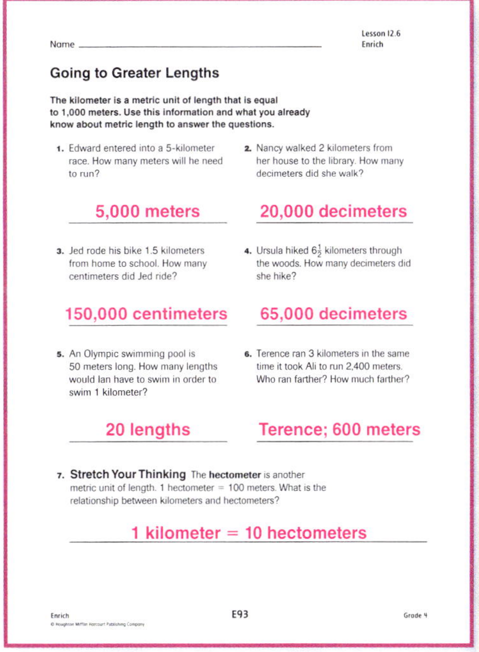

Enrich 12.6

Name ______ Lesson 12.6 Enrich

Going to Greater Lengths

The kilometer is a metric unit of length that is equal to 1,000 meters. Use this information and what you already know about metric length to answer the questions.

1. Edward entered into a 5-kilometer race. How many meters will he need to run? 5,000 meters
2. Nancy walked 2 kilometers from her house to the library. How many decimeters did she walk? 20,000 decimeters
3. Jed rode his bike 1.5 kilometers from home to school. How many centimeters did Jed ride? 150,000 centimeters
4. Ursula hiked $6\frac{1}{2}$ kilometers through the woods. How many decimeters did she hike? 65,000 decimeters
5. An Olympic swimming pool is 50 meters long. How many lengths would Ian have to swim in order to swim 1 kilometer? 20 lengths
6. Terence ran 3 kilometers in the same time it took Ali to run 2,400 meters. Who ran farther? How much farther? Terence; 600 meters
7. **Stretch Your Thinking** The **hectometer** is another metric unit of length. 1 hectometer = 100 meters. What is the relationship between kilometers and hectometers? 1 kilometer = 10 hectometers

Enrich © Houghton Mifflin Harcourt Publishing Company E93 Grade 4

H.O.T. Problem Exercise 3 requires students to apply their knowledge of unit comparisons and determine the operation needed to change from larger units to smaller units.

Make Connections

Have students find 30 centimeters on their metersticks. Then ask them to find 3 decimeters. Discuss how both measurements represent the same length, although they use different units.

Make sure students understand how to write equivalent units as fractions and decimals. Write the following fractions on the board:

1 centimeter = $\frac{1}{100}$ meter;

1 decimeter = $\frac{1}{10}$ meter.

- **If 1 centimeter is $\frac{1}{100}$ meter, what part of a meter is 51 centimeters?** $\frac{51}{100}$ meter
- **How do you write $\frac{51}{100}$ as a decimal?** 0.51

Use similar comparisons for 8 decimeters and for 82 centimeters.

Use Math Talk to focus on students' understanding of how to relate centimeters and decimeters to meters.

COMMON ERRORS

Error Students may write fractions of a meter incorrectly.

Example In Make Connections, students write 8 decimeters as $\frac{8}{100}$ and 0.08 of a meter.

Springboard to Learning Remind students that there are only 10 decimeters in a meter, so the fraction and decimal should both show tenths.

Share and Show • Guided Practice

The first problem connects to the learning model. Have students use the MathBoard to explain their thinking.

Use Exercises 1 and 8 for Quick Check. Students should show their answers for the Quick Check on the MathBoard.

Quick Check

If a student misses Exercises 1 and 8

Then Differentiate Instruction with

- RtI Tier 1 Activity, p. 467B
- Reteach 12.6
- Soar to Success Math 44.32

Problem Solving

H.O.T. Problem Exercise 13 requires students to analyze the relationship between meters and decimeters. Remind students that 1 meter is equivalent to 10 decimeters.

Name ________________________________

Share and Show

Metric Units of Length
1 centimeter (cm) = 10 millimeters (mm)
1 decimeter (dm) = 10 centimeters
1 meter (m) = 10 decimeters
1 meter (m) = 100 centimeters
1 meter (m) = 1,000 millimeters

Complete.

1. 2 meters = 200 centimeters
2. 3 centimeters = 30 millimeters
3. 5 decimeters = 50 centimeters

Algebra Compare using <, >, or =.

4. 4 meters = 40 decimeters
5. 5 centimeters > 5 millimeters
6. 6 decimeters < 65 centimeters
7. 7 meters > 700 millimeters

Describe the length in meters. Write your answer as a fraction and as a decimal.

8. 65 centimeters = $\frac{65}{100}$ or 0.65 meter
9. 47 centimeters = $\frac{47}{100}$ or 0.47 meter
10. 9 decimeters = $\frac{9}{10}$ or 0.9 meter
11. 2 decimeters = $\frac{2}{10}$ or 0.2 meter

Problem Solving REAL WORLD

12. Lucille runs the 50-meter dash in her track meet. How many decimeters long is the race?
    500 decimeters

13. H.O.T. Alexis is knitting a blanket 2 meters long. Every 2 decimeters, she changes the color of the yarn to make stripes. How many stripes will the blanket have? **Explain.**
    10; possible explanation: 2 meters = 20 decimeters; if she changes the color of the yarn every 2 decimeters, she will make 10 stripes; 2 decimeters × 10 = 20 decimeters.

© Houghton Mifflin Harcourt Publishing Company

COMMON CORE PROFESSIONAL DEVELOPMENT

Math Talk in Action

Teacher: How did you solve Exercise 12?

Viranda: I knew to multiply since I wanted to change meters to decimeters.

Teacher: Good thinking. What was the next step?

Johnna: I multiplied 50 times 10 since there are 10 decimeters in a meter.

Damion: Yes, and the product is 500.

Teacher: That product is correct. What units should be used?

Damion: Decimeters.

Teacher: So, how far did Lucille run?

Damion: She ran 500 decimeters.

Teacher: Perfect!

Model • Reason • Make Sense

14. Write Math **Explain** how you know that a line that is 8 centimeters long is longer than a line that is 75 millimeters long.

Possible explanation: I know that 8 centimeters equals 80 millimeters, and 80 is greater than 75, so 8 centimeters is longer than 75 millimeters.

15. H.O.T. **What's the Error?** Julianne's desk is 75 centimeters long. She says her desk is 7.5 meters long. **Describe** her error.

Possible description: a centimeter is $\frac{1}{100}$ or 0.01 of a meter, so 75 centimeters is $\frac{75}{100}$ or 0.75 of a meter.

Pose a Problem

16. Aruna was writing a report on pecan trees. She made the table of information to the right.

Write a problem that can be solved by using the data.

Pecan Tree	
Average Measurements	
Length of nuts	3 cm to 5 cm
Height	21 m to 30 m
Width of trunk	18 dm
Width of leaf	10 cm to 20 cm

Pose a problem.

Answers will vary.

Solve your problem.

Check students' work.

- **Describe** how you could change the problem by changing a unit in the problem. Then solve the problem.

Check students' work.

© Houghton Mifflin Harcourt Publishing Company

FOR MORE PRACTICE:
Standards Practice Book, pp. P231–P232

Go Deeper

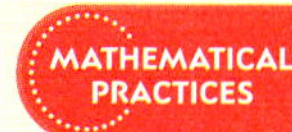

Have students compare the measurements in Exercise 14 to 2 decimeters.

- **Which measure is longest?** 2 decimeters

Discuss how to write each length as a part of a meter and compare the fractions. Have students explain how they can prove their answers using a meterstick.

H.O.T. Problem Exercise 16 requires students to create a new problem using existing data. Check students' problems for reasonableness. Allow them to trade problems with a partner and have partners solve each other's problems.

4 SUMMARIZE

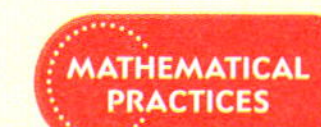

Essential Question

How can you use models to compare metric units of length? Possible answer: I can use a meterstick to find a measurement of different units: millimeters, centimeters, decimeters, or meters. Then I can compare the measurements.

Math Journal

Find a measurement, in centimeters, of an object. Look through books, magazines, or the Internet. Then write the measurement as parts of a meter.

Differentiated Instruction

INDEPENDENT ACTIVITIES

Differentiated Centers Kit

Activities

Measure Up

Students complete blue Activity Card 1 by comparing lengths.

Literature

A Trip to the Pond

Students read about using metric units to measure and identify insects.

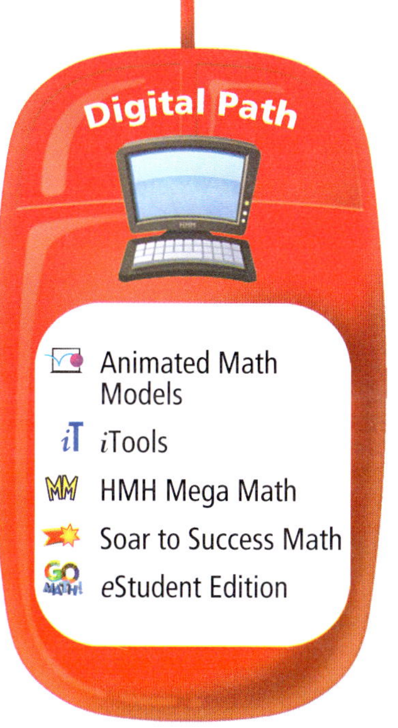

LESSON 12.7

Metric Units of Mass and Liquid Volume

LESSON AT A GLANCE

Common Core Standard

Solve problems involving measurement and conversion of measurements from a larger unit to a smaller unit.

CC.4.MD.1 Know relative sizes of measurement units within one system of units including km, m, cm; kg, g; lb, oz.; l, ml; hr, min, sec. Within a single system of measurement, express measurements in a larger unit in terms of a smaller unit. Record measurement equivalents in a two-column table.

CC.4.MD.2 Use the four operations to solve word problems involving distances, intervals of time, liquid volumes, masses of objects, and money, including problems involving simple fractions or decimals, and problems that require expressing measurements given in a larger unit in terms of a smaller unit. Represent measurement quantities using diagrams such as number line diagrams that feature a measurement scale.

Lesson Objective

Use models to compare metric units of mass and liquid volume.

Essential Question

How can you use models to compare metric units of mass and liquid volume?

Vocabulary

milliliter

Materials

MathBoard

Digital Path

Animated Math Models

HMH Mega Math

eStudent Edition

COMMON CORE PROFESSIONAL DEVELOPMENT

About the Math

Why Teach This The use of metric units in our society has increased dramatically in recent years. As students encounter real-world measurement situations, they will need to be comfortable working with both metric and customary units.

An important skill students need to learn in working with metric units is how to change from a larger unit to a smaller unit, using powers of 10. They should understand that a larger unit can be changed to a related smaller unit by multiplying by 10, 100, or 1,000. Guide them to see that the digits in the measurement remain the same, but the number of zeros increases.

Professional Development Video Podcasts

Daily Routines

Common Core

SPIRAL REVIEW

Problem of the Day

Test Prep John's store sold 8 packs of T-shirts for $64. If each pack cost the same amount, how much did each pack cost?

Ⓐ $6   Ⓒ $8
Ⓑ $7   Ⓓ $9

Fluency Builder

Multiplication Facts Have students complete the multiplication facts for 9 as quickly as possible.

9 × 1 = 9	9 × 7 = 63
9 × 2 = 18	9 × 8 = 72
9 × 3 = 27	9 × 9 = 81
9 × 4 = 36	9 × 10 = 90
9 × 5 = 45	9 × 11 = 99
9 × 6 = 54	9 × 12 = 108

Differentiated Instruction Activities

ELL Language Support

Visual
Small Group

Strategy: Explore Concepts

Materials 2-liter bottle, measuring cup

- Students will better understand liquid volume units if they explore the concept using an actual object.
- Have students measure and pour two liters of water in a bottle. Explain that there are 2 liters of water in the bottle.
- **If 1 liter is 1,000 milliliters, how many milliliters are in 2 liters?** 2,000 milliliters
- Write the problem on the board: $2 \times 1{,}000 = 2{,}000$.
- **There are 2 liters of water in the bottle. That is the same as 2,000 milliliters.** Have students repeat your statement.

See ELL Activity Guide for leveled activities.

Enrich

Visual / Individual
Partners

Materials various objects measured in kilograms or liters

- Give each student one object, such as a juice carton or cereal box, showing a metric measurement of mass or liquid volume.
- Have students write the measurement on their papers. Then have pairs work together to change the measurements in kilograms to grams, or liters to milliliters.
- Once they have completed the change for their measurements, have students pass their objects around and repeat the activity with the next object they receive.
- Repeat until each student has had every object.
- Have students discuss their findings. Remind them to be sure they multiplied by 1,000 for each change.

Response to Intervention

Reteach Tier 1

Kinesthetic / Visual
Whole Class / Small Group

Materials MathBoards

- Write the following measurements on the board: 3 kilogram, 9 liters
- **How can we change kilograms to grams?** multiply by 1,000
- Have students work out the problem on their MathBoards. **How many grams are in 3 kilograms?** 3,000 grams
- Have students write a comparison statement on their MathBoards: 3 kilograms = 3,000 grams
- Repeat the activity with 9 liters. Have students write the measurement in milliliters.
- Discuss the results of each unit change.

Tier 2

Kinesthetic / Visual
Small Group

Materials Mathboards

- Have students write the following on their MathBoards: 1 kilogram = 1,000 grams; 1 liter = 1,000 milliliters.
- **How many grams are in 9 kilograms?** 9,000 grams Write $9 \times 1{,}000 = 9{,}000$ and have students copy it on their MathBoards.
- **How many milliliters are in 7 liters?** 7,000 milliliters Guide students to write $7 \times 1{,}000 = 7{,}000$ on their MathBoards.
- On the board, write a comparison statement for each change: 9 kilograms = 9,000 grams; 7 liters = 7,000 milliliters. Discuss the statements.

LESSON 12.7

CC.4.MD.1 Know relative sizes of measurement units within one system of units including km, m, cm; kg, g; lb, oz.; l, ml; hr, min, sec. Within a single system of measurement, express measurements in a larger unit in terms of a smaller unit. Record measurement equivalents in a two-column table.

1 ENGAGE

Access Prior Knowledge Show students a 2-liter bottle of seltzer water. Have students describe the bottle. Point out that the amount of liquid in these bottles is described in metric units of liquid volume, rather than customary units.

2 TEACH and TALK

Animated Math Models

Unlock the Problem

Ask students to suggest common objects that they have seen measured in grams and kilograms. Then have them suggest liquids they have seen measured in liters or milliliters.

Example 1

- **Which unit is larger, grams or kilograms?** kilograms
- **How do you change from larger units to smaller units?** multiply

Write the following comparison statement on the board: 9 kilograms = 9,000 grams.

Example 2

- **Which unit is larger, liters or milliliters?** liters

Be sure students multiply and include units with each measurement.

Use **Math Talk** to focus on students' understanding of the relative sizes of smaller and larger metric units of mass and liquid volume.

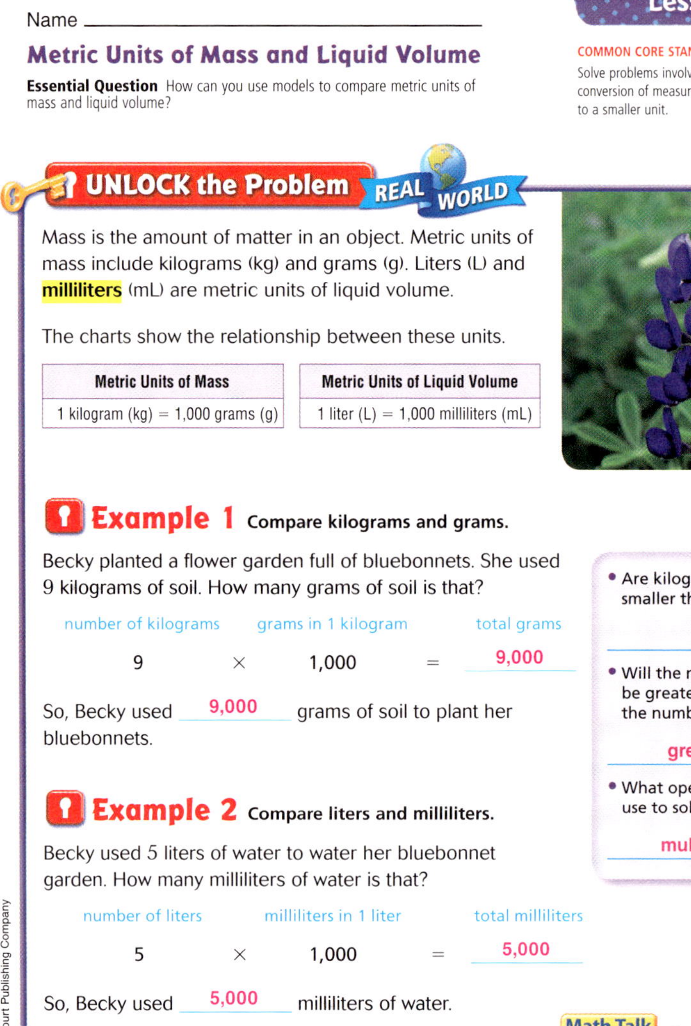

Name ______________________

Lesson 12.7

Metric Units of Mass and Liquid Volume

Essential Question How can you use models to compare metric units of mass and liquid volume?

COMMON CORE STANDARDS CC.4.MD.1, CC.4.MD.2
Solve problems involving measurement and conversion of measurements from a larger unit to a smaller unit.

UNLOCK the Problem REAL WORLD

Mass is the amount of matter in an object. Metric units of mass include kilograms (kg) and grams (g). Liters (L) and **milliliters** (mL) are metric units of liquid volume.

The charts show the relationship between these units.

Metric Units of Mass
1 kilogram (kg) = 1,000 grams (g)

Metric Units of Liquid Volume
1 liter (L) = 1,000 milliliters (mL)

Example 1 Compare kilograms and grams.

Becky planted a flower garden full of bluebonnets. She used 9 kilograms of soil. How many grams of soil is that?

number of kilograms		grams in 1 kilogram		total grams
9	×	1,000	=	9,000

So, Becky used 9,000 grams of soil to plant her bluebonnets.

- Are kilograms larger or smaller than grams? larger
- Will the number of grams be greater than or less than the number of kilograms? greater than
- What operation will you use to solve the problem? multiplication

Example 2 Compare liters and milliliters.

Becky used 5 liters of water to water her bluebonnet garden. How many milliliters of water is that?

number of liters		milliliters in 1 liter		total milliliters
5	×	1,000	=	5,000

So, Becky used 5,000 milliliters of water.

Math Talk MATHEMATICAL PRACTICES Compare the size of a kilogram to the size of a gram. Then compare the size of a liter to the size of a milliliter.

Possible answer: 1 kilogram is 1,000 times as much as 1 gram. 1 liter is 1,000 times as much as 1 milliliter.

© Houghton Mifflin Harcourt Publishing Company

Chapter 12 471

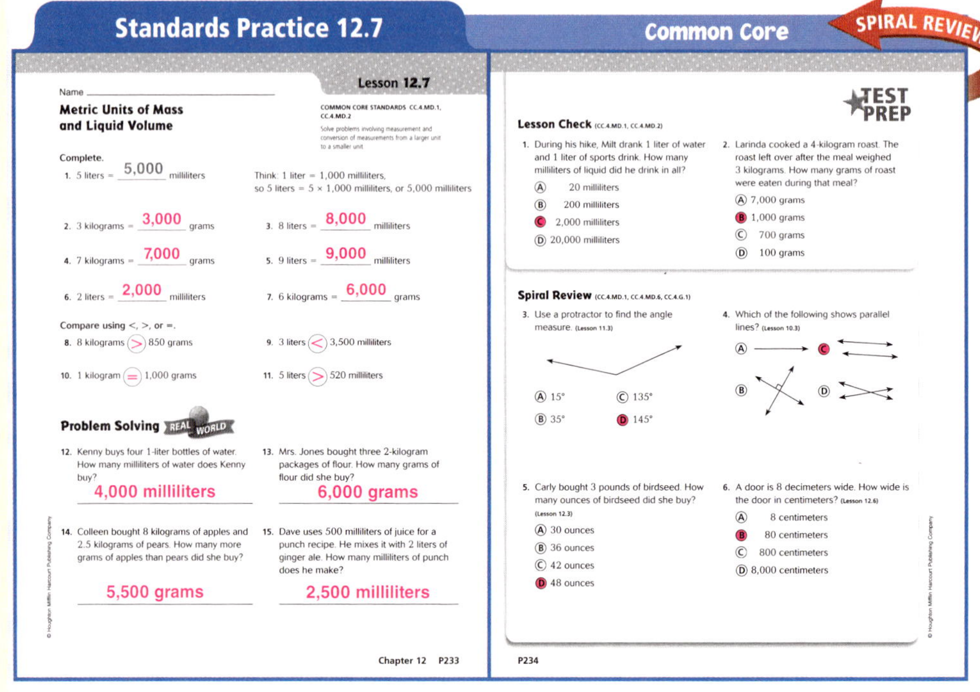

Standards Practice 12.7

Name ______________________

Lesson 12.7

Metric Units of Mass and Liquid Volume

COMMON CORE STANDARDS CC.4.MD.1, CC.4.MD.2
Solve problems involving measurement and conversion of measurements from a larger unit to a smaller unit.

Complete.

1. 5 liters = 5,000 milliliters
Think: 1 liter = 1,000 milliliters, so 5 liters = 5 × 1,000 milliliters, or 5,000 milliliters
2. 3 kilograms = 3,000 grams
3. 8 liters = 8,000 milliliters
4. 7 kilograms = 7,000 grams
5. 9 liters = 9,000 milliliters
6. 2 liters = 2,000 milliliters
7. 6 kilograms = 6,000 grams

Compare using <, >, or =.

8. 8 kilograms (>) 850 grams
9. 3 liters (<) 3,500 milliliters
10. 1 kilogram (=) 1,000 grams
11. 5 liters (>) 520 milliliters

Problem Solving REAL WORLD

12. Kenny buys four 1-liter bottles of water. How many milliliters of water does Kenny buy? 4,000 milliliters
13. Mrs. Jones bought three 2-kilogram packages of flour. How many grams of flour did she buy? 6,000 grams
14. Colleen bought 8 kilograms of apples and 2.5 kilograms of pears. How many more grams of apples than pears did she buy? 5,500 grams
15. Dave uses 500 milliliters of juice for a punch recipe. He mixes it with 2 liters of ginger ale. How many milliliters of punch does he make? 2,500 milliliters

© Houghton Mifflin Harcourt Publishing Company

Chapter 12 P233

Common Core SPIRAL REVIEW

TEST PREP

Lesson Check (CC.4.MD.1, CC.4.MD.2)

1. During his hike, Milt drank 1 liter of water and 1 liter of sports drink. How many milliliters of liquid did he drink in all?
Ⓐ 20 milliliters
Ⓑ 200 milliliters
Ⓒ 2,000 milliliters
Ⓓ 20,000 milliliters
2. Larinda cooked a 4-kilogram roast. The roast left over after the meal weighed 3 kilograms. How many grams of roast were eaten during that meal?
Ⓐ 7,000 grams
Ⓑ 1,000 grams
Ⓒ 700 grams
Ⓓ 100 grams

Spiral Review (CC.4.MD.1, CC.4.MD.6, CC.4.G.1)

3. Use a protractor to find the angle measure. (Lesson 11.3)
Ⓐ 15°
Ⓑ 35°
Ⓒ 135°
Ⓓ 145°
4. Which of the following shows parallel lines? (Lesson 10.3)
Ⓐ Ⓑ Ⓒ Ⓓ
5. Carly bought 3 pounds of birdseed. How many ounces of birdseed did she buy? (Lesson 12.3)
Ⓐ 30 ounces
Ⓑ 36 ounces
Ⓒ 42 ounces
Ⓓ 48 ounces
6. A door is 8 decimeters wide. How wide is the door in centimeters? (Lesson 12.6)
Ⓐ 8 centimeters
Ⓑ 80 centimeters
Ⓒ 800 centimeters
Ⓓ 8,000 centimeters

© Houghton Mifflin Harcourt Publishing Company

P234

Share and Show 

1. There are 3 liters of water in a pitcher. How many milliliters of water are in the pitcher?

   There are 1,000 milliliters in 1 liter. Since I am changing from a larger unit to a smaller unit, I can multiply 3 by 1,000 to find the number of milliliters in 3 liters.

   So, there are 3,000 milliliters of water in the pitcher.

Complete.

2. 4 liters = 4,000 milliliters
3. 6 kilograms = 6,000 grams

Possible explanation: I multiplied the number of kilograms, 6, by the number of grams in 1 kilogram, 1,000. $6 \times 1{,}000 = 6{,}000$ grams

Math Talk MATHEMATICAL PRACTICES Explain how you found the number of grams in 6 kilograms in Exercise 3.

On Your Own

Complete.

4. 8 kilograms = 8,000 grams
5. 7 liters = 7,000 milliliters

Algebra Compare using <, >, or =.

6. 1 kilogram > 900 grams
7. 2 liters = 2,000 milliliters

Algebra Complete.

8.

Liters	Milliliters
1	1,000
2	2,000
3	3,000
4	4,000
5	5,000
6	6,000
7	7,000
8	8,000
9	9,000
10	10,000

9.

Kilograms	Grams
1	1,000
2	2,000
3	3,000
4	4,000
5	5,000
6	6,000
7	7,000
8	8,000
9	9,000
10	10,000

© Houghton Mifflin Harcourt Publishing Company

472

Reteach 12.7

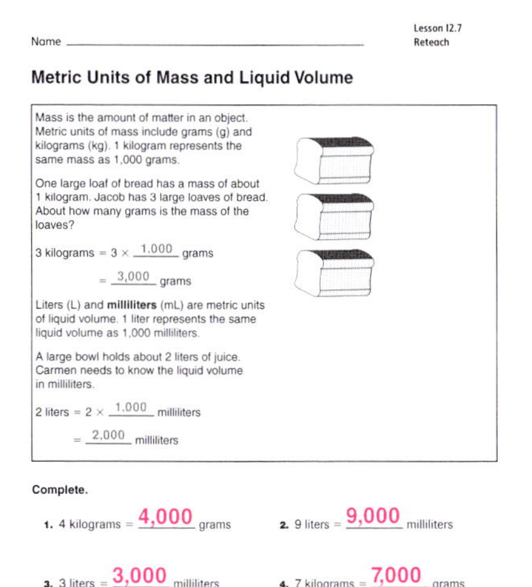

Name ______ Lesson 12.7 Reteach

Metric Units of Mass and Liquid Volume

Mass is the amount of matter in an object. Metric units of mass include grams (g) and kilograms (kg). 1 kilogram represents the same mass as 1,000 grams.

One large loaf of bread has a mass of about 1 kilogram. Jacob has 3 large loaves of bread. About how many grams is the mass of the loaves?

3 kilograms = 3 × 1,000 grams

= 3,000 grams

Liters (L) and **milliliters** (mL) are metric units of liquid volume. 1 liter represents the same liquid volume as 1,000 milliliters.

A large bowl holds about 2 liters of juice. Carmen needs to know the liquid volume in milliliters.

2 liters = 2 × 1,000 milliliters

= 2,000 milliliters

Complete.

1. 4 kilograms = 4,000 grams
2. 9 liters = 9,000 milliliters
3. 3 liters = 3,000 milliliters
4. 7 kilograms = 7,000 grams
5. 5 kilograms = 5,000 grams
6. 8 liters = 8,000 milliliters

Reteach R94 Grade 4

© Houghton Mifflin Harcourt Publishing Company

Enrich 12.7

Name ______ Lesson 12.7 Enrich

More Volume, Less Mass

The milligram is a metric unit of mass. One gram is equal to 1,000 milligrams. The kiloliter is a unit of metric volume that is equal to 1,000 liters. Use this information and what you know about metric units to answer the questions.

1. A small swimming pool contains 6 kiloliters of water. How many liters of water does the pool contain? 6,000 liters
2. A scientist has a 3-gram sample of soil to analyze. How many milligrams is the soil sample? 3,000 milligrams
3. About 1 kiloliter of water runs past a certain point in a freshwater stream each minute. How many 2-liter bottles could be filled from 1 kiloliter of water? 500 bottles
4. A pill contains 200 milligrams of medicine. If Barb takes one pill each day, how many grams of medicine does she take in 10 days? 2 grams
5. Helen places a 2-gram mass on one side of a scale. How many milligrams would it take to balance the scale? 2,000 milligrams
6. A storage tank holds 4 kiloliters of water. How many liters of water does the tank hold? 4,000 liters
7. Write Math **Explain** how you found the answer to Problem 4.

   Possible answer: I multiplied 200 by 10 to find the mass of the pills she takes in 10 days, 2,000 milligrams. Every gram is 1,000 milligrams, so 2,000 milligrams is 2 grams.

Enrich E94 Grade 4

© Houghton Mifflin Harcourt Publishing Company

3 PRACTICE 

Share and Show • Guided Practice

The first problem connects to the learning model. Have students use the MathBoard to explain their thinking.

Use Exercises 2 and 3 for **Quick Check**. Students should show their answers for the Quick Check on the MathBoard.

Use **Math Talk** to focus on students' understanding of changing from larger units to smaller units.

Quick Check

If a student misses Exercises 2 and 3

Then Differentiate Instruction with

- RtI Tier 1 Activity, p. 471B
- Reteach 12.7
- Soar to Success Math 42.07, 42.09, 45.26, 46.32

On Your Own

If students complete Exercises 2 and 3 correctly, they may continue with Independent Practice.

COMMON ERRORS

Error Students may write the wrong number of zeros in the product.

Example In Exercise 2, students write 400 milliliters rather than 4,000 milliliters as the equivalent of 4 liters.

Springboard to Learning Remind students that there are 3 zeros in 1,000, so they should add 3 zeros in the product when multiplying by 1,000.

Problem Solving 

H.O.T. Problem Exercise 14 is a multi-step problem that requires students to compare the costs of a product sold in two different units. Make sure students find the number of grams in 2 kilograms, and determine the number of 500-gram bags that would equal 2,000 kilograms.

For Exercise 15, have volunteers read their explanations aloud. Discuss their reasoning.

Go Deeper 

Have students suggest how they would compare 2,400 milliliters to 2 liters. Remind them to write 2 liters as milliliters first. Then have them write a comparison statement to show the answer: 2,400 milliliters $>$ 2 liters or 2 liters $<$ 2,400 milliliters.

Name ______________________________

Problem Solving REAL WORLD

10. Frank wants to fill a fish tank with 8 liters of water. How many milliliters is that?

    8,000 milliliters

11. Kim has 3 water bottles. She fills each bottle with 1 liter of water. How many milliliters of water does she have?

    3,000 milliliters

12. Jared's empty backpack has a mass of 3 kilograms. He doesn't want to carry more than 7 kilograms on a trip. How many grams of equipment can Jared pack?

    4,000 grams

13. A large cooler contains 20 liters of iced tea and a small cooler contains 5 liters of iced tea. How many more milliliters of iced tea does the large cooler contain than the small cooler?

    15,000 more milliliters

14. H.O.T. A 500-gram bag of granola costs $4, and a 2-kilogram bag of granola costs $15. What is the cheapest way to buy 2,000 grams of granola? **Explain.**

    A 2-kilogram bag; possible explanation: 2 kilograms is equal to 2,000 grams, and a 2-kilogram bag costs $15. Four 500-gram bags are equal to 2,000 grams and cost $16: $4 \times \$4 = \$16$. $\$15 < \$16$

15. **Sense or Nonsense?** The world's largest apple had a mass of 1,849 grams. Sue said the mass was greater than 2 kilograms. Does Sue's statement make sense? **Explain.**

    No. Possible explanation: I know that 1 kilogram = 1,000 grams, so 2 kilograms = 2,000 grams. Since 1,849 grams $<$ 2,000 grams, Sue's statement does not make sense. The mass of the world's largest apple is less that 2 kilograms.

© Houghton Mifflin Harcourt Publishing Company

Cross-Curricular

SCIENCE

- Scientists use metric units for mass and liquid volume when performing experiments. For example, scientists in chemistry labs have studied the properties of soap bubbles by floating them on carbon dioxide, a gas slightly more dense than the air inside the bubbles themselves.
- One example of such an experiment requires 125 milliliters of baking soda and 250 milliliters of vinegar.
- How many times could the experiment be performed with 1 liter of vinegar? 4

SOCIAL STUDIES

- Many countries use the "gold standard" to determine the value of their money. This means that the value of money is based on the value of a certain fixed amount of gold.
- On June 5, 1933, the United States system officially left the gold standard. Gold is still very valuable, but the value of a U.S. dollar is no longer based on the price of gold.
- If 1 gram of gold is worth $32, how much would 1 kilogram of gold be worth? $32,000

Model • Reason • Make Sense

UNLOCK the Problem REAL WORLD

16. Lori bought 600 grams of cayenne pepper and 2 kilograms of black pepper. How many grams of pepper did she buy?

black pepper   cayenne pepper

a. What are you asked to find?

how many grams of pepper Lori bought in all

b. What information will you use?

She bought 600 grams of cayenne pepper and 2 kilograms of black pepper.

c. Tell how you might solve the problem.

I will find how many grams of black pepper Lori bought. Then I will add the mass of the cayenne pepper and the mass of the black pepper to find how many grams of pepper she bought in all.

d. Show how you solved the problem.

2 kilograms × 1,000 = 2,000 grams.

Lori has 2,000 grams of black pepper.

600 grams + 2,000 grams = 2,600 grams.

e. Complete the sentences.

Lori bought 600 grams of cayenne pepper.

She bought 2,000 grams of black pepper.

600 + 2,000 = 2,600 grams

So, Lori bought 2,600 grams of pepper in all.

17. Write Math Jill has two rocks. One has a mass of 20 grams and the other has a mass of 20 kilograms. Which rock has the greater mass? **Explain.**

The rock with the mass of 20 kilograms; possible explanation: a kilogram is a larger unit than a gram.

18. Test Prep Caroline bought a bag of onions that was labeled 5 kilograms. She needs to know how many grams that is for her recipe. How many grams is 5 kilograms?

Ⓐ 50 grams
Ⓑ 500 grams
Ⓒ 5,000 grams
Ⓓ 50,000 grams

© Houghton Mifflin Harcourt Publishing Company

FOR MORE PRACTICE:
Standards Practice Book, pp. P233–P234

Unlock the Problem

Exercise 16 provides a scaffolded approach to solving multi-step problems that involve metric units of mass. As students complete step d, make sure they include the units of measurement in their explanation.

Test Prep Coach

Test Prep Coach helps teachers to identify common errors that students can make.

In Exercise 18, if students selected:

A They multiplied the number of kilograms by 10.

B They multiplied the number of kilograms by 100.

D They multiplied the number of kilograms by 10,000.

4 SUMMARIZE

Essential Question

How can you use models to compare metric units of mass and liquid volume? Possible answer: for metric units of mass, I can multiply the number of kilograms by the number of grams in 1 kilogram, or 1,000. For metric units of liquid volume, I can multiply the number liters by the number of milliliters in 1 liter, or 1,000.

Math Journal

Write a problem that involves changing kilograms to grams. Explain how to find the solution.

Differentiated Instruction INDEPENDENT ACTIVITIES

Differentiated Centers Kit

Activities
Mass Match-Up

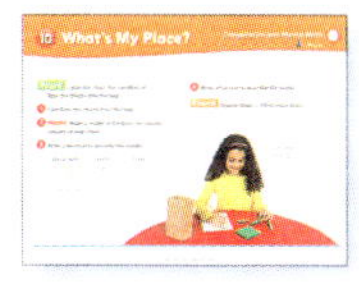

Students complete orange Activity Card 14 by estimating and measuring mass and weight.

Activities
Balancing Act

Students complete blue Activity Card 14 by measuring mass and weight.

Activities
Capacity Overload!

Students complete orange Activity Card 16 by estimating liquid volume of real-world containers.

Digital Path

- Animated Math Models
- *i*Tools
- HMH Mega Math
- Soar to Success Math
- *e*Student Edition

LESSON 12.8

Units of Time

LESSON AT A GLANCE

Common Core Standard

Solve problems involving measurement and conversion of measurements from a larger unit to a smaller unit.

CC.4.MD.1 Know relative sizes of measurement units within one system of units including km, m, cm; kg, g; lb, oz.; l, ml; hr, min, sec. Within a single system of measurement, express measurements in a larger unit in terms of a smaller unit. Record measurement equivalents in a two-column table.

Also CC.4.MD.2

Lesson Objective

Use models to compare units of time.

Essential Question

How can you use models to compare units of time?

Vocabulary

second

Materials

MathBoard

Digital Path

- Animated Math Models
- *i*Tools: Measurement
- *e*Student Edition

COMMON CORE PROFESSIONAL DEVELOPMENT — About the Math

Why Teach This Students need to understand the units of time and how to compare and use each unit because almost everything they do is based on schedules. Using multiplication to find the number of seconds in an hour or the number of days in 3 months is a skill that will prove invaluable in real-world applications.

Students need to have a concrete knowledge of how units compare, such as knowing that minutes are longer than seconds, weeks are longer than days, and years are longer than months. This will help them quickly determine which units to multiply to make comparisons.

Professional Development Video Podcasts

Daily Routines

Common Core

SPIRAL REVIEW

Problem of the Day

eTransparency 12.8

Test Prep Jerome had 500 grams of birdseed for his parakeets. He got a new parakeet and bought another kilogram of birdseed. How much birdseed does he have now?

Ⓐ 1,500 grams Ⓒ 500 kilograms
Ⓑ 2,000 grams Ⓓ 1,500 kilograms

Vocabulary Builder

Units of Time Have students draw their own diagrams like the ones shown below to associate units of time. For example, ask students to start with a circle that reads 1 hour. Have them write equivalent amounts of time in the other parts of the diagram.

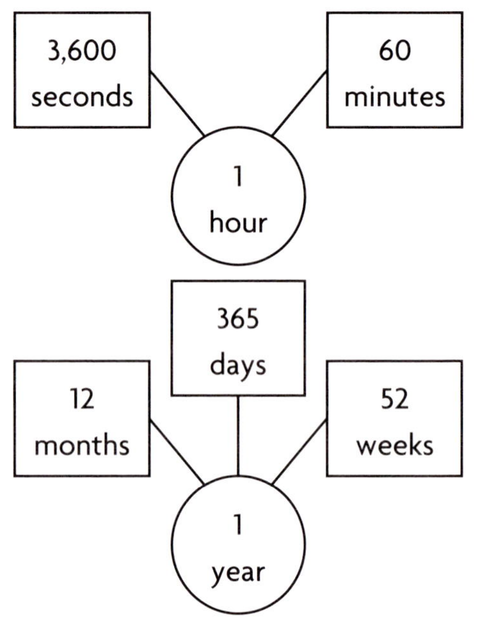

Differentiated Instruction Activities

ELL Language Support  Visual / Small Group

Strategy: Draw

Materials tape, scissors, Number Lines (see *eTeacher Resources*)

- Work with students to create a number line from 0 to 24. Label the top of the number line "Days" and the bottom "Hours."
- **There are 24 hours in 1 day.** Have students count aloud the ticks on the number line as they shade the bottom of the number line from 0 to 24. Write 1 above the number 24, to show 1 day. Then have them shade from 0 to 1 on the top to show 1 day.

See ELL Activity Guide for leveled activities.

Enrich  Visual / Partners / Small Group

Materials markers, poster board

- Have a small group work together to create one poster showing the various units of time.
- Then have partners choose one pair of units to compare, such as days and weeks. They should create a second poster with a model comparing the two units, such as a number line with shading, clocks, or a table.
- Display the poster showing all the units of time. Then allow each pair to present their poster to the group and explain how their model demonstrates the comparison of the two units of time.

Response to Intervention

Reteach Tier 1  Kinesthetic / Visual / Whole Class / Small Group

- Write the following comparison statement on the board. Have students copy the statement.

  4 minutes ◯ 200 seconds
- **How many seconds are in 1 minute?** 60
- **How can we find the number of seconds in 4 minutes?** Multiply by 60. Have students multiply 4×60. 240
- **How many seconds are in 4 minutes?** 240 seconds
- **Which is greater, 240 or 200?** 240
- Have students complete the comparison statement using $<$, $>$, or $=$. Repeat the activity with other comparison statements using various units of time.

Tier 2  Kinesthetic / Visual / Small Group

- Write the following comparison statement on the board: 36 days ◯ 5 weeks.
- **How can you compare these two times?** Possible answer: change weeks to days and compare the numbers of days.
- Guide students to rewrite the comparison statement under the original using days:

  36 days ◯ ________________ days.
- **How can you write 5 weeks as days?** Multiply 5 times the number of days in 1 week, or 7.
- Have students multiply 5×7. 35 Direct students to complete their new comparison statement: 36 days $>$ 35 days.

LESSON 12.8

COMMON CORE

CC.4.MD.1 Know relative sizes of measurement units within one system of units including km, m, cm; kg, g; lb, oz.; l, ml; hr, min, sec. Within a single system of measurement, express measurements in a larger unit in terms of a smaller unit. Record measurement equivalents in a two-column table.

1 ENGAGE

Access Prior Knowledge Ask students to look at the classroom clock and tell what time it is. Discuss how to use the short hand for hours and the long hand for minutes. Write the time on the board.

2 TEACH and TALK

▶ Unlock the Problem

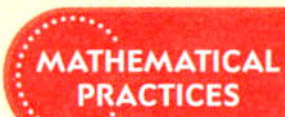

Talk about the top clock. Identify the minute and hour hands. Tell students that the red hand is called the second hand, because it shows the time unit *seconds*. Explain that the shaded region on each clock shows elapsed time. Emphasize that the shaded region for 1 second and 1 minute are the same, but they represent different times.

▶ Example 1

- **How many minutes are in 1 hour?** 60
- **How many seconds are in 1 minute?** 60
- **How can we find the number of seconds in 1 hour?** Multiply 60 times 60.

Write the multiplication on the board. Review how to multiply by a two-digit number, if needed.

Use **Math Talk** to focus on students' understanding of how the minute hand's movement relates to hours.

Name ____________________

Lesson 12.8

Units of Time

Essential Question How can you use models to compare units of time?

COMMON CORE STANDARD CC.4.MD.1
Solve problems involving measurement and conversion of measurements from a larger unit to a smaller unit.

UNLOCK the Problem

The analog clock below has an hour hand, a minute hand, and a **second** hand to measure time. The time is 4:30:12.

Read Math
Read 4:30:12 as 4:30 and 12 seconds, or 30 minutes and 12 seconds after 4.

- Are there more minutes or seconds in one hour? seconds

There are 60 seconds in a minute and 60 minutes in an hour. The clocks below show the length of a second, a minute, and an hour.

Start Time: 3:00:00

1 second elapses.

The time is now 3:00:01.

1 minute, or 60 seconds, elapses. The second hand has made a full turn clockwise.

The time is now 3:01:00.

1 hour, or 60 minutes, elapses. The minute hand has made a full turn clockwise.

The time is now 4:00:00.

Example 1 How does the size of an hour compare to the size of a second?

There are __60__ minutes in an hour.

There are __60__ seconds in a minute.

60 minutes × __60__ = __3,600__ seconds

Think: Multiply the number of minutes in a hour by the number of seconds in a minute.

There are __3,600__ seconds in a hour.

So, 1 hour is __3,600__ times as long as 1 second.

MATHEMATICAL PRACTICES
Math Talk How many full turns clockwise does a minute hand make in 3 hours? **Explain.**

3 full turns clockwise; possible explanation: when a minute hand makes 1 full turn clockwise, 60 minutes, or 1 hour, elapse. So, when a minute hand makes 3 full turns clockwise, 3 hours elapse.

© Houghton Mifflin Harcourt Publishing Company

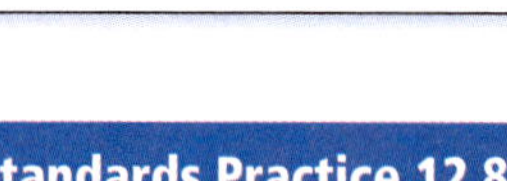

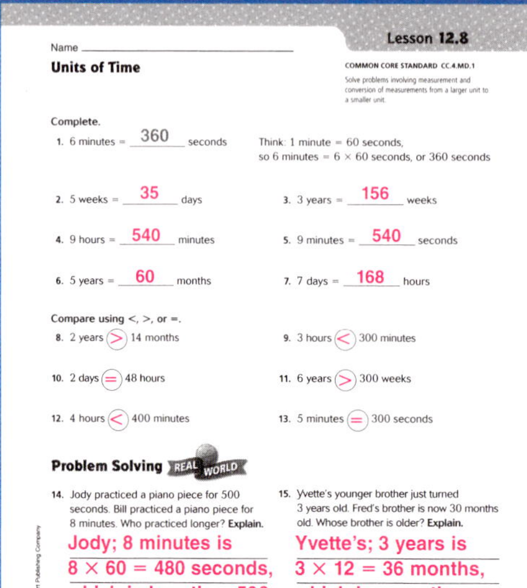

Name ____________________

Lesson 12.8

Units of Time

COMMON CORE STANDARD CC.4.MD.1
Solve problems involving measurement and conversion of measurements from a larger unit to a smaller unit.

Complete.

1. 6 minutes = __360__ seconds

Think: 1 minute = 60 seconds, so 6 minutes = 6 × 60 seconds, or 360 seconds

2. 5 weeks = __35__ days
3. 3 years = __156__ weeks
4. 9 hours = __540__ minutes
5. 9 minutes = __540__ seconds
6. 5 years = __60__ months
7. 7 days = __168__ hours

Compare using <, >, or =.

8. 2 years (>) 14 months
9. 3 hours (<) 300 minutes
10. 2 days (=) 48 hours
11. 6 years (>) 300 weeks
12. 4 hours (<) 400 minutes
13. 5 minutes (=) 300 seconds

Problem Solving REAL WORLD

14. Jody practiced a piano piece for 500 seconds. Bill practiced a piano piece for 8 minutes. Who practiced longer? **Explain.**
Jody; 8 minutes is 8 × 60 = 480 seconds, which is less than 500 seconds.

15. Yvette's younger brother just turned 3 years old. Fred's brother is now 30 months old. Whose brother is older? **Explain.**
Yvette's; 3 years is 3 × 12 = 36 months, which is more than 30 months.

© Houghton Mifflin Harcourt Publishing Company

Chapter 12 P235

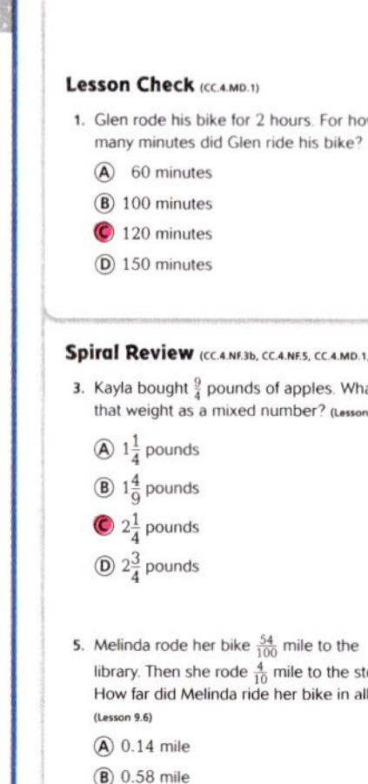

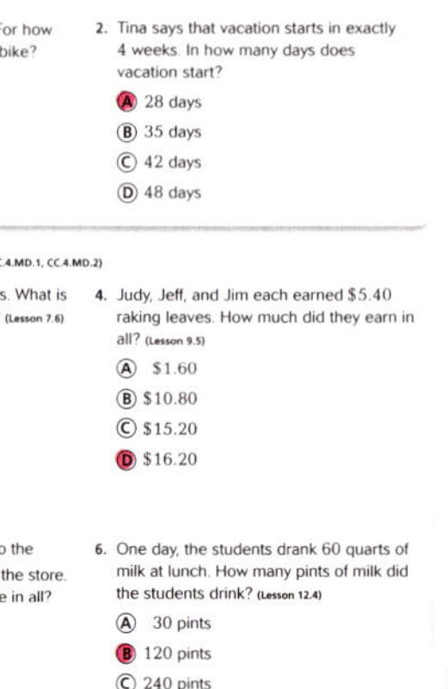

TEST PREP

Lesson Check (CC.4.MD.1)

1. Glen rode his bike for 2 hours. For how many minutes did Glen ride his bike?
Ⓐ 60 minutes
Ⓑ 100 minutes
Ⓒ 120 minutes
Ⓓ 150 minutes

2. Tina says that vacation starts in exactly 4 weeks. In how many days does vacation start?
Ⓐ 28 days
Ⓑ 35 days
Ⓒ 42 days
Ⓓ 48 days

Spiral Review (CC.4.NF.3b, CC.4.NF.5, CC.4.MD.1, CC.4.MD.2)

3. Kayla bought $\frac{9}{4}$ pounds of apples. What is that weight as a mixed number? (Lesson 7.6)
Ⓐ $1\frac{1}{4}$ pounds
Ⓑ $1\frac{4}{9}$ pounds
Ⓒ $2\frac{1}{4}$ pounds
Ⓓ $2\frac{3}{4}$ pounds

4. Judy, Jeff, and Jim each earned $5.40 raking leaves. How much did they earn in all? (Lesson 9.5)
Ⓐ $1.60
Ⓑ $10.80
Ⓒ $15.20
Ⓓ $16.20

5. Melinda rode her bike $\frac{54}{100}$ mile to the library. Then she rode $\frac{4}{10}$ mile to the store. How far did Melinda ride her bike in all? (Lesson 9.6)
Ⓐ 0.14 mile
Ⓑ 0.58 mile
Ⓒ 0.94 mile
Ⓓ 1.04 miles

6. One day, the students drank 60 quarts of milk at lunch. How many pints of milk did the students drink? (Lesson 12.4)
Ⓐ 30 pints
Ⓑ 120 pints
Ⓒ 240 pints
Ⓓ 480 pints

© Houghton Mifflin Harcourt Publishing Company

P236

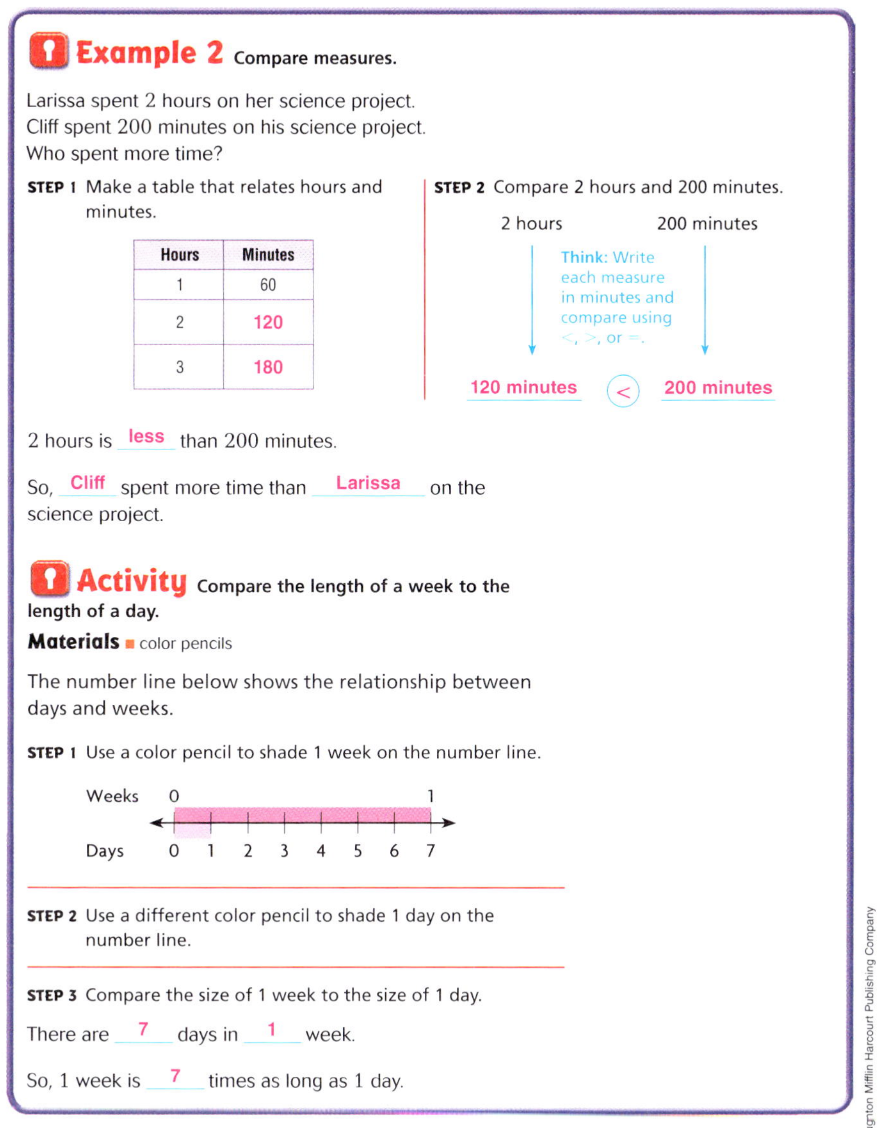

Example 2 Compare measures.

Larissa spent 2 hours on her science project.
Cliff spent 200 minutes on his science project.
Who spent more time?

STEP 1 Make a table that relates hours and minutes.

Hours	Minutes
1	60
2	120
3	180

STEP 2 Compare 2 hours and 200 minutes.

2 hours 200 minutes

Think: Write each measure in minutes and compare using <, >, or =.

120 minutes < 200 minutes

2 hours is less than 200 minutes.

So, Cliff spent more time than Larissa on the science project.

Activity Compare the length of a week to the length of a day.

Materials ■ color pencils

The number line below shows the relationship between days and weeks.

STEP 1 Use a color pencil to shade 1 week on the number line.

STEP 2 Use a different color pencil to shade 1 day on the number line.

STEP 3 Compare the size of 1 week to the size of 1 day.

There are 7 days in 1 week.

So, 1 week is 7 times as long as 1 day.

© Houghton Mifflin Harcourt Publishing Company

▶ Example 2

Read through the problem with students. Have students underline the measurements of time given in the problem.

For Step 1, guide students to complete the table and find the number of minutes in 2 hours and 3 hours.

For Step 2, have students explain how they know that 2 hours is the same as 120 minutes. Have them compare 120 minutes to 200 minutes.

▶ Activity

Review how to use the number line. Have students shade 7 days to show 1 week, and then shade 1 day. Discuss how the two shaded areas compare.

Go Deeper

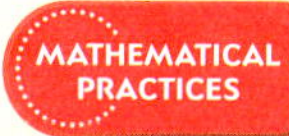

Have students write a fraction to compare days to weeks. Since there are 7 days in 1 week, guide students to see that 1 day is $\frac{1}{7}$ of a week. Have them write a fraction to show other numbers of days as part of a week, such as 3 days = $\frac{3}{7}$ week.

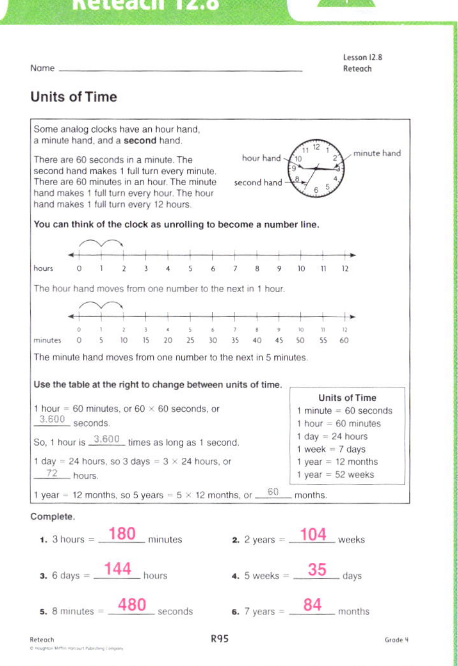

Reteach 12.8

Name ____________ Lesson 12.8 Reteach

Units of Time

Some analog clocks have an hour hand, a minute hand, and a **second** hand.

There are 60 seconds in a minute. The second hand makes 1 full turn every minute. There are 60 minutes in an hour. The minute hand makes 1 full turn every hour. The hour hand makes 1 full turn every 12 hours.

You can think of the clock as unrolling to become a number line.

The hour hand moves from one number to the next in 1 hour.

The minute hand moves from one number to the next in 5 minutes.

Use the table at the right to change between units of time.

Units of Time
1 minute = 60 seconds
1 hour = 60 minutes
1 day = 24 hours
1 week = 7 days
1 year = 12 months
1 year = 52 weeks

1 hour = 60 minutes, or 60 × 60 seconds, or 3,600 seconds.

So, 1 hour is 3,600 times as long as 1 second.

1 day = 24 hours, so 3 days = 3 × 24 hours, or 72 hours.

1 year = 12 months, so 5 years = 5 × 12 months, or 60 months.

Complete.

1. 3 hours = 180 minutes
2. 2 years = 104 weeks
3. 6 days = 144 hours
4. 5 weeks = 35 days
5. 8 minutes = 480 seconds
6. 7 years = 84 months

Reteach R95 Grade 4

© Houghton Mifflin Harcourt Publishing Company

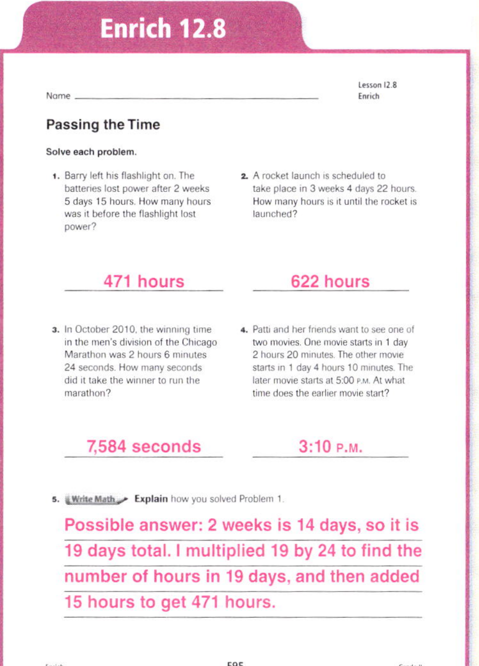

Enrich 12.8

Name ____________ Lesson 12.8 Enrich

Passing the Time

Solve each problem.

1. Barry left his flashlight on. The batteries lost power after 2 weeks 5 days 15 hours. How many hours was it before the flashlight lost power?
   471 hours
2. A rocket launch is scheduled to take place in 3 weeks 4 days 22 hours. How many hours is it until the rocket is launched?
   622 hours
3. In October 2010, the winning time in the men's division of the Chicago Marathon was 2 hours 6 minutes 24 seconds. How many seconds did it take the winner to run the marathon?
   7,584 seconds
4. Patti and her friends want to see one of two movies. One movie starts in 1 day 2 hours 20 minutes. The other movie starts in 1 day 4 hours 10 minutes. The later movie starts at 5:00 P.M. At what time does the earlier movie start?
   3:10 P.M.
5. Write Math **Explain** how you solved Problem 1.
   Possible answer: 2 weeks is 14 days, so it is 19 days total. I multiplied 19 by 24 to find the number of hours in 19 days, and then added 15 hours to get 471 hours.

Enrich E95 Grade 4

© Houghton Mifflin Harcourt Publishing Company

COMMON ERRORS

Error Students may not change units before comparing.

Example In Exercise 6, students may fail to change units and compare the numbers 3 and 35.

3 years < 35 months

Springboard to Learning Make sure students recognize that they must only compare values with the same units, such as months and months. Suggest students circle the larger unit and make sure they record the change from the larger unit to the smaller unit.

3 PRACTICE

▶ Share and Show • Guided Practice

The first problem connects to the learning model. Have students use the MathBoard to explain their thinking.

Use Exercises 2 and 3 for **Quick Check.** Students should show their answers for the Quick Check on the MathBoard.

Quick Check

If a student misses Exercises 2 and 3

Then Differentiate Instruction with

- RtI Tier 1 Activity, p. 475B
- Reteach 12.8
- Soar to Success Math 51.12, 51.14

▶ On Your Own • Independent Practice

If students complete Exercises 2 and 3 correctly, they may continue with Independent Practice.

▶ Problem Solving

H.O.T. Problem Exercise 9 requires students to apply their knowledge of hours to larger units. Have them multiply the number of hours in a day by the number of days in a week to find the number of hours in a week.

Name ____________________

Share and Show

Units of Time
1 minute (min) = 60 seconds (s)
1 hour (hr) = 60 minutes
1 day (d) = 24 hours
1 week (wk) = 7 days
1 year (yr) = 12 months (mo)
1 year (yr) = 52 weeks

1. Compare the length of a year to the length of a month. Use a model to help.

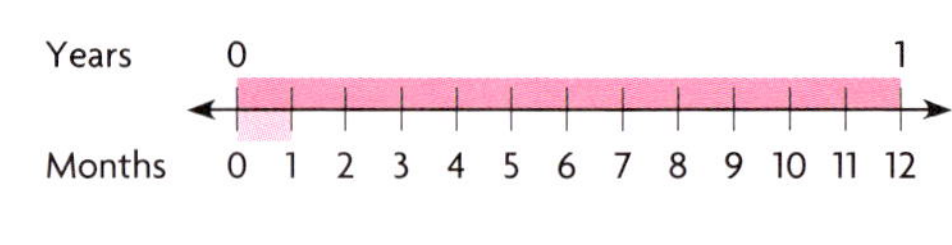

1 year is __12__ times as long as __1__ month.

Math Talk MATHEMATICAL PRACTICES **Explain** how the number line helped you compare the length of a year and the length of a month.

Complete.

2. 2 minutes = __120__ seconds
3. 4 years = __48__ months

On Your Own

Complete.

4. 3 minutes = __180__ seconds
5. 4 hours = __240__ minutes

Algebra Compare using $>$, $<$, or $=$.

6. 3 years $>$ 35 months
7. 2 days $>$ 40 hours

Math Talk: Possible explanation: the number line makes it easy to see that there are 12 months in a year, so 1 year is 12 times as long as 1 month.

Problem Solving REAL WORLD

8. Damien has lived in the apartment building for 5 years. Ken has lived there for 250 weeks. Who has lived in the building longer? **Explain.** Make a table to help.

Damien; possible explanation: 5 years is 260 weeks. 260 weeks $>$ 250 weeks, so Damien has lived in the building longer.

Years	Weeks
1	52
2	104
3	156
4	208
5	260

9. H.O.T. How many hours are in a week? **Explain.**

168 hours; possible explanation: there are 7 days in 1 week and 24 hours in 1 day. 7 days × 24 = 168 hours.

© Houghton Mifflin Harcourt Publishing Company

Extend the Math Activity

Make a Table

Investigate Students have learned to use models to solve problems involving different units of time. In this activity, they will make a table to compare hours and days.

Tell students that they need to make a table to determine which amount of time is longer: 8 days or 340 hours. Remind them to draw a table with two columns. Have pairs work together to determine how to label each column. Then, have students complete the table.

Ask questions such as the following:

- **How many hours are in 1 day?** 24
- **How can you find the number of hours in 2 days?** Multiply 2 × 24

Summarize Discuss how students found the number of hours in 8 days. Have them explain how they used their tables to compare the number of hours in 8 days to 340 hours. Then have them write the comparison statement: 8 days $<$ 340 hours.

Days	Hours
1	24
2	48
3	72
4	96
5	120
6	144
7	168
8	192

MATHEMATICAL PRACTICES **Model • Reason • Make Sense**

10. **Write Math** Explain how you know that 9 minutes is less than 600 seconds.

Possible explanation: I know 9 minutes is equal to 540 seconds. 540 is less than 600, so 9 minutes is less than 600 seconds.

11. **H.O.T.** Football practice lasts 3 hours. The coach wants to spend an equal number of minutes on each of 4 different plays. How many minutes will the team spend on each play?

45 minutes

12. **Test Prep** Martin's brother just turned 2 years old. What is his brother's age in months?

Ⓐ 2 months
Ⓑ 14 months
Ⓒ 24 months
Ⓓ 104 months

Connect to Science

One day is the length of time it takes Earth to make one complete rotation. One year is the time it takes Earth to revolve around the sun. To make the calendar match Earth's orbit time, there are leap years. Leap years add one extra day to the year. A leap day, February 29, is added to the calendar every four years.

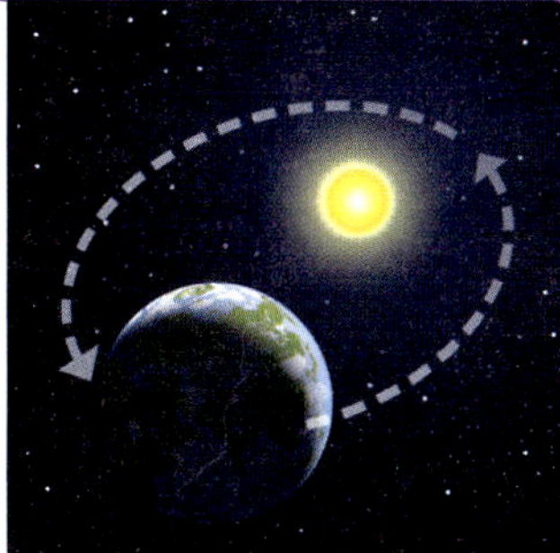

1 year = 365 days
1 leap year = 366 days

13. How many days are there in 4 years, if the fourth year is a leap year? **Explain.** Make a table to help.

1,461 days; possible explanation: there are 365 days in 1 year. 4 years × 365 = 1,460 days. 1 more day is added for leap year.

Years	Days
1	365
2	730
3	1,095
4	1,461

14. Parker was born on February 29, 2008. The second time he is able to celebrate on his actual birthday is in 2016. How many days old will Parker be on February 29, 2016? **Explain.**

2,922 days; possible explanation: Parker will be 8 years old when he celebrates his second actual birthday in 2016. There are 365 days in 1 year. 8 years × 365 = 2,920 days. 2 more days are added for the 2 leap years.

© Houghton Mifflin Harcourt Publishing Company

FOR MORE PRACTICE: Standards Practice Book, pp. P235–P236

FOR EXTRA PRACTICE: Standards Practice Book, p. P244

H.O.T. Problem Exercise 11 is a multi-step problem that requires students to determine the number of minutes in 3 hours and then divide by 4 to find the number of minutes spent on each play.

Test Prep Coach

In Exercise 12, if students selected:

A They chose the same number of months as years.
B They added 2 to the number of months in a year.
D They found the number of weeks in 2 years.

Connect to Science

Guide students to complete the table. Discuss the difference between a normal year and a leap year.

4 SUMMARIZE

MATHEMATICAL PRACTICES

Essential Question

How can you use models to compare units of time? Possible answer: I can draw a number line to compare days to weeks, or I can use a table to compare seconds, minutes, and hours.

Math Journal

Explain how you can prove that 3 weeks is less than 24 days.

Differentiated Instruction

INDEPENDENT ACTIVITIES

Grab-and-Go!™

Differentiated Centers Kit

Activities
Ultimate Units

Students complete blue Activity Card 16 by identifying the appropriate unit of measure.

Games
Time to Go

Students practice finding elapsed time to move along the game path.

LESSON 12.9

Problem Solving • Elapsed Time

LESSON AT A GLANCE

Common Core Standard

Solve problems involving measurement and conversion of measurements from a larger unit to a smaller unit.

CC.4.MD.2 Use the four operations to solve word problems involving distances, intervals of time, liquid volumes, masses of objects, and money, including problems involving simple fractions or decimals, and problems that require expressing measurements given in a larger unit in terms of a smaller unit. Represent measurement quantities using diagrams such as number line diagrams that feature a measurement scale.

Also CC.4.MD.1

Lesson Objective

Use the strategy *draw a diagram* to solve elapsed time problems.

Essential Question

How can you use the strategy *draw a diagram* to solve elapsed time problems?

Materials MathBoard

Digital Path

- Animated Math Models
- *i*Tools: Measurement
- HMH Mega Math
- *e*Student Edition

COMMON CORE PROFESSIONAL DEVELOPMENT

About the Math

Teaching for Depth In this lesson, students learn how to use a diagram of a number line with a measurement scale to find either the start or end time of an event, given one of those times and the event's elapsed time. It is important to take note of whether the start and end times given are in A.M. or P.M. All elapsed times in this lesson are limited to two hours or less.

Students need repeated reinforcement with the real-world skill of telling an event's start time, elapsed time, or end time. Throughout the day, ask time questions such as: *How long is it until we have recess?*

Professional Development Video Podcasts

Daily Routines

Common Core

SPIRAL REVIEW

Problem of the Day

*e*Transparency 12.9

Test Prep Gary wants to find the length of his horse barn using customary units. Which tool should he use to measure the length of the barn?

Ⓐ clock
Ⓑ meterstick
Ⓒ yardstick
Ⓓ pan balance

Vocabulary Builder

Abbreviations A.M. is the abbreviation for *ante meridiem*, which is Latin for *before midday*. P.M. is the abbreviation for *post meridiem*, which is Latin for *after midday*. Often instead of using A.M. or P.M., other words are given to indicate which time of day it is. Ask students to make word webs for A.M. and P.M. showing words that indicate these times of the day. Sample word webs are shown below.

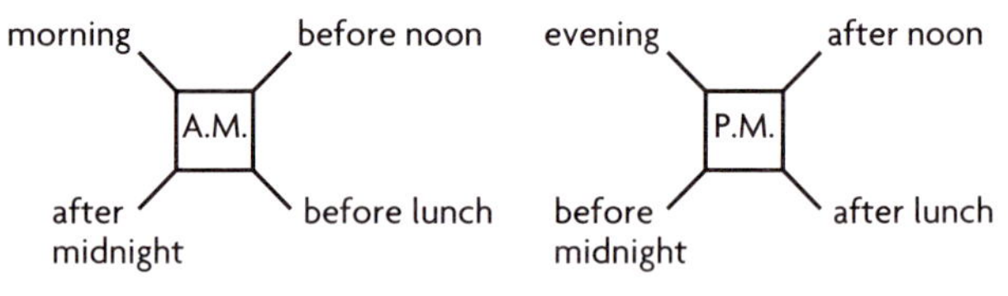

Differentiated Instruction Activities

ELL Language Support  Interpersonal / Social, Small Group

Strategy: Creative Grouping

- Partner advanced English learners or students who are fluent in English with beginning and intermediate English learners to assist in language acquisition and practice.
- Have students draw a diagram of a time line and then practice explaining how to find elapsed time using the diagram.
- Make sure students can explain the process of counting by fives, as well as by fives followed by ones, to find a start time or end time, given one of the times and the elapsed time. Be sure students can verbalize when they must count forward or backward along the time line.

See ELL Activity Guide for leveled activities.

Enrich  Visual / Logical, Partners

- Tell students that a clock tower rings one bell at 1:00 every afternoon. It proceeds to ring one additional bell as each half hour passes. So, at 1:30 two bells are rung, and so on. Ask students to determine the time when nine bells are rung. 5:00 P.M.
- Have partners create their own clock tower problems, modifying the start time, as well as the numbers of bells and times bells are rung. Partners can trade problems to solve and check.

RtI Response to Intervention

Reteach Tier 1  Visual / Mathematical, Whole Class / Small Group

- On the board, draw a T-chart with the left side labeled *Time* and the right side labeled *Minutes*. Have students copy the chart. Then present the following problem:

  Liz started reading a book at 3:35 P.M. and she read for 17 minutes. What time did she stop reading?
- Have students write 3:35 under *Time* and 0 under *Minutes* to show the starting time.
- Under 0 in the *Minutes* column, skip-count by 5s and then by 1s. Next to each number (5, 10, 15, and so on), write the corresponding time (3:40, 3:45, 3:50, and so on) in the *Time* column. **What time did Liz stop reading?** 3:52 P.M.

Tier 2  Visual / Kinesthetic, Small Group

Materials Analog Clockfaces (see *eTeacher Resources*)

- Present the following problem: **Aaron and Zack finished a game of checkers at 3:43 P.M. They played for 22 minutes. What time did they start?**
- **Do you need to move forward or backward along a time line to solve this problem?** backward
- Have students label the end time and draw the backward moves on their time lines to find the start time. **What time did Aaron and Zack start the game?** 3:21 P.M
- Repeat the activity with a problem that can be solved by moving forward.

LESSON 12.9

CC.4.MD.2 Use the four operations to solve word problems involving distances, intervals of time, liquid volumes, masses of objects, and money, including problems involving simple fractions or decimals, and problems that require expressing measurements given in a larger unit in terms of a smaller unit. Represent measurement quantities using diagrams such as number line diagrams that feature a measurement scale.

1 ENGAGE

Access Prior Knowledge Have students tell how many minutes are in an hour. 60 minutes
Then ask:

- **How many minutes is 3 hours?** 180 minutes
- **How many minutes is 1 hour 10 minutes?** 70 minutes

2 TEACH and TALK

▶ Unlock the Problem

Read the problem with the class.

Outline the three parts to elapsed time problems: start time, elapsed time, and end time. Explain that students need two of those three times in order to solve an elapsed time problem.

- **Which two times are we given in this problem?** elapsed time: 1 hour and 35 min; end time: 1:20 P.M.
- **Which time do you need to find to solve this problem?** start time
- **How do you know which way to count along the time line to solve this problem?** Because this problem is about finding the start time when you know the end time and elapsed time, you start at the end time and count backward along the time line.
- **Explain how you might use a time line to find the end time if you know the start time and the elapsed time.** You would start at the start time and count forward the elapsed time.

Students may demonstrate finding elapsed time by using *i*Tools: Measurement.

Name ____________________

PROBLEM SOLVING
Lesson 12.9

Problem Solving • Elapsed Time

Essential Question How can you use the strategy *draw a diagram* to solve elapsed time problems?

COMMON CORE STANDARD CC.4.MD.2
Solve problems involving measurement and conversion of measurements from a larger unit to a smaller unit.

UNLOCK the Problem REAL WORLD

Dora and her brother Kyle spent 1 hour and 35 minutes doing yard work. Then they stopped for lunch at 1:20 P.M. At what time did they start doing yard work?

Use the graphic organizer to help you solve the problem.

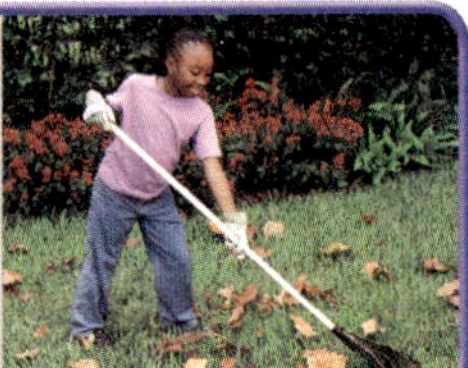

Read the Problem

What do I need to find?	What information do I need to use?	How will I use the information?
I need to find the time that Dora and Kyle started doing yard work.	I need to use the elapsed time and the time that they stopped for lunch.	I can draw a time line to help me count backward and find the start time.

Solve the Problem

I draw a time line that shows the end time 1:20 P.M. Next, I count backward 1 hour and then 5 minutes at a time until I have 35 minutes.

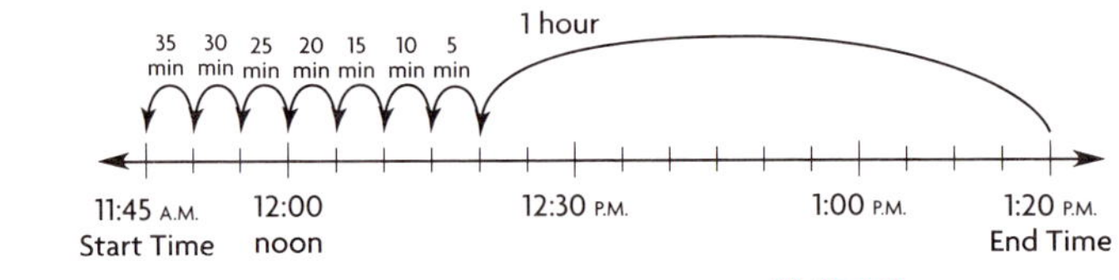

So, Dora and her brother Kyle started doing yard work at 11:45 A.M..

1. **What if** Dora and Kyle spent 50 minutes doing yard work and they stopped for lunch at 12:30 P.M.? What time would they have started doing yard work?

 11:40 A.M.

© Houghton Mifflin Harcourt Publishing Company

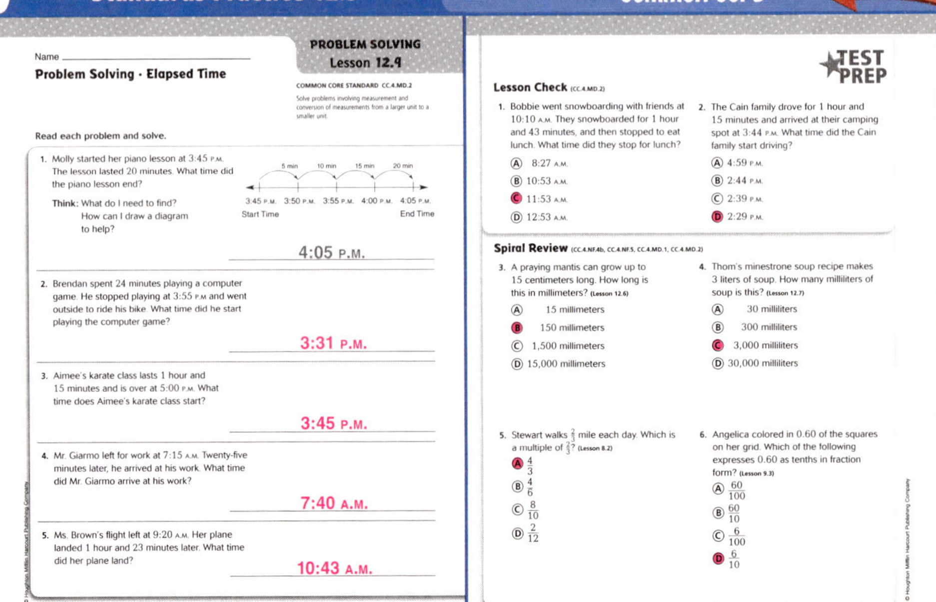

Standards Practice 12.9

Name ____________________

PROBLEM SOLVING
Lesson 12.9

Problem Solving • Elapsed Time

COMMON CORE STANDARD CC.4.MD.2
Solve problems involving measurement and conversion of measurements from a larger unit to a smaller unit.

Read each problem and solve.

1. Molly started her piano lesson at 3:45 P.M. The lesson lasted 20 minutes. What time did the piano lesson end?

 Think: What do I need to find? How can I draw a diagram to help?

 5 min, 10 min, 15 min, 20 min
 3:45 P.M. (Start Time), 3:50 P.M., 3:55 P.M., 4:00 P.M., 4:05 P.M. (End Time)

 4:05 P.M.

2. Brendan spent 24 minutes playing a computer game. He stopped playing at 3:55 P.M and went outside to ride his bike. What time did he start playing the computer game?

 3:31 P.M.

3. Aimee's karate class lasts 1 hour and 15 minutes and is over at 5:00 P.M. What time does Aimee's karate class start?

 3:45 P.M.

4. Mr. Giarmo left for work at 7:15 A.M. Twenty-five minutes later, he arrived at his work. What time did Mr. Giarmo arrive at his work?

 7:40 A.M.

5. Ms. Brown's flight left at 9:20 A.M. Her plane landed 1 hour and 23 minutes later. What time did her plane land?

 10:43 A.M.

© Houghton Mifflin Harcourt Publishing Company

Chapter 7 P237

Common Core SPIRAL REVIEW

TEST PREP

Lesson Check (CC.4.MD.2)

1. Bobbie went snowboarding with friends at 10:10 A.M. They snowboarded for 1 hour and 43 minutes, and then stopped to eat lunch. What time did they stop for lunch?
 Ⓐ 8:27 A.M.
 Ⓑ 10:53 A.M.
 Ⓒ 11:53 A.M.
 Ⓓ 12:53 A.M.

2. The Cain family drove for 1 hour and 15 minutes and arrived at their camping spot at 3:44 P.M. What time did the Cain family start driving?
 Ⓐ 4:59 P.M.
 Ⓑ 2:44 P.M.
 Ⓒ 2:39 P.M.
 Ⓓ 2:29 P.M.

Spiral Review (CC.4.NF.4b, CC.4.NF.5, CC.4.MD.1, CC.4.MD.2)

3. A praying mantis can grow up to 15 centimeters long. How long is this in millimeters? (Lesson 12.6)
 Ⓐ 15 millimeters
 Ⓑ 150 millimeters
 Ⓒ 1,500 millimeters
 Ⓓ 15,000 millimeters

4. Thom's minestrone soup recipe makes 3 liters of soup. How many milliliters of soup is this? (Lesson 12.7)
 Ⓐ 30 milliliters
 Ⓑ 300 milliliters
 Ⓒ 3,000 milliliters
 Ⓓ 30,000 milliliters

5. Stewart walks $\frac{2}{3}$ mile each day. Which is a multiple of $\frac{2}{3}$? (Lesson 8.2)
 Ⓐ $\frac{4}{3}$
 Ⓑ $\frac{4}{6}$
 Ⓒ $\frac{8}{10}$
 Ⓓ $\frac{2}{12}$

6. Angelica colored in 0.60 of the squares on her grid. Which of the following expresses 0.60 as tenths in fraction form? (Lesson 9.3)
 Ⓐ $\frac{60}{100}$
 Ⓑ $\frac{60}{10}$
 Ⓒ $\frac{6}{100}$
 Ⓓ $\frac{6}{10}$

© Houghton Mifflin Harcourt Publishing Company

P238

Try Another Problem

Ben started riding his bike at 10:05 A.M. He stopped 23 minutes later when his friend Robbie asked him to play kickball. At what time did Ben stop riding his bike?

Read the Problem

What do I need to find?	What information do I need to use?	How will I use the information?
I need to find the time that Ben stopped riding his bike.	I need to use the elapsed time and the time that he started riding his bike.	I can draw a time line to help me count forward and find the end time.

Solve the Problem

I can draw a time line that shows the start time 10:05 and then count forward 5 minutes at a time until I have counted 20 minutes. Then I can count forward 3 more minutes to find the time that is 23 minutes after 10:05.

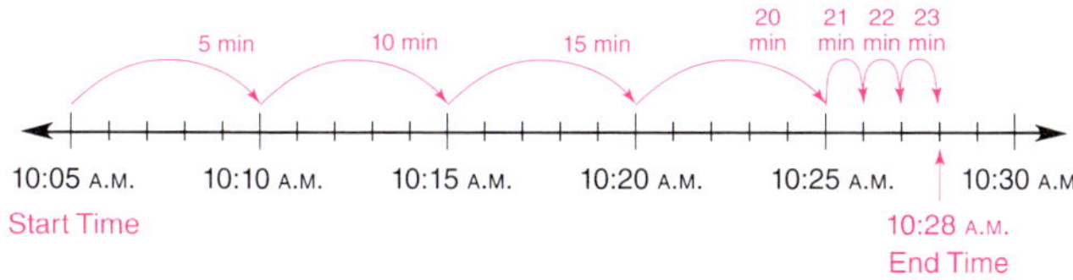

23 minutes after 10:05 is 10:28. So, Ben stopped riding his bike at 10:28 A.M.

2. How did your diagram help you solve the problem?

Possible answer: a time line helps me count the minutes from the start time to the end time by 5s and then by 1s.

Math Talk MATHEMATICAL PRACTICES **Describe** another way you could find the time an activity started or ended given the elapsed time and either the start or end time.

Math Talk: Possible answer: instead of counting backward on a time line, you can subtract the given elapsed time from the end time to find the start time. Instead of counting forward on a time line, you can add the given elapsed time to the start time to find the end time.

© Houghton Mifflin Harcourt Publishing Company

Reteach 12.9

Name ____ Lesson 12.9 Reteach

Problem Solving • Elapsed Time

Opal finished her art project at 2:25 P.M. She spent 50 minutes working on her project. What time did she start working on her project?

Read the Problem		
What do I need to find?	What information do I need to use?	How will I use the information?
I need to find Opal's start time.	End time: 2:25 P.M. Elapsed time: 50 minutes	I can draw a diagram of a clock. I can then count back 5 minutes at a time until I reach 50 minutes.

Solve the Problem

I start by showing 2:25 P.M. on the clock. Then I count back 50 minutes by 5s.
Think: As I count back, I go past the 12. The hour must be 1 hour less than the ending time.
The hour will be 1 o'clock.
So, Opal started on her project at 1:35 P.M.

Draw hands on the clock to help you solve the problem.

1. Bill wants to be at school at 8:05 A.M. It takes him 20 minutes to walk to school. At what time should Bill leave his house?

Bill should leave his house at 7:45 A.M.

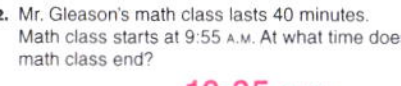

2. Mr. Gleason's math class lasts 40 minutes. Math class starts at 9:55 A.M. At what time does math class end?

Math class ends at 10:35 A.M.

3. Hannah rode her bike for 1 hour and 15 minutes until she got a flat tire at 2:30 P.M. What time did Hannah start riding her bike?

Hannah started riding her bike at 1:15 P.M.

Reteach R96 Grade 4

Enrich 12.9

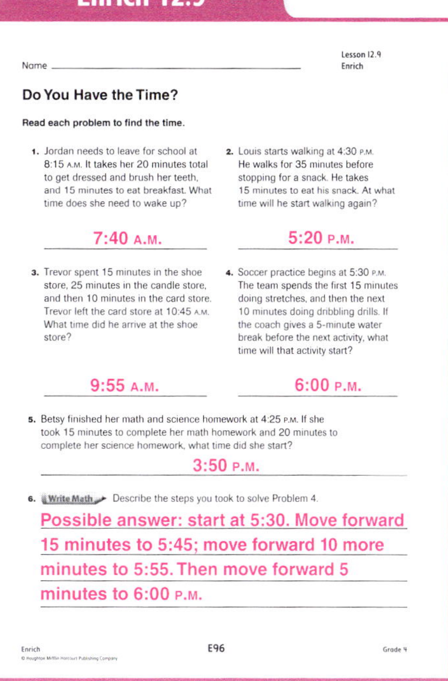

Name ____ Lesson 12.9 Enrich

Do You Have the Time?

Read each problem to find the time.

1. Jordan needs to leave for school at 8:15 A.M. It takes her 20 minutes total to get dressed and brush her teeth, and 15 minutes to eat breakfast. What time does she need to wake up? 7:40 A.M.

2. Louis starts walking at 4:30 P.M. He walks for 35 minutes before stopping for a snack. He takes 15 minutes to eat his snack. At what time will he start walking again? 5:20 P.M.

3. Trevor spent 15 minutes in the shoe store, 25 minutes in the candle store, and then 10 minutes in the card store. Trevor left the card store at 10:45 A.M. What time did he arrive at the shoe store? 9:55 A.M.

4. Soccer practice begins at 5:30 P.M. The team spends the first 15 minutes doing stretches, and then the next 10 minutes doing dribbling drills. If the coach gives a 5-minute water break before the next activity, what time will that activity start? 6:00 P.M.

5. Betsy finished her math and science homework at 4:25 P.M. If she took 15 minutes to complete her math homework and 20 minutes to complete her science homework, what time did she start? 3:50 P.M.

6. Write Math Describe the steps you took to solve Problem 4.

Possible answer: start at 5:30. Move forward 15 minutes to 5:45; move forward 10 more minutes to 5:55. Then move forward 5 minutes to 6:00 P.M.

Enrich E96 Grade 4

Try Another Problem

Have students answer the questions in the graphic organizer and complete the time line to solve the problem. Invite students to describe the steps they used to solve the problem. Have them explain how the time line helped.

Go Deeper

To extend their thinking, ask students to explain how they know the time that Ben stopped riding his bike was in the A.M. and not in the P.M. Possible explanation: P.M. is used for times after noon. From 10 A.M. to noon is 2 hours, or 120 minutes. Ben rode his bike for 23 minutes, so he could not have stopped after noon.

Use Math Talk to focus on students' understanding of possible methods for finding start time or end time given elapsed time.

You may suggest that students place completed Try Another Problem graphic organizers in their portfolios.

COMMON ERRORS

Error Students may forget to change time from A.M to P.M. or P.M. to A.M. when calculating elapsed time.

Example Lunch begins at 11:30 A.M. and lasts 1 hour and 15 minutes. Student thinks that lunch ends at 12:45 A.M.

A.M

P.M

Springboard to Learning Remind students that anytime they count elapsed time past noon, the time label changes from A.M. to P.M., and anytime they pass midnight, the time label changes from P.M. to A.M.

3 PRACTICE 

▶ Share and Show • Guided Practice

The first problem connects to the learning model. Have students use the MathBoard to explain their thinking.

H.O.T. Problem Exercise 2 requires students to use higher order thinking skills to conclude that they have the start time and the elapsed time and need to find the end time to solve the problem.

Use Exercises 3 and 4 for Quick Check. Students should show their answers for the Quick Check on the MathBoard.

 **Quick Check** 

If a student misses Exercises 3 and 4

Then Differentiate Instruction with

- RtI Tier 1 Activity, p. 479B
- Reteach 12.9
- Soar to Success Math 51.16

Name ____________________

Share and Show 

UNLOCK the Problem Tips

- √ Use the Problem Solving MathBoard.
- √ Choose a strategy you know.
- √ Underline important facts.

1. Evelyn has dance class every Saturday. It lasts 1 hour and 15 minutes and is over at 12:45 P.M. At what time does Evelyn's dance class begin?

First, write the problem you need to solve.

At what time does Evelyn's dance class begin?

Next, draw a time line to show the end time and the elapsed time. Possible drawing is given.

15 min, 10 min, 5 min, 1 hour

11:00 A.M. — 12:00 noon — 1:00 P.M.

11:30 A.M. Start Time — 12:45 P.M. End Time

Finally, find the start time.

Evelyn's dance class begins at 11:30 A.M..

2. H.O.T. What if Evelyn's dance class started at 11:00 A.M. and lasted 1 hour and 25 minutes? At what time would her class end? Describe how this problem is different from Problem 1.

Her class would end at 12:25 P.M. Possible description: this problem provides the start time and the elapsed time, while Problem 1 provides the end time and the elapsed time.

3. Beth got on the bus at 8:06 A.M. Thirty-five minutes later, she arrived at school. At what time did Beth arrive at school?

Beth arrived at school at 8:41 A.M.

4. Lyle went fishing for 1 hour and 30 minutes until he ran out of bait at 6:40 P.M. At what time did Lyle start fishing?

Lyle started fishing at 5:10 P.M.

© Houghton Mifflin Harcourt Publishing Company

Model • Reason • Make Sense

On Your Own

Choose a STRATEGY
- Act It Out
- Draw a Diagram
- Find a Pattern
- Make a Table or List
- Solve a Simpler Problem

5. Mike and Jed went skiing at 10:30 A.M. They skied for 1 hour and 55 minutes before stopping for lunch. At what time did Mike and Jed stop for lunch?

12:25 P.M.

6. H.O.T. What's the Question? One hour and 10 minutes later, it was 6:20 P.M.

Possible answer: Shalani's class began at 5:10 P.M. If her class lasted for 1 hour and 10 minutes, what time was it when her class ended?

SHOW YOUR WORK

7. Write Math Explain how you can use a diagram to determine the start time when the end time is 9:00 A.M. and the elapsed time is 26 minutes. What is the start time?

8:34 A.M.; possible explanation: I can draw a time line that shows 9:00, and then I can count backward 5 minutes at a time until I get to 25 minutes. Then I count backward one more minute for a total elapsed time of 26 minutes.

8. H.O.T. Bethany finished her math homework at 4:20 P.M. She did 25 multiplication problems in all. If each problem took her 3 minutes to do, at what time did Bethany start her math homework?

3:05 P.M.

9. Test Prep Vincent began his weekly chores on Saturday morning at 11:20. He finished 1 hour and 15 minutes later. At what time did Vincent finish his chores?

Ⓐ 12:35 A.M.　Ⓒ 12:35 P.M.
Ⓑ 10:05 A.M.　Ⓓ 1:05 P.M.

© Houghton Mifflin Harcourt Publishing Company

 FOR MORE PRACTICE: Standards Practice Book, pp. P237–P238

On Your Own • Independent Practice

H.O.T. Problem Exercise 8 requires students to use higher order thinking skills as they solve the multi-step problem. Make sure students think of 75 minutes as 1 hour 15 minutes.

Test Prep Coach

Test Prep Coach helps teachers identify common errors that students can make.

In Exercise 9, if students selected:

A They chose the time in the morning and not the afternoon.
B They counted backward instead of forward.
D They included an extra half hour of elapsed time.

4 SUMMARIZE

Essential Question

How can you use the strategy *draw a diagram* to solve elapsed time problems?
A time line is a diagram that helps to count the number of hours and minutes of the elapsed time forward or backward from the given start or end time to find the unknown time.

Math Journal

Explain why it is important to know if a time is in the A.M. or in the P.M. when figuring out how much time has elapsed.

Differentiated Instruction
INDEPENDENT ACTIVITIES

Differentiated Centers Kit

Activities
Ultimate Units

Students complete blue Activity Card 16 by identifying the appropriate unit of measure.

Games
Time to Go

Students practice finding elapsed time to move along the game path.

Digital Path
- Animated Math Models
- *i*Tools
- HMH Mega Math
- Soar to Success Math
- *e*Student Edition

LESSON 12.10

Mixed Measures

LESSON AT A GLANCE

Common Core Standard

Solve problems involving measurement and conversion of measurements from a larger unit to a smaller unit.

CC.4.MD.2 Use the four operations to solve word problems involving distances, intervals of time, liquid volumes, masses of objects, and money, including problems involving simple fractions or decimals, and problems that require expressing measurements given in a larger unit in terms of a smaller unit. Represent measurement quantities using diagrams such as number line diagrams that feature a measurement scale.

Also CC.4.MD.1

Lesson Objective

Solve problems involving mixed measures.

Essential Question

How can you solve problems involving mixed measures?

Materials

MathBoard

Digital Path

- Read World Video, Ch.12
- *i*Tools: Measurement
- HMH Mega Math
- *e*Student Edition

About the Math

Teaching for Depth Using mixed measures in addition and subtraction problems requires students to draw upon their knowledge of mathematical operations and of measurement units. Regrouping becomes more involved, as students must first consider the units being used before determining how to rename the units.

Students need to understand the difference between the base-ten addition/subtraction model and the addition/subtraction of mixed measures. Demonstrate this by solving various problems of each type on the board. Guide students to see how the basic algorithm remains the same, but the regrouped units change based on the number of smaller units in each larger unit.

Professional Development Video Podcasts

Daily Routines

Common Core

SPIRAL REVIEW

Problem of the Day

eTransparency 12.10

Test Prep Quinn wants to know the mass of a bag of flour. Which units should he use?

Ⓐ pounds Ⓒ cups
Ⓑ liters Ⓓ grams

Fluency Builder

Addition Have students practice addition with 3-digit and 4-digit addends. Write the following problems on the board and ask students to complete them as quickly as possible. Provide students with the sums and have students check their answers. Make sure students can explain if and how they regrouped in each of the problems.

1. 235 + 158 = 393
2. 114 + 672 = 786
3. 823 + 107 = 930
4. 339 + 401 = 740
5. 1,863 + 3,540 = 5,403
6. 3,917 + 2,138 = 6,055
7. 7,550 + 6,081 = 13,631
8. 9,446 + 5,872 = 15,318

Differentiated Instruction Activities

ELL Language Support

Visual
Small Group

Strategy: Explore Context

Materials ruler, gallon jug or container

- Students can explore measures to reinforce the concept of working with mixed measures.
- Show students a ruler. **How many inches are in 1 foot?** 12
- Show a gallon jug. **How many quarts are in 1 gallon?** 4
- Discuss how the larger units compare to the smaller units.
- Explain how regrouping in subtraction is the same as changing from larger to smaller units, so the renamed number must be based on the units. For example, 2 gallons 3 quarts could be renamed as 1 gallon 7 quarts.

See ELL Activity Guide for leveled activities.

Enrich

Visual
Partners

Materials markers, poster board

- Assign pairs different units, such as pounds, gallons, or feet. Have each pair write a subtraction problem using the given unit.
- Give students markers and poster board and have them draw models to illustrate their subtraction problems.
- Make sure students show any necessary regrouping. Have them look at subtraction models in previous chapters as a guide.
- Remind students to write the units in the problem and answer. Have them present their posters to the group and explain their models.

RtI Response to Intervention

Reteach Tier 1

Kinesthetic / Visual
Whole Class / Small Group

Materials MathBoards

- **Molly's sister weighed 7 pounds 4 ounces when she was born. She weighed 9 pounds 3 ounces at her two-week checkup. How much weight had she gained?**
- Have students copy the problem as you write it on the board and guide them through each step.

  9 pounds 3 ounces
  −7 pounds 4 ounces

- Discuss how to regroup pounds to ounces. Remind students that measures do not regroup in tens as in regular subtraction. Solve the problem and discuss the results.

  8 (regrouped from ~~9~~) pounds 19 (regrouped from ~~3~~) ounces
  − 7 pounds 4 ounces
  1 pound 15 ounces

Tier 2

Kinesthetic / Visual
Small Group

- Write: 6 pounds 2 ounces; 3 pounds 9 ounces. **Which measure is larger?** 6 pounds 2 ounces
- Write the following on the board. Have students use given measurements to create two problems.

  □ pounds □ ounces
  − □ pounds □ ounces

  □ pounds □ ounces
  + □ pounds □ ounces

- Work with students to complete each problem. Discuss how to regroup pounds to ounces in the subtraction problem.

  5 (regrouped from ~~6~~) pounds 18 (regrouped from ~~2~~) ounces
  − 3 pounds 9 ounces
  2 pounds 9 ounces

  6 pounds 2 ounces
  + 3 pounds 9 ounces
  9 pounds 11 ounces

LESSON 12.10

CCC.4.MD.2 Use the four operations to solve word problems involving distances, intervals of time, liquid volumes, masses of objects, and money, including problems involving simple fractions or decimals, and problems that require expressing measurements given in a larger unit in terms of a smaller unit. Represent measurement quantities using diagrams such as number line diagrams that feature a measurement scale.

1 ENGAGE

GO Online — Real World Video, Ch. 12

Access Prior Knowledge Show the Real-World Video *Designing a Campground*. Ask students to name any units of measure they heard or saw in the video. Review units used to measure length, time, weight, and liquid volume.

2 TEACH and TALK

GO Online — *i*Tools

▶ Unlock the Problem

Post charts showing the relationship between the units and unit abbreviations used in the lesson for student reference.

Read through the problem with students. Have them identify the measurement given in the problem. Students should recognize that the measurement has two units, feet and inches.

- **How many inches are in 1 foot?** 12

Guide students to see that 5 feet is 60 inches, so 5 feet 10 inches is the same as 60 + 10 inches, or 70 inches.

▶ Example 1

- **How do you add hours and minutes?** Add the minutes, and then add the hours.
- **When should you regroup when adding minutes?** Possible answer: if the sum is equal to or more than 60, regroup 60 minutes as 1 hour.

Use **Math Talk** to focus on students' understanding of how base-ten addition compares to the addition of mixed measures.

Lesson 12.10

Name ______________

Mixed Measures

Essential Question How can you solve problems involving mixed measures?

COMMON CORE STANDARD CC.4.MD.2
Solve problems involving measurement and conversion of measurements from a larger unit to a smaller unit.

UNLOCK the Problem REAL WORLD

Herman is building a picnic table for a new campground. The picnic table is 5 feet 10 inches long. How long is the picnic table in inches?

- Is the mixed measure greater than or less than 6 feet? less
- How many inches are in 1 foot? 12

Change a mixed measure.

Think of 5 feet 10 inches as 5 feet + 10 inches.

Write feet as inches.

5 feet
+ 10 inches

Think: 5 feet × 12 = 60 inches

60 inches
+ 10 inches
70 inches

So, the picnic table is 70 inches long.

Example 1 Add mixed measures.

Herman built the picnic table in 2 days. The first day he worked for 3 hours 45 minutes. The second day he worked for 2 hours 10 minutes. How long did it take him to build the table?

STEP 1 Add the minutes.

3 hr 45 min
+ 2 hr 10 min
55 min

STEP 2 Add the hours.

3 hr 45 min
+ 2 hr 10 min
5 hr 55 min

So, it took Herman 5 hours 55 minutes to build the table.

Possible explanation: similar: you add from right to left; different: you don't necessarily regroup when you have 10 of the smaller unit. Instead, you regroup when you have enough of the smaller unit to make 1 of the larger unit.

Math Talk MATHEMATICAL PRACTICES How is adding mixed measures similar to adding tens and ones? How is it different? Explain.

- **What if** Herman worked an extra 5 minutes on the picnic table? How long would he have worked on the table then? **Explain.**

6 hours; possible explanation: there are 60 minutes in 1 hour. 55 minutes + 5 minutes = 60 minutes, or 1 hour. 5 hours + 1 hour = 6 hours

© Houghton Mifflin Harcourt Publishing Company

Standards Practice 12.10 — Common Core — SPIRAL REVIEW

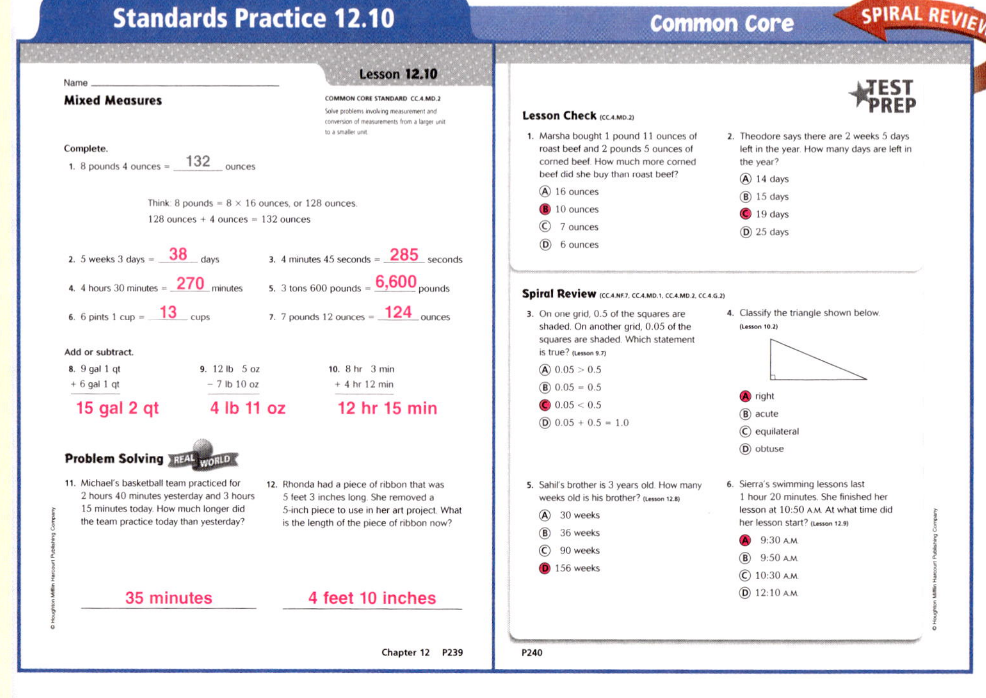

Lesson 12.10

Name ______

Mixed Measures

COMMON CORE STANDARD CC.4.MD.2 Solve problems involving measurement and conversion of measurements from a larger unit to a smaller unit.

Complete.

1. 8 pounds 4 ounces = 132 ounces

Think: 8 pounds = 8 × 16 ounces, or 128 ounces. 128 ounces + 4 ounces = 132 ounces

2. 5 weeks 3 days = 38 days
3. 4 minutes 45 seconds = 285 seconds
4. 4 hours 30 minutes = 270 minutes
5. 3 tons 600 pounds = 6,600 pounds
6. 6 pints 1 cup = 13 cups
7. 7 pounds 12 ounces = 124 ounces

Add or subtract.

8. 9 gal 1 qt + 6 gal 1 qt = 15 gal 2 qt
9. 12 lb 5 oz − 7 lb 10 oz = 4 lb 11 oz
10. 8 hr 3 min + 4 hr 12 min = 12 hr 15 min

Problem Solving REAL WORLD

11. Michael's basketball team practiced for 2 hours 40 minutes yesterday and 3 hours 15 minutes today. How much longer did the team practice today than yesterday? 35 minutes
12. Rhonda had a piece of ribbon that was 5 feet 3 inches long. She removed a 5-inch piece to use in her art project. What is the length of the piece of ribbon now? 4 feet 10 inches

Chapter 12 P239

TEST PREP

Lesson Check (CC.4.MD.2)

1. Marsha bought 1 pound 11 ounces of roast beef and 2 pounds 5 ounces of corned beef. How much more corned beef did she buy than roast beef?
   Ⓐ 16 ounces
   Ⓑ 10 ounces
   Ⓒ 7 ounces
   Ⓓ 6 ounces
2. Theodore says there are 2 weeks 5 days left in the year. How many days are left in the year?
   Ⓐ 14 days
   Ⓑ 15 days
   Ⓒ 19 days
   Ⓓ 25 days

Spiral Review (CC.4.NF.7, CC.4.MD.1, CC.4.MD.2, CC.4.G.2)

3. On one grid, 0.5 of the squares are shaded. On another grid, 0.05 of the squares are shaded. Which statement is true? (Lesson 9.7)
   Ⓐ 0.05 > 0.5
   Ⓑ 0.05 = 0.5
   Ⓒ 0.05 < 0.5
   Ⓓ 0.05 + 0.5 = 1.0
4. Classify the triangle shown below. (Lesson 10.2)
   Ⓐ right
   Ⓑ acute
   Ⓒ equilateral
   Ⓓ obtuse
5. Sahil's brother is 3 years old. How many weeks old is his brother? (Lesson 12.8)
   Ⓐ 30 weeks
   Ⓑ 36 weeks
   Ⓒ 90 weeks
   Ⓓ 156 weeks
6. Sierra's swimming lessons last 1 hour 20 minutes. She finished her lesson at 10:50 A.M. At what time did her lesson start? (Lesson 12.9)
   Ⓐ 9:30 A.M.
   Ⓑ 9:50 A.M.
   Ⓒ 10:30 A.M.
   Ⓓ 12:10 A.M.

P240

Example 2 Subtract mixed measures.

Alicia is building a fence around the picnic area. She has a pole that is 6 feet 6 inches long. She cuts off 1 foot 7 inches from one end. How long is the pole now?

STEP 1 Subtract the inches.

Think: 7 inches is greater than 6 inches. You need to regroup to subtract.

6 ft 6 in. = 5 ft 6 in. + 12 in.

= 5 ft 18 in.

```
  5   18
  6 ft 6 in.
– 1 ft 7 in.
      11 in.
```

STEP 2 Subtract the feet.

```
  5   18
  6 ft 6 in.
– 1 ft 7 in.
  4 ft 11 in.
```

So, the pole is now 4 feet 11 inches long.

ERROR Alert

Be sure to check that you are regrouping correctly. There are 12 inches in 1 foot.

Try This! Subtract.

3 pounds 5 ounces − 1 pound 2 ounces

```
  3 lb 5 oz
– 1 lb 2 oz
  2 lb 3 oz
```

Share and Show MATH BOARD

1. A truck is carrying 2 tons 500 pounds of steel. How many pounds of steel is the truck carrying?

Think of 2 tons 500 pounds as 2 tons + 500 pounds. Write tons as pounds.

2 tons — Think: 2 tons × 2,000 = 4,000 pounds → 4,000 pounds

+ 500 pounds → + 500 pounds

4,500 pounds

So, the truck is carrying 4,500 pounds of steel.

© Houghton Mifflin Harcourt Publishing Company

▶ Example 2

Work through Step 1 with students by writing the given measurements as a subtraction problem on the board.

- **How can you regroup the units in order to subtract?** I can regroup 6 feet 6 inches as 5 feet 18 inches because there are 12 inches in 1 foot.

Complete the subtraction problem in Step 2. Discuss how to check the difference by adding it to the subtracted amount. The sum should be the top value, 6 ft 6 in., in the subtraction problem.

Try This!

Have a volunteer write the subtraction problem on the board. Discuss how to subtract pounds and ounces. Since there is no need to regroup, students should subtract ounces, then pounds. Remind students that they should subtract smaller units first so that they can regroup if necessary.

3 PRACTICE

▶ Share and Show • Guided Practice

The first problem connects to the learning model. Have students use the MathBoard to explain their thinking.

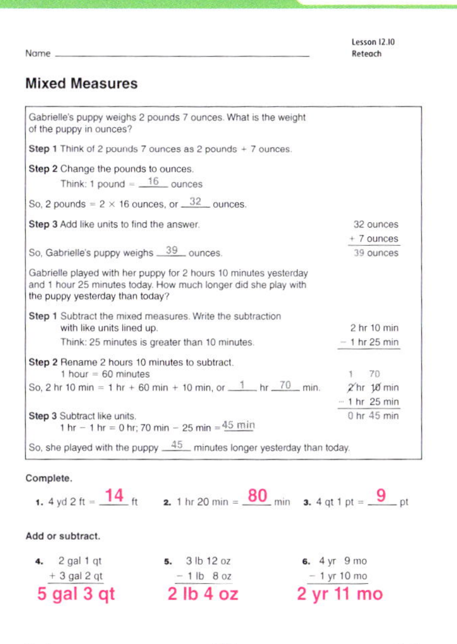

Reteach 12.10

Name ____________ Lesson 12.10 Reteach

Mixed Measures

Gabrielle's puppy weighs 2 pounds 7 ounces. What is the weight of the puppy in ounces?

Step 1 Think of 2 pounds 7 ounces as 2 pounds + 7 ounces.

Step 2 Change the pounds to ounces.
Think: 1 pound = 16 ounces

So, 2 pounds = 2 × 16 ounces, or 32 ounces.

Step 3 Add like units to find the answer.

32 ounces
+ 7 ounces
39 ounces

So, Gabrielle's puppy weighs 39 ounces.

Gabrielle played with her puppy for 2 hours 10 minutes yesterday and 1 hour 25 minutes today. How much longer did she play with the puppy yesterday than today?

Step 1 Subtract the mixed measures. Write the subtraction with like units lined up.
Think: 25 minutes is greater than 10 minutes.

2 hr 10 min
− 1 hr 25 min

Step 2 Rename 2 hours 10 minutes to subtract.
1 hour = 60 minutes
So, 2 hr 10 min = 1 hr + 60 min + 10 min, or 1 hr 70 min.

1 hr 70 min
− 1 hr 25 min
0 hr 45 min

Step 3 Subtract like units.
1 hr − 1 hr = 0 hr; 70 min − 25 min = 45 min

So, she played with the puppy 45 minutes longer yesterday than today.

Complete.

1. 4 yd 2 ft = 14 ft
2. 1 hr 20 min = 80 min
3. 4 qt 1 pt = 9 pt

Add or subtract.

4. 2 gal 1 qt + 3 gal 2 qt = 5 gal 3 qt
5. 3 lb 12 oz − 1 lb 8 oz = 2 lb 4 oz
6. 4 yr 9 mo − 1 yr 10 mo = 2 yr 11 mo

Reteach R97 Grade 4

© Houghton Mifflin Harcourt Publishing Company

Enrich 12.10

Name ____________ Lesson 12.10 Enrich

Mixed Measures

Solve each problem.

1. Ted's new puppy weighed 8 pounds 11 ounces two months ago. One month later, the puppy had gained 2 pounds 7 ounces. During the second month, the puppy gained 3 pounds 5 ounces. How much does Ted's puppy weigh now?

   14 pounds 7 ounces

2. Gilda made 2 gallons of lemonade to sell at her lemonade stand. At the end of the day, she had 2 quarts 1 pint left over. How many 1-cup servings did Gilda sell?

   22 1-cup servings

3. Four friends competed in a relay race. Each friend ran one leg of the race. Ann ran her leg in 2 minutes 15 seconds. Kyra ran her leg in 1 minute 53 seconds. Marie ran her leg in 2 minutes 9 seconds. Zoe ran the final leg in 1 minute 58 seconds. What was the total time for the relay team?

   8 minutes 15 seconds

4. Ron timed his flight from Los Angeles to New York. The plane was in the air for 4 hours 52 minutes 45 seconds. The return trip took longer because of a headwind. Ron recorded the flight time as 5 hours 34 minutes 14 seconds. How much longer was the return flight?

   41 minutes 29 seconds

5. Write Math **Explain** how you converted units to solve Problem 2.

   Possible answer: I converted the measures to cups: 2 gallons = 32 cups; 2 quarts 1 pint = 8 cups + 2 cups, or 10 cups. I subtracted 32 − 10 = 22. So, 22 cups were sold.

Enrich E97 Grade 4

© Houghton Mifflin Harcourt Publishing Company

COMMON ERRORS

Error Students may regroup using tens instead of the measurement unit in the problem.

Example In Exercise 6, students may regroup 1 gallon as 10 quarts.

```
  2     14
  3 gal 4 qt
– 1 gal 5 qt
```

Springboard to Learning Remind students that regrouping must be based on the units being used. So, 1 gallon must be regrouped as 4 quarts.

Use Exercises 4 and 6 for Quick Check. Students should show their answers for the Quick Check on the MathBoard.

 a student misses Exercises 4 and 6

 Differentiate Instruction with
- RtI Tier 1 Activity, p. 483B
- Reteach 12.10
- Soar to Success Math 44.36, 45.30, 46.37

If students complete Exercises 4 and 6 correctly, they may continue with Independent Practice.

Problem Solving

H.O.T. Problems Exercises 14 and 15 require students to multiply or divide mixed measures. Remind them to use the correct units for each measure when regrouping to write the solution.

Exercise 16 requires students to critique given answers and explain whether the answers make sense. Draw a number line on the board with tick marks for feet and inches. Have one student mark 4 feet 18 inches and another student mark 5 feet 6 inches; discuss how the measurements are the same.

Name ______

Rewrite each measure in the given unit.

2. 1 yard 2 feet
5 feet

3. 3 pints 1 cup
7 cups

4. 3 weeks 1 day
22 days

Add or subtract.

5. 2 lb 4 oz + 1 lb 6 oz = 3 lb 10 oz

6. 3 gal 4 qt − 1 gal 5 qt = 1 gal 3 qt

7. 5 hr 20 min − 3 hr 15 min = 2 hr 5 min

MATHEMATICAL PRACTICES **Math Talk** How do you know when you need to regroup to subtract? Explain.

On Your Own

Rewrite each measure in the given unit.

8. 1 hour 15 minutes
75 minutes

9. 4 quarts 2 pints
10 pints

10. 10 feet 10 inches
130 inches

Add or subtract.

11. 2 tons 300 lb − 1 ton 300 lb = 1 ton

12. 10 gal 8 c + 8 gal 9 c = 19 gal 1 c

13. 7 lb 6 oz − 2 lb 12 oz = 4 lb 10 oz

Math Talk: Possible explanation: you need to regroup if you do not have enough of the unit from which you are subtracting. Then you regroup 1 larger unit as an equivalent amount of the smaller unit.

Problem Solving REAL WORLD

14. H.O.T. Jackson has a rope 1 foot 8 inches long. He cuts it into 4 equal pieces. How many inches long is each piece?

5 inches

15. H.O.T. Ahmed fills 6 pitchers with juice. Each pitcher contains 2 quarts 1 pint. How many pints of juice does he have?

30 pints

16. H.O.T. Sense or Nonsense? Sam and Dave each solve the problem at the right. Sam says the sum is 4 feet 18 inches. Dave says the sum is 5 feet 6 inches. Whose answer makes sense? Whose answer is nonsense? Explain.

2 ft 10 in. + 2 ft 8 in.

Both answers make sense; possible explanation: the sum is 4 feet 18 inches, which is the same as 5 feet 6 inches.

© Houghton Mifflin Harcourt Publishing Company

Extend the Math Activity

Finding Elapsed Time Beyond Adjacent Hours

Investigate A movie started at 4:35 P.M. and ended at 7:05 P.M. How long did the movie last?

Use a Diagram Display the diagram below. Explain that the first clock is used to find the minutes needed to take the start time to the next hour. The middle clocks are used to find the elapsed whole hours. The last clock is used to take the hour to the end time.

4:35 to 5:00

25 minutes

5:00 to 6:00

1 hour

6:00 to 7:00

1 hour

7:00 to 7:05
5 minutes

25 minutes + 1 hour + 1 hour + 5 minutes = 2 hours 30 minutes

Use Subtraction Show students how to rename and subtract to find the elapsed time.

~~7 hr 05 min~~
− 4 hr 35 min

6 hr 65 min
~~7 hr 05 min~~
− 4 hr 35 min
2 hr 30 min

Think: 7 hours is the same as 6 hr 60 min. So, 7 hr 05 min is the same as 6 hr 65 min.

Summarize Ask students to choose a method, diagram, or algorithm to solve the following problem.

What is the length of a flight if the plane took off at 1:50 P.M. and landed at 6:25 P.M.?

10 min + 4 hr + 25 min = 4 hr 35 min

 Model • Reason • Make Sense

UNLOCK the Problem REAL WORLD

TEST PREP

17. Theo is practicing for a 5-kilometer race. He runs 5 kilometers every day and records his time. His normal time is 25 minutes 15 seconds. Yesterday it took him only 23 minutes 49 seconds. How much faster was his time yesterday than his normal time?

(A) 1 minute 26 seconds (C) 2 minutes 26 seconds
(B) 1 minute 64 seconds (D) 2 minutes 34 seconds

a. What are you asked to find?

how much faster Theo's time was yesterday than his normal time

b. What information do you know?

His normal time is 25 minutes 15 seconds. It took him only 23 minutes 49 seconds yesterday.

c. How will you solve the problem?

I will subtract his time yesterday from his normal time.

d. Solve the problem.

24 min 75 sec (25 min 15 sec regrouped)
− 23 min 49 sec
1 min 26 sec

e. Fill in the bubble for the correct answer choice above.

18. H.O.T. Don has 5 pieces of pipe. Each piece is 3 feet 6 inches long. If Don joins the pieces end to end to make one long pipe, how long will the new pipe be?

(A) 8 feet 11 inches
(B) 15 feet 6 inches
(C) 15 feet 11 inches
(D) 17 feet 6 inches

19. Maya's cat weighed 7 pounds 2 ounces last year. The cat gained 1 pound 8 ounces this year. What is the weight of Maya's cat now?

(A) 5 pounds 10 ounces
(B) 8 pounds 2 ounces
(C) 8 pounds 10 ounces
(D) 9 pounds

© Houghton Mifflin Harcourt Publishing Company

 FOR MORE PRACTICE: Standards Practice Book, pp. P239–P240

FOR EXTRA PRACTICE: Standards Practice Book, p. P244

Unlock the Problem 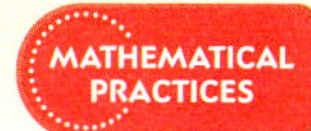

H.O.T. Problem Exercise 18 requires students to multiply mixed measures. Make sure students multiply inches, then feet, and regroup the inches correctly. Have them use repeated addition to check their answer.

Test Prep Coach

Test Prep Coach helps teachers to identify common errors that students can make.

In Exercise 19, if students selected:

A They subtracted instead of adding.
B They added the pounds but not the ounces.
D They regrouped the sum of ounces, 10 ounces, as 1 pound.

4 SUMMARIZE 

Essential Question

How can you solve problems involving mixed measures? Possible answer: I start by adding or subtracting the smaller units and then the larger units. I can regroup using the correct numbers of units.

Math Journal 

Write a subtraction problem involving pounds and ounces. Solve the problem and show your work.

Differentiated Instruction

INDEPENDENT ACTIVITIES

Grab-and-Go!™

Differentiated Centers Kit

Activities
Balancing Act

Students complete blue Activity Card 14 by measuring mass and weight.

Activities
Ultimate Units

Students complete blue Activity Card 16 by identifying the appropriate unit of measure.

Literature
A Trip to the Pond

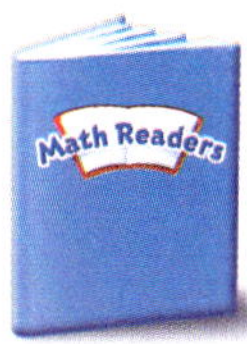

Students read about using metric units to measure and identify insects.

Digital Path

- Animated Math Models
- *i*Tools
- HMH Mega Math
- Soar to Success Math
- *e*Student Edition

LESSON 12.11

Algebra • Patterns in Measurement Units

LESSON AT A GLANCE

Common Core Standard

Solve problems involving measurement and conversion of measurements from a larger unit to a smaller unit.

CC.4.MD.1 Know relative sizes of measurement units within one system of units including km, m, cm; kg, g; lb, oz.; l, ml; hr, min, sec. Within a single system of measurement, express measurements in a larger unit in terms of a smaller unit. Record measurement equivalents in a two-column table.

Lesson Objective

Use patterns to write number pairs for measurement units.

Essential Question

How can you use patterns to write number pairs for measurement units?

Materials

MathBoard

Digital Path

*i*Tools: Measurement

*e*Student Edition

COMMON CORE PROFESSIONAL DEVELOPMENT

Building Mathematical Practices

CC.K–12.MP.2 Reason abstractly and quantitatively.
In this lesson, students will identify relationships between number pairs of measurement units. Students must use reasoning to select the correct measurement units based on their previous knowledge of their numerical relationship. Then they use a table to show the pattern of number pairs and label the columns of the table.

As students work with the tables and number pairs, they understand that measurement units involve a direct relationship and how mathematical relationships can often be irreversible.

Daily Routines

Math Board

Common Core

SPIRAL REVIEW

Problem of the Day

Test Prep Eric swam 4 laps in 3 minutes. How many seconds did it take him to swim 4 laps?

Ⓐ 180 seconds Ⓒ 220 seconds
Ⓑ 200 seconds Ⓓ 240 seconds

Fluency Builder

Counting Tape

Materials Counting Tape

Continue to have students identify and mark multiples with Multiple Markers each day.

- **What is the least number on the Tape that can be broken up evenly into twos or threes?** 132
- **What is the least number on the Tape that is a common multiple of 2 and 4?** 132
- **What is the least number on the Tape that is a common multiple of 2, 3, and 4?** 132
- **How many 2s are in 134?** 67 **How can you figure that out?** divide

132 133 134 135 136 137 138 139 140

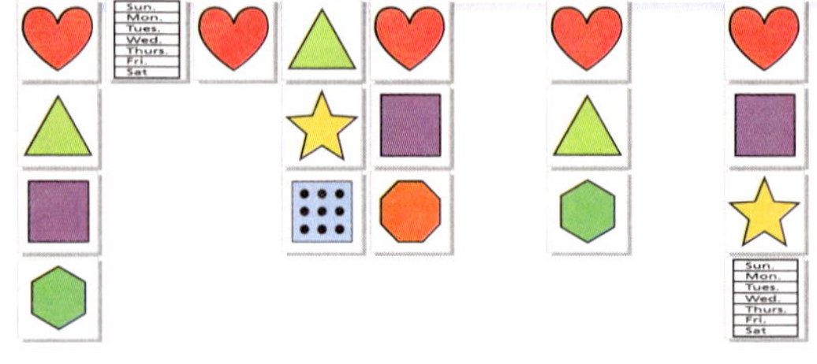

Differentiated Instruction Activities

ELL Language Support  Visual / Small Group

Strategy: Identify Patterns

Materials MathBoards

- Students can identify patterns in mathematical relationships to reinforce math concepts.
- Show students the table below. **How many decimeters in 1 meter?** 10
- Write 10 in the first row under Decimeters. Ask students to suggest the correct number for each of the following rows.
- Discuss any patterns students see in the columns. Then discuss how the numbers in each pair are related.

Meters	Decimeters
1	10
2	20
3	30
4	40
5	50
6	60
7	70
8	80

See ELL Activity Guide for leveled activities.

Enrich  Visual / Small Group

- Have each student draw a blank table with 2 columns and 6 rows. Tell students to choose two related measurement units and label the columns as such.
- Have students pass their tables to the next person in the group. The receiving student should complete the first row of the table, using 1 as the larger unit.
- Continue to pass the tables, with students completing another row of each table they receive.
- When all of the tables are completed, have students discuss their work.

Response to Intervention

Reteach Tier 1  Kinesthetic / Visual · Whole Class / Small Group

- Have students draw a blank table with 2 columns.
- **What is the relationship between minutes and hours?** 1 hour = 60 minutes
- Have students label the first column of the table *Hours* and the second column *Minutes*. Then have them write the numbers 1 through 5, one number in each row of the left column.
- **How many minutes are in 1 hour?** 60 Have students write 60 under *Minutes*, in the row next to 1. Have them complete the remaining rows. Discuss the finished table.
- **Could you reverse the order of the numbers in a row? Why or why not?** No; possible answer: it would be incorrect because that would mean there was 1 minute in 60 hours.

Tier 2  Kinesthetic / Visual · Small Group

- Draw a large blank table with two columns and 6 rows on the board.
- **How many cups are in 1 pint?** 2
- **How can we show the relationship between cups and pints on this table?** Possible answer: use one column for pints and one column for cups.
- Allow volunteers to write in the labels for the table. Then write 1 in the first blank row under *Pints*.
- Have volunteers take turns writing the remaining numbers in the table. Discuss why each number does or does not fit, and why the columns cannot be reversed.

LESSON 12.11

CCC.4.MD.1 Know relative sizes of measurement units within one system of units including km, m, cm; kg, g; lb, oz.; l, ml; hr, min, sec. Within a single system of measurement, express measurements in a larger unit in terms of a smaller unit. Record measurement equivalents in a two-column table.

1 ENGAGE

*i*Tools

Materials *i*Tools: Measurement

Access Prior Knowledge Ask students to tell how many inches are in 1 foot. 12
Write *1 foot = 12 inches* on the board.

- **How many inches are in 2 feet?** 24

Write *2 feet = 24* inches on the board.
Ask how to find the number of inches in any number of feet. Multiply the number of feet by 12 to find inches.

2 TEACH and TALK

Connect Have students read the numbers in the table using the following sentence pattern: "There are ____ feet in ____ yards." 3, 1; 6, 2; 9, 3; 12, 4; 15, 5

Discuss how the table shows pairs that compare yards to feet.

▶ Unlock the Problem

Read through the problem with students. Explain that they will be analyzing the pattern in this table to determine what labels to include in each column.

▶ Activity

- **What units of time have a relationship of 1 to 7?** Possible answer: days and weeks
- **What is represented by the number pair 4 and 28?** Possible answer: there are 28 days in 4 weeks.

Discuss how the table shows the relationship between the numbers in each pair. It may be helpful to post charts showing the relationship between various units for student reference.

Use **Math Talk** to focus on students' understanding of the relationship between the numbers in number pairs.

Name ____________________

ALGEBRA
Lesson 12.11

Patterns in Measurement Units

Essential Question How can you use patterns to write number pairs for measurement units?

COMMON CORE STANDARD CC.4.MD.1
Solve problems involving measurement and conversion of measurements from a larger unit to a smaller unit.

CONNECT The table at the right relates yards and feet. You can think of the numbers in the table as number pairs. 1 and 3, 2 and 6, 3 and 9, 4 and 12, and 5 and 15 are number pairs.

The number pairs show the relationship between yards and feet. 1 yard is equal to 3 feet, 2 yards is equal to 6 feet, 3 yards is equal to 9 feet, and so on.

Yards	Feet
1	3
2	6
3	9
4	12
5	15

UNLOCK the Problem REAL WORLD

Lillian made the table below to relate two units of time. What units of time does the pattern in the table show?

Activity Use the relationship between the number pairs to label the columns of the table.

Weeks	Days
1	7
2	14
3	21
4	28
5	35

- List the number pairs.
  1 and 7, 2 and 14, 3 and 21, 4 and 28, 5 and 35
- **Describe** the relationship between the numbers in each pair.
  Possible description: the second number in each pair is 7 times as great as the first number in each pair.
- Label the columns of the table. **Think:** What unit of time is 7 times as great as another unit?

Math Talk MATHEMATICAL PRACTICES Look at each number pair in the table. Could you change the order of the numbers in the number pairs? **Explain** why or why not.

Yes. Possible explanation: you can change the order of the numbers if you also change the order of the column labels.

© Houghton Mifflin Harcourt Publishing Company

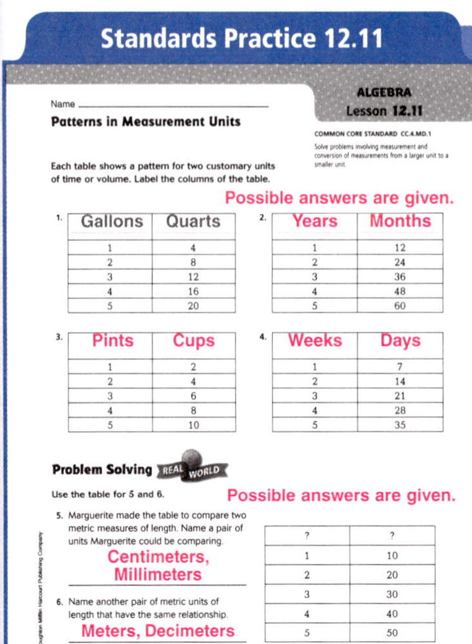

Standards Practice 12.11

Name ____________________

ALGEBRA
Lesson 12.11

Patterns in Measurement Units

COMMON CORE STANDARD CC.4.MD.1
Solve problems involving measurement and conversion of measurements from a larger unit to a smaller unit.

Each table shows a pattern for two customary units of time or volume. Label the columns of the table.

Possible answers are given.

1.

Gallons	Quarts
1	4
2	8
3	12
4	16
5	20

2.

Years	Months
1	12
2	24
3	36
4	48
5	60

3.

Pints	Cups
1	2
2	4
3	6
4	8
5	10

4.

Weeks	Days
1	7
2	14
3	21
4	28
5	35

Problem Solving REAL WORLD

Use the table for 5 and 6. Possible answers are given.

?	?
1	10
2	20
3	30
4	40
5	50

5. Marguerite made the table to compare two metric measures of length. Name a pair of units Marguerite could be comparing.
Centimeters, Millimeters

6. Name another pair of metric units of length that have the same relationship.
Meters, Decimeters

© Houghton Mifflin Harcourt Publishing Company

Chapter 12 P241

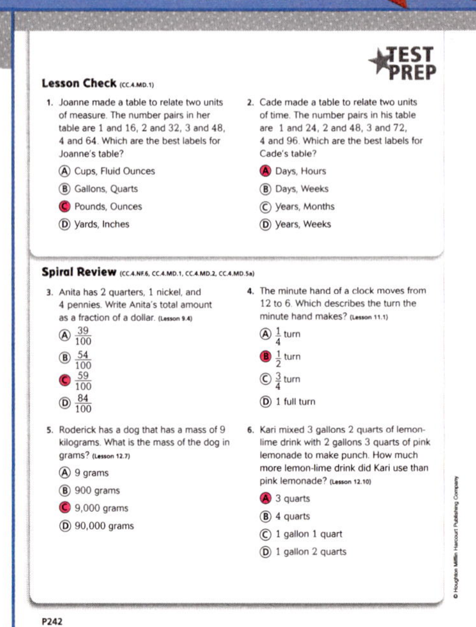

Common Core SPIRAL REVIEW

TEST PREP

Lesson Check (CC.4.MD.1)

1. Joanne made a table to relate two units of measure. The number pairs in her table are 1 and 16, 2 and 32, 3 and 48, 4 and 64. Which are the best labels for Joanne's table?
   - (A) Cups, Fluid Ounces
   - (B) Gallons, Quarts
   - **(C) Pounds, Ounces**
   - (D) Yards, Inches

2. Cade made a table to relate two units of time. The number pairs in his table are 1 and 24, 2 and 48, 3 and 72, 4 and 96. Which are the best labels for Cade's table?
   - **(A) Days, Hours**
   - (B) Days, Weeks
   - (C) Years, Months
   - (D) Years, Weeks

Spiral Review (CC.4.NF.6, CC.4.MD.1, CC.4.MD.2, CC.4.MD.5a)

3. Anita has 2 quarters, 1 nickel, and 4 pennies. Write Anita's total amount as a fraction of a dollar. (Lesson 9.4)
   - (A) $\frac{39}{100}$
   - (B) $\frac{54}{100}$
   - **(C) $\frac{59}{100}$**
   - (D) $\frac{84}{100}$

4. The minute hand of a clock moves from 12 to 6. Which describes the turn the minute hand makes? (Lesson 11.1)
   - (A) $\frac{1}{4}$ turn
   - **(B) $\frac{1}{2}$ turn**
   - (C) $\frac{3}{4}$ turn
   - (D) 1 full turn

5. Roderick has a dog that has a mass of 9 kilograms. What is the mass of the dog in grams? (Lesson 12.7)
   - (A) 9 grams
   - (B) 900 grams
   - **(C) 9,000 grams**
   - (D) 90,000 grams

6. Kari mixed 3 gallons 2 quarts of lemon-lime drink with 2 gallons 3 quarts of pink lemonade to make punch. How much more lemon-lime drink did Kari use than pink lemonade? (Lesson 12.10)
   - **(A) 3 quarts**
   - (B) 4 quarts
   - (C) 1 gallon 1 quart
   - (D) 1 gallon 2 quarts

© Houghton Mifflin Harcourt Publishing Company

P242

Try This! Jasper made the table below to relate two customary units of liquid volume. What customary units of liquid volume does the pattern in the table show?

- List the number pairs.
  1 and 4, 2 and 8, 3 and 12, 4 and 16, 5 and 20
- **Describe** the relationship between the numbers in each pair.
  Possible description: the second number in each pair is 4 times as great as the first number in each pair.
- Label the columns of the table. Possible answer is given.

Gallons	Quarts
1	4
2	8
3	12
4	16
5	20

Think: What customary unit of liquid volume is 4 times as great as another unit?

- What other units could you have used to label the columns of the table above? **Explain.**
  Possible answer: quarts and cups; possible explanation: 1 quart is 4 times as much as 1 cup.

Share and Show 

1. The table shows a pattern for two units of time. Label the columns of the table with the units of time.

Think: What unit of time is 24 times as great as another unit?

Days	Hours
1	24
2	48
3	72
4	96
5	120

Possible explanation: I know that there are 24 hours in 1 day, 48 hours in 2 days, and so on. The number pairs show a pattern for the relationship between days and hours.

Math Talk MATHEMATICAL PRACTICES **Explain** how you labeled the columns of the table.

© Houghton Mifflin Harcourt Publishing Company

Try This!

Have students name different customary units of liquid volume, such as cups, pints, quarts, and gallons. Write each unit on the board as students suggest it.

- **Which of these units could be shown using the numbers in the table?** Possible answers: gallons and quarts, quarts and cups
- **What relationship is shown in the number pair of 5 and 20?** Possible answer: there are 20 quarts in 5 gallons.

Guide students to describe the relationship between cups and quarts.

3 PRACTICE 

Share and Show • Guided Practice

The first problem connects to the learning model. Have students use the MathBoard to explain their thinking.

Use **Math Talk** to focus on students' understanding of how to identify and label columns in a table of number pairs involving measurement units.

Reteach 12.11

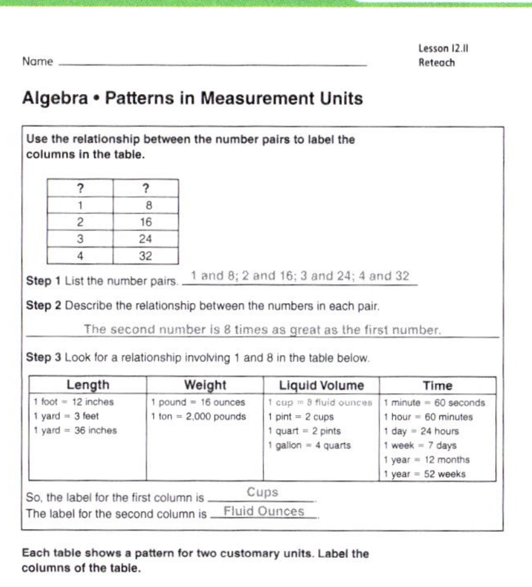

Name ______ Lesson 12.11 Reteach

Algebra • Patterns in Measurement Units

Use the relationship between the number pairs to label the columns in the table.

?	?
1	8
2	16
3	24
4	32

Step 1 List the number pairs. 1 and 8; 2 and 16; 3 and 24; 4 and 32

Step 2 Describe the relationship between the numbers in each pair.
The second number is 8 times as great as the first number.

Step 3 Look for a relationship involving 1 and 8 in the table below.

Length	Weight	Liquid Volume	Time
1 foot = 12 inches 1 yard = 3 feet 1 yard = 36 inches	1 pound = 16 ounces 1 ton = 2,000 pounds	1 cup = 8 fluid ounces 1 pint = 2 cups 1 quart = 2 pints 1 gallon = 4 quarts	1 minute = 60 seconds 1 hour = 60 minutes 1 day = 24 hours 1 week = 7 days 1 year = 12 months 1 year = 52 weeks

So, the label for the first column is Cups.
The label for the second column is Fluid Ounces.

Each table shows a pattern for two customary units. Label the columns of the table.

1.

Feet	Inches
1	12
2	24
3	36
4	48

2.

Tons	Pounds
1	2,000
2	4,000
3	6,000
4	8,000

Reteach R98 Grade 4
© Houghton Mifflin Harcourt Publishing Company

Enrich 12.11

Name ______ Lesson 12.11 Enrich

Two-Step Patterns

Use unit relationships and write a pattern to solve each problem.

1. Jessie hops for 1 minute then rests for 15 seconds. She repeats this pattern for several minutes. Write a pattern showing the number of seconds when Jessie switches from one activity to the next. After how many seconds will she start resting for the fourth time?
   60, 75, 135, 150, 210, 225, 285...; 285 seconds
2. A snail creeps up a plank 8 centimeters each day and slides back down 15 millimeters each night. Write a numerical pattern showing the number of millimeters where the snail changes direction. On which day will the snail have moved 275 millimeters up from its starting point?
   80, 65, 145, 130, 210, 195, 275...; fourth day
3. Joel is doing an experiment. He adds 2 gallons of water to a large tub each week. During the week, 1 quart 1 cup of water evaporates. Write a numerical pattern showing the number of cups of water before and after Joel adds water. How long will it take until there are more than 100 cups of water in the tub?
   32, 27, 59, 54, 86, 81, 113...; 4 weeks
4. **Stretch Your Thinking** In Problem 2, after how many days will the snail be 65 centimeters ahead? **Explain.**
   10 days; 65 centimeters is 650 millimeters. Each day the snail gains 65 millimeters, $80 - 15$. Since $650 \div 65 = 10$, it will take the snail 10 days.

Enrich E98 Grade 4
© Houghton Mifflin Harcourt Publishing Company

COMMON ERRORS

Error Students may reverse the column labels for a table.

Example In Exercise 4, students label the left column "Seconds" and the right column "Minutes."

Springboard to Learning Ask students to use the data from one row of the table in a sentence starter such as the following: There are ____ in ____. Have them check the reasonableness of the sentence to be sure they labeled the columns correctly.

Use Exercises 2 and 3 for Quick Check. Students should show their answers for the Quick Check on the MathBoard.

Quick Check

If a student misses Exercises 2 and 3

Then Differentiate Instruction with
- RtI Tier 1 Activity, p. 487B
- Reteach 12.11

On Your Own

If students complete Exercises 2 and 3 correctly, they may continue with Independent Practice. Have them explain how they labeled each column of the table in Exercise 6.

Name ____________________

Each table shows a pattern for two customary units. Label the columns of the table. Possible answers are given.

2.

Quarts	Pints
1	2
2	4
3	6
4	8
5	10

3.

Pounds	Ounces
1	16
2	32
3	48
4	64
5	80

On Your Own

Each table shows a pattern for two units of time. Label the columns of the table.

4.

Minutes	Seconds
1	60
2	120
3	180
4	240
5	300

Possible answer is given.

5.

Years	Months
1	12
2	24
3	36
4	48
5	60

Each table shows a pattern for two metric units of length. Label the columns of the table. Possible answers are given.

6.

Centimeters	Millimeters
1	10
2	20
3	30
4	40
5	50

7.

Meters	Centimeters
1	100
2	200
3	300
4	400
5	500

8. Write Math List the number pairs for the table in Exercise 6. Describe the relationship between the numbers in each pair.

1 and 10, 2 and 20, 3 and 30, 4 and 40, 5 and 50; possible description: the second number in each pair is 10 times as great as the first number in each pair.

© Houghton Mifflin Harcourt Publishing Company

COMMON CORE PROFESSIONAL DEVELOPMENT

Math Talk in Action

Teacher: How did you label the columns of the table in Exercise 4?

Vic: I labeled the first column Minutes and the second column Seconds.

Teacher: Why did you choose those labels?

Vic: I saw that the first column had a 1 and the second column had a 60. Since there are 60 seconds in 1 minute, I knew I could label the columns Seconds and Minutes.

Teacher: Are there any other labels that might fit as well?

Sarah: Yes, you could use minutes and hours.

Teacher: Yes, you could. Why would those labels fit?

Sarah: There are 60 minutes in an hour.

Teacher: Which column would get each label?

Vic: The first column would have to have the larger unit label, so it would be labeled Hours.

Sarah: The second column would be labeled Minutes, because there are 60 minutes in 1 hour.

Teacher: You are both correct. Great work!

MATHEMATICAL PRACTICES **Model • Reason • Make Sense**

Problem Solving REAL WORLD

9. H.O.T. **What's the Error?** Maria wrote *Weeks* as the label for the first column of the table and *Years* as the label for the second column. **Describe** her error.

?	?
1	52
2	104
3	156
4	208
5	260

Possible description: Maria wrote the labels in the wrong order. *Years* is the label for the first column and *Weeks* is the label for the second column because there are 52 weeks in 1 year.

10. H.O.T. **Sense or Nonsense?** The table shows a pattern for two metric units. Lou labels the columns *Meters* and *Millimeters*. Zayna labels them *Liters* and *Milliliters*. Whose answer makes sense? Whose answer is nonsense? **Explain.**

?	?
1	1,000
2	2,000
3	3,000
4	4,000
5	5,000

Both answers make sense; possible explanation: 1 meter is 1,000 times as long as 1 millimeter. 1 liter is 1,000 times as much as 1 milliliter. The number pairs in the table show the relationship between meters and millimeters and also liters and milliliters.

11. Look back at Problem 10. What other labels for metric units could you write for the columns of the table? **Explain.**

Possible answer: *Kilograms* and *Grams*; possible explanation: 1 kilogram is 1,000 times as much as 1 gram.

12. H.O.T. Look at the following number pairs: 1 and 365, 2 and 730, 3 and 1,095. The number pairs describe the relationship between which two units of time? **Explain.**

Years and days; possible explanation: 1 year is 365 times as long as 1 day.

13. **Test Prep** The table shows a pattern for two customary units of length. Which are the best labels?

?	?
1	12
2	24
3	36
4	48
5	60

Ⓐ Years, Months
Ⓑ Feet, Inches
Ⓒ Yards, Inches
Ⓓ Yards, Feet

© Houghton Mifflin Harcourt Publishing Company

FOR MORE PRACTICE: Standards Practice Book, pp. P241–P242

FOR EXTRA PRACTICE: Standards Practice Book, p. P244

Problem Solving

H.O.T. Problems Exercises 9, 10, and 12 require students to identify the correct relationship between numbers. Exercises 9 and 10 also require students to critique the reasoning of others.

Test Prep Coach

Test Prep Coach helps teachers to identify common errors that students can make.

In Exercise 13, if students selected:

A They chose units of time instead of units of length.

C or **D** They do not understand the relationship between yards, feet, and inches.

4 SUMMARIZE

Essential Question

How can you use patterns to write number pairs for measurement units? Possible answer: I can make a table with one column for each unit in the pair. I can list the measurements that have the same relationship in the column by units. Then I label each column with the name for that unit.

Math Journal

Draw a table to represent months and years. Explain how you labeled each column.

Differentiated Instruction

INDEPENDENT ACTIVITIES

Grab-and-Go!™

Differentiated Centers Kit

Activities
Challenging Changes

Students complete purple Activity Card 14 by performing simple conversions between different units of weight within the customary measurement system.

Activities
Ultimate Units

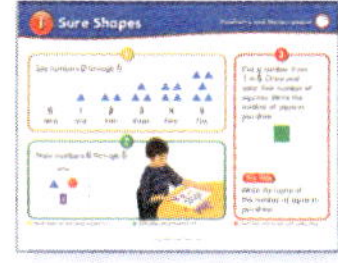

Students complete blue Activity Card 16 by identifying the appropriate unit of measure.

Activities
Capacity Challenge

Students complete purple Activity Card 16 by changing customary units of liquid volume.

Chapter 12 Review/Test

Summative Assessment

Use the **Chapter Review/Test** to assess students' progress in Chapter 12.

You may want to review with students the essential question for the chapter.

Chapter Essential Question

How can you use relative sizes of measurements to solve problems and to generate measurement tables that show a relationship?

Ask the following to focus students' thinking:

- **How can you compare metric units of length, mass, or liquid volume?**
- **How can you compare customary units of length, weight, or liquid volume?**

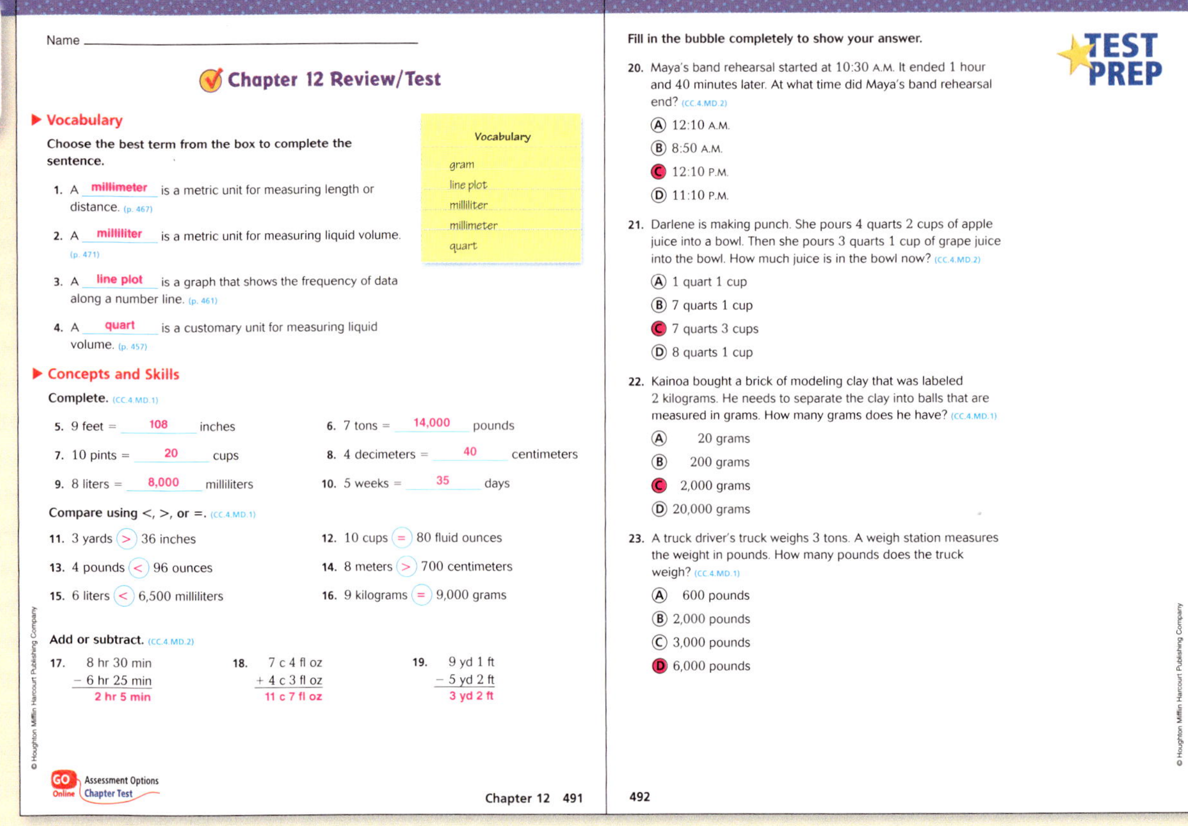

Name ______________________

Chapter 12 Review/Test

Vocabulary

Choose the best term from the box to complete the sentence.

Vocabulary
gram
line plot
milliliter
millimeter
quart

1. A millimeter is a metric unit for measuring length or distance. (p. 467)
2. A milliliter is a metric unit for measuring liquid volume. (p. 471)
3. A line plot is a graph that shows the frequency of data along a number line. (p. 461)
4. A quart is a customary unit for measuring liquid volume. (p. 457)

Concepts and Skills

Complete. (CC.4.MD.1)

5. 9 feet = 108 inches
6. 7 tons = 14,000 pounds
7. 10 pints = 20 cups
8. 4 decimeters = 40 centimeters
9. 8 liters = 8,000 milliliters
10. 5 weeks = 35 days

Compare using <, >, or =. (CC.4.MD.1)

11. 3 yards > 36 inches
12. 10 cups = 80 fluid ounces
13. 4 pounds < 96 ounces
14. 8 meters > 700 centimeters
15. 6 liters < 6,500 milliliters
16. 9 kilograms = 9,000 grams

Add or subtract. (CC.4.MD.2)

17. 8 hr 30 min − 6 hr 25 min = 2 hr 5 min
18. 7 c 4 fl oz + 4 c 3 fl oz = 11 c 7 fl oz
19. 9 yd 1 ft − 5 yd 2 ft = 3 yd 2 ft

GO Online Assessment Options Chapter Test

Chapter 12 491

TEST PREP

Fill in the bubble completely to show your answer.

20. Maya's band rehearsal started at 10:30 A.M. It ended 1 hour and 40 minutes later. At what time did Maya's band rehearsal end? (CC.4.MD.2)
    - Ⓐ 12:10 A.M.
    - Ⓑ 8:50 A.M.
    - Ⓒ 12:10 P.M.
    - Ⓓ 11:10 P.M.
21. Darlene is making punch. She pours 4 quarts 2 cups of apple juice into a bowl. Then she pours 3 quarts 1 cup of grape juice into the bowl. How much juice is in the bowl now? (CC.4.MD.2)
    - Ⓐ 1 quart 1 cup
    - Ⓑ 7 quarts 1 cup
    - Ⓒ 7 quarts 3 cups
    - Ⓓ 8 quarts 1 cup
22. Kainoa bought a brick of modeling clay that was labeled 2 kilograms. He needs to separate the clay into balls that are measured in grams. How many grams does he have? (CC.4.MD.1)
    - Ⓐ 20 grams
    - Ⓑ 200 grams
    - Ⓒ 2,000 grams
    - Ⓓ 20,000 grams
23. A truck driver's truck weighs 3 tons. A weigh station measures the weight in pounds. How many pounds does the truck weigh? (CC.4.MD.1)
    - Ⓐ 600 pounds
    - Ⓑ 2,000 pounds
    - Ⓒ 3,000 pounds
    - Ⓓ 6,000 pounds

492

© Houghton Mifflin Harcourt Publishing Company

Based on the results of the Chapter Review/Test use the following resources to review skills.

Item	Lesson	*CCSS	Common Error	Intervene With	Soar to Success Math
5–7, 11–13, 23, 27	12.2, 12.3, 12.4	CC.4.MD.1	May multiply by the wrong number of customary units	**R**—12.2, 12.3, 12.4; **TE**—pp. 449B, 453B, 457B	41.09, 42.05, 44.36, 45.30, 43.07, 46.37
8, 9, 14–16, 22, 25, 26	12.6, 12.7	CC.4.MD.1	May multiply by the wrong number of metric units	**R**—12.6, 12.7; **TE**—pp. 467B, 471B	42.07, 43.09, 44.32, 45.26, 46.32
10	12.8	CC.4.MD.1	May multiply by the wrong number for units of time	**R**—12.8; **TE**—p. 475B	51.12, 51.14
20, 24	12.9	CC.4.MD.2	May not correctly add or subtract across A.M. or P.M.	**R**—12.9; **TE**—p. 479B	51.16
17–19, 21	12.10	CC.4.MD.2	May regroup incorrectly	**R**—12.10; **TE**—p. 483B	44.36, 45.30, 46.37
27	12.1	CC.4.MD.1	May choose an inappropriate unit of length	**R**—12.1; **TE**—p. 445B	41.16, 41.17, 42.09, 42.10, 43.11, 43.12

***CCSS**—Common Core State Standards

Key: R—Reteach Book; **TE**—RtI Activities

Name ______________________________

TEST PREP

Fill in the bubble completely to show your answer.

24. Brody and Amanda canoed for 1 hour and 20 minutes before stopping to fish at 1:15 P.M. At what time did they start canoeing? (CC.4.MD.2)

- Ⓐ 11:55 A.M. (filled in)
- Ⓑ 12:05 P.M.
- Ⓒ 2:35 P.M.
- Ⓓ 11:55 P.M.

25. Lewis fills his thermos with 2 liters of water. Garret fills his thermos with 1 liter of water. How many more milliliters of water does Lewis have than Garret? (CC.4.MD.1)

- Ⓐ 1 more milliliter
- Ⓑ 100 more milliliters
- Ⓒ 1,000 more milliliters (filled in)
- Ⓓ 2,000 more milliliters

26. Lola won the 100-meter freestyle event at her swim meet. How many decimeters did Lola swim? (CC.4.MD.1)

- Ⓐ 1 decimeter
- Ⓑ 10 decimeters
- Ⓒ 100 decimeters
- Ⓓ 1,000 decimeters (filled in)

27. What is the best estimate for the length of an ant's leg? (CC.4.MD.1)

- Ⓐ 2 millimeters (filled in)
- Ⓑ 2 centimeters
- Ⓒ 2 decimeters
- Ⓓ 2 meters

© Houghton Mifflin Harcourt Publishing Company

▶ **Constructed Response**

28. Sabita made this table to relate two customary units of liquid volume. List the number pairs for the table. Describe the relationship between the numbers in each pair. (CC.4.MD.1)

Pints	Cups
1	2
2	4
3	6
4	8
5	10

1 and 2, 2 and 4, 3 and 6, 4 and 8, 5 and 10; possible description: the second number in each pair is two times as great as the first number in each pair.

29. Label the columns of the table. Explain your answer. (CC.4.MD.1)

Possible labels are given; possible explanation: pints and cups are both customary units of liquid volume. The table shows a pattern for the relationship between pints and cups, since 1 pint is two times as much as 1 cup.

▶ **Performance Task** (CC.4.MD.4)

30. Landon borrowed a book from the library. The data show the lengths of time Landon read the book each day until he finished it.

Time Reading Book (in hours)
$\frac{1}{4}, \frac{1}{4}, 1, \frac{1}{4}, \frac{1}{2}, \frac{3}{4}, \frac{1}{2}, \frac{1}{4}$

A Make a tally table and a line plot to show the data.

Time Reading Book	
Time (in hours)	Tally
$\frac{1}{4}$	||||
$\frac{1}{2}$	||
$\frac{3}{4}$	|
1	|

B Explain how you used the tally table to label the numbers and plot the Xs on the line plot.

Possible explanation: I ordered the data from least to greatest time to complete the tally table. Then I labeled the fraction lengths on the number line from the least value to the greatest value. Finally, I plotted an X for each data point.

C What is the difference between the longest time and shortest time Landon spent reading the book? $\frac{3}{4}$ hour

© Houghton Mifflin Harcourt Publishing Company

Constructed Response

Score student's responses with a 2–1–0 rubric (see *Assessment Guide*). For a level 2 the answer would include:

For Problem 28, students should recognize that the numbers in the right column are twice as large as the numbers in the left column.

For Problem 29, students should realize that pints are twice as large as cups, so the columns should be labeled Pints and Cups.

Performance Indicators

A student with a Level 3 paper:

- ____ correctly organizes and plots data on the line plot.
- ____ explains steps clearly and accurately.
- ____ identifies the data needed to solve each problem.
- ____ correctly finds the difference between requested data.

Performance Task

Use the performance indicators, scoring rubric, and DOK level to evaluate conceptual understanding.

Depth of Knowledge

Item	DOK Level
30A	2
30B	3
30C	3

Performance Task Scoring Rubric

3	**Generally accurate, complete, and clear:** All of the parts of the task are successfully completed. The student demonstrates sound reasoning and an understanding of the key concepts and procedures. Explanations are complete and clear with no meaningful errors.
2	**Accurate results without sufficient support:** All parts of the task are completed. While correct answers may indicate some understanding of the key concepts and procedures, explanations are lacking in reasoning and mathematical justification.
1	**Partially accurate:** Part of the task is successfully completed while other parts may be attempted, but not successfully completed. The student demonstrates minimal understanding of key concepts and procedures.
0	**Not accurate, complete, and clear:** No part of the task is completed with any success. There is little, if any, evidence that the student understands key concepts and procedures.

Performance Assessment

Chapters 10–13

See *Assessment Guide* for Performance Assessment Tasks to be completed at the end of each critical area.

Chapter 12 Test

Summative Assessment

Use the **Chapter Test** to assess students' progress in Chapter 12.

Chapter Tests are provided in multiple-choice and mixed-response format in the *Assessment Guide*.

GO Online Chapter 12 Test is available online.

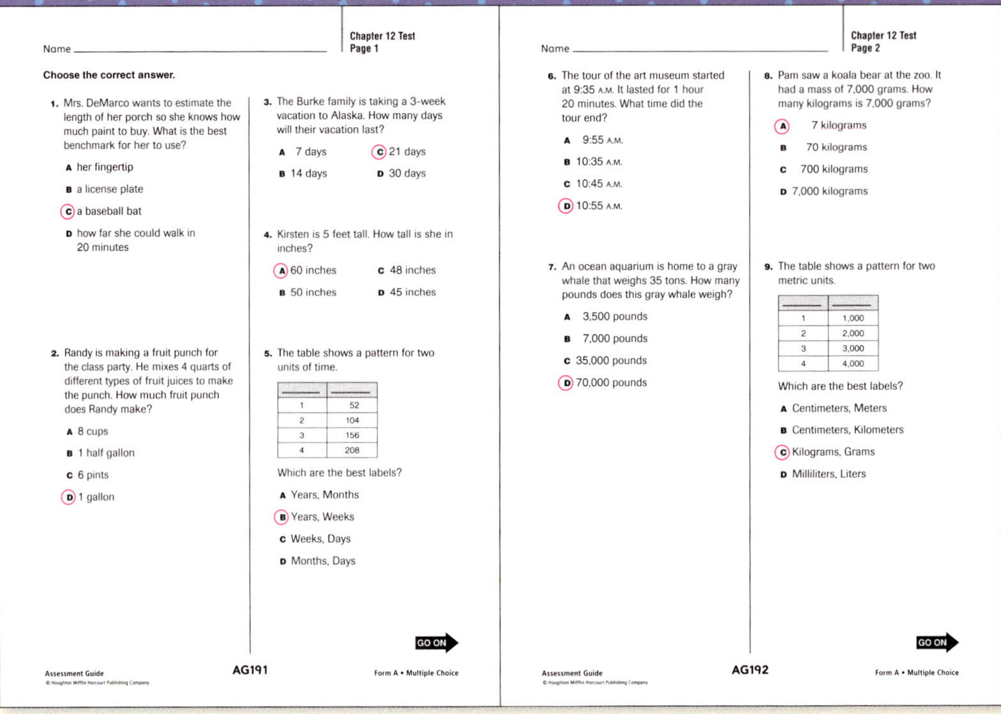

Name ______ Chapter 12 Test Page 1

Choose the correct answer.

1. Mrs. DeMarco wants to estimate the length of her porch so she knows how much paint to buy. What is the best benchmark for her to use?
   - A her fingertip
   - B a license plate
   - (C) a baseball bat
   - D how far she could walk in 20 minutes

2. Randy is making a fruit punch for the class party. He mixes 4 quarts of different types of fruit juices to make the punch. How much fruit punch does Randy make?
   - A 8 cups
   - B 1 half gallon
   - C 6 pints
   - (D) 1 gallon

3. The Burke family is taking a 3-week vacation to Alaska. How many days will their vacation last?
   - A 7 days
   - (C) 21 days
   - B 14 days
   - D 30 days

4. Kirsten is 5 feet tall. How tall is she in inches?
   - (A) 60 inches
   - C 48 inches
   - B 50 inches
   - D 45 inches

5. The table shows a pattern for two units of time.

____	____
1	52
2	104
3	156
4	208

Which are the best labels?
   - A Years, Months
   - (B) Years, Weeks
   - C Weeks, Days
   - D Months, Days

GO ON

Assessment Guide © Houghton Mifflin Harcourt Publishing Company AG191 Form A • Multiple Choice

Name ______ Chapter 12 Test Page 2

6. The tour of the art museum started at 9:35 A.M. It lasted for 1 hour 20 minutes. What time did the tour end?
   - A 9:55 A.M.
   - B 10:35 A.M.
   - C 10:45 A.M.
   - (D) 10:55 A.M.

7. An ocean aquarium is home to a gray whale that weighs 35 tons. How many pounds does this gray whale weigh?
   - A 3,500 pounds
   - B 7,000 pounds
   - C 35,000 pounds
   - (D) 70,000 pounds

8. Pam saw a koala bear at the zoo. It had a mass of 7,000 grams. How many kilograms is 7,000 grams?
   - (A) 7 kilograms
   - B 70 kilograms
   - C 700 kilograms
   - D 7,000 kilograms

9. The table shows a pattern for two metric units.

____	____
1	1,000
2	2,000
3	3,000
4	4,000

Which are the best labels?
   - A Centimeters, Meters
   - B Centimeters, Kilometers
   - (C) Kilograms, Grams
   - D Milliliters, Liters

GO ON

Assessment Guide © Houghton Mifflin Harcourt Publishing Company AG192 Form A • Multiple Choice

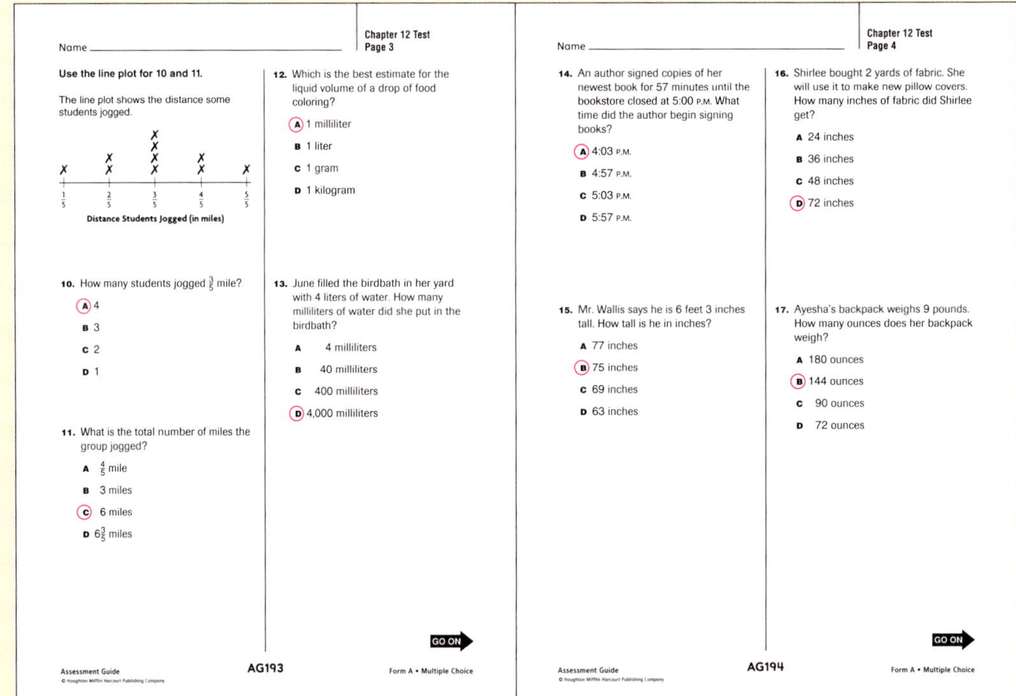

Name ______ Chapter 12 Test Page 3

Use the line plot for 10 and 11.

The line plot shows the distance some students jogged.

10. How many students jogged $\frac{3}{5}$ mile?
   - (A) 4
   - B 3
   - C 2
   - D 1

11. What is the total number of miles the group jogged?
   - A $\frac{4}{5}$ mile
   - B 3 miles
   - (C) 6 miles
   - D $6\frac{3}{5}$ miles

12. Which is the best estimate for the liquid volume of a drop of food coloring?
   - (A) 1 milliliter
   - B 1 liter
   - C 1 gram
   - D 1 kilogram

13. June filled the birdbath in her yard with 4 liters of water. How many milliliters of water did she put in the birdbath?
   - A 4 milliliters
   - B 40 milliliters
   - C 400 milliliters
   - (D) 4,000 milliliters

GO ON

Assessment Guide © Houghton Mifflin Harcourt Publishing Company AG193 Form A • Multiple Choice

Name ______ Chapter 12 Test Page 4

14. An author signed copies of her newest book for 57 minutes until the bookstore closed at 5:00 P.M. What time did the author begin signing books?
   - (A) 4:03 P.M.
   - B 4:57 P.M.
   - C 5:03 P.M.
   - D 5:57 P.M.

15. Mr. Wallis says he is 6 feet 3 inches tall. How tall is he in inches?
   - A 77 inches
   - (B) 75 inches
   - C 69 inches
   - D 63 inches

16. Shirlee bought 2 yards of fabric. She will use it to make new pillow covers. How many inches of fabric did Shirlee get?
   - A 24 inches
   - B 36 inches
   - C 48 inches
   - (D) 72 inches

17. Ayesha's backpack weighs 9 pounds. How many ounces does her backpack weigh?
   - A 180 ounces
   - (B) 144 ounces
   - C 90 ounces
   - D 72 ounces

GO ON

Assessment Guide © Houghton Mifflin Harcourt Publishing Company AG194 Form A • Multiple Choice

Data-Driven Decision Making

Item	Lesson	*CCSS	Common Error	Intervene With	Soar to Success Math
1, 12	12.1	CC.4.MD.1	May not understand the relative sizes of benchmarks	**R**—12.1; **TE**—p. 445B	42.09, 42.10, 43.11, 43.12
2, 19, 23	12.4	CC.4.MD.1	May not correctly identify or sort units of measure	**R**—12.4; **TE**—p. 457B	43.07, 46.37
3, 25	12.8	CC.4.MD.1	May not correctly compare or convert units of time (years/months/weeks/days/hours)	**R**—12.8; **TE**—p. 475B	51.12, 51.14
4, 16	12.2	CC.4.MD.1	May not correctly convert customary units of length (feet/inches/yards)	**R**—12.2; **TE**—p. 449B	41.09, 44.36

***CCSS**—Common Core State Standards **Key: R**—Reteach Book; **TE**—RtI Activities

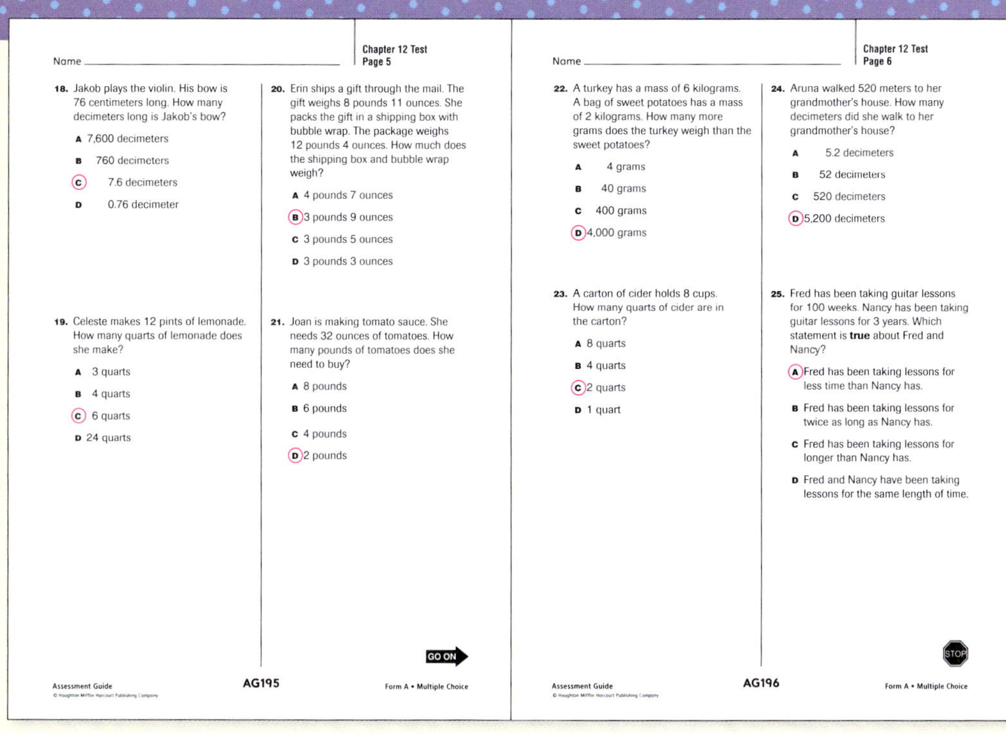

Name ______________________ **Chapter 12 Test Page 5**

18. Jakob plays the violin. His bow is 76 centimeters long. How many decimeters long is Jakob's bow?

A 7,600 decimeters
B 760 decimeters
(C) 7.6 decimeters
D 0.76 decimeter

19. Celeste makes 12 pints of lemonade. How many quarts of lemonade does she make?

A 3 quarts
B 4 quarts
(C) 6 quarts
D 24 quarts

20. Erin ships a gift through the mail. The gift weighs 8 pounds 11 ounces. She packs the gift in a shipping box with bubble wrap. The package weighs 12 pounds 4 ounces. How much does the shipping box and bubble wrap weigh?

A 4 pounds 7 ounces
(B) 3 pounds 9 ounces
C 3 pounds 5 ounces
D 3 pounds 3 ounces

21. Joan is making tomato sauce. She needs 32 ounces of tomatoes. How many pounds of tomatoes does she need to buy?

A 8 pounds
B 6 pounds
C 4 pounds
(D) 2 pounds

GO ON

Assessment Guide AG195 Form A • Multiple Choice

© Houghton Mifflin Harcourt Publishing Company

Name ______________________ **Chapter 12 Test Page 6**

22. A turkey has a mass of 6 kilograms. A bag of sweet potatoes has a mass of 2 kilograms. How many more grams does the turkey weigh than the sweet potatoes?

A 4 grams
B 40 grams
C 400 grams
(D) 4,000 grams

23. A carton of cider holds 8 cups. How many quarts of cider are in the carton?

A 8 quarts
B 4 quarts
(C) 2 quarts
D 1 quart

24. Aruna walked 520 meters to her grandmother's house. How many decimeters did she walk to her grandmother's house?

A 5.2 decimeters
B 52 decimeters
C 520 decimeters
(D) 5,200 decimeters

25. Fred has been taking guitar lessons for 100 weeks. Nancy has been taking guitar lessons for 3 years. Which statement is **true** about Fred and Nancy?

(A) Fred has been taking lessons for less time than Nancy has.
B Fred has been taking lessons for twice as long as Nancy has.
C Fred has been taking lessons for longer than Nancy has.
D Fred and Nancy have been taking lessons for the same length of time.

STOP

Assessment Guide AG196 Form A • Multiple Choice

© Houghton Mifflin Harcourt Publishing Company

Portfolio **Portfolio Suggestions** The portfolio represents the growth, talents, achievements, and reflections of the mathematics learner. Students might spend a short time selecting work samples for their portfolios and completing A Guide to My Math Portfolio from the *Assessment Guide*.

You many want to have students respond to the following questions:

- What new understanding of math have I developed in the past several weeks?
- What growth in understanding or skills can I see in my work?
- What can I do to improve my understanding of math ideas?
- What would I like to learn more about?

For information about how to organize, share, and evaluate portfolios, see the *Assessment Guide*.

Data-Driven Decision Making RtI

Item	Lesson	*CCSS	Common Error	Intervene With	Soar to Success Math
5, 9	12.11	CC.4.MD.1	May not recognize or apply patterns in related units of measure	**R**—12.11; **TE**—p. 487B	
6, 14	12.9	CC.4.MD.2	May not understand how to solve problems involving elapsed time	**R**—12.9; **TE**—p. 479B	51.16
7, 17, 21	12.3	CC.4.MD.1	May not correctly convert customary units of weight (tons/pounds/ounces)	**R**—12.3; **TE**—p. 453B	42.05, 45.30
8, 13, 22	12.7	CC.4.MD.1 CC.4.MD.2	May not correctly convert metric units of mass or liquid volume (grams/kilograms; liters/milliliters)	**R**—12.7; **TE**—p. 471B	42.07, 42.09, 45.26, 46.32
10, 11	12.5	CC.4.MD.4	May not understand how to read or interpret a line plot, or use its data to solve problems	**R**—12.5; **TE**—p. 461B	54.17
15, 20	12.10	CC.4.MD.2	May incorrectly convert between or compute in problems involving mixed units of measure	**R**—12.10; **TE**—p. 483B	44.36, 45.30, 46.37
18, 24	12.6	CC.4.MD.1	May not correctly convert metric units of length (millimeters, centimeters, decimeters, meters, kilometers)	**R**—12.6; **TE**—p. 467B	44.32

***CCSS**—Common Core State Standards **Key: R**—Reteach Book; **TE**—RtI Activities